Sustaining
European
Monetary Union

Studies on the European Polity

BRENT NELSEN, SERIES EDITOR

Sustaining
European
Monetary Union

Confronting
the Cost of Diversity

TAL SADEH

LYNNE
RIENNER
PUBLISHERS

BOULDER
LONDON

Published in the United States of America in 2006 by
Lynne Rienner Publishers, Inc.
1800 30th Street, Boulder, Colorado 80301
www.rienner.com

and in the United Kingdom by
Lynne Rienner Publishers, Inc.
3 Henrietta Street, Covent Garden, London WC2E 8LU

Library of Congress Cataloging-in-Publication Data
Sadeh, Tal, 1964–
   Sustaining European Monetary Union : confronting the
costs of diversity / Tal Sadeh.
   (Studies on the European polity)
   Includes bibliographical references and index.
   ISBN 13: 978-1-58826-478-7 (hardcover : alk. paper)
   ISBN 10: 1-58826-478-5 (hardcover : alk. paper)
   1. Economic and Monetary Union. 2. Economic and
Monetary Union—Economic aspects. 3. Economic and
Monetary Union—Political aspects. 4. Europe—Economic
integration. 5. Monetary policy—European Union
countries. I. Title. II. Series.
HG3942.S23 2006
332.4'94—dc22

                                       2006011922

British Cataloguing in Publication Data
A Cataloguing in Publication record for this book
is available from the British Library.

Printed and bound in the United States of America

          The paper used in this publication meets the requirements
   ∞   of the American National Standard for Permanence of
          Paper for Printed Library Materials Z39.48-1992.

   5 4 3 2 1

To my wife, Iris
and my kids, Avishay, Hadas, and Naomi

and

To my parents, Ruthanne and Amichi
and my in-laws, Sarah and Ariel

Contents

Illustrations

Tables

Figure

Boxes

Preface

In the fall of 1992, I was a foreign exchange dealer at Union Bank of Israel, a fresh university graduate, and an enthusiast of European monetary integration. I believed that policymakers would never break their promises to maintain declared exchange rate parities. When the skies fell on the European Monetary System (EMS), making my advice to the bank's management very costly, I realized that I had a lot more to learn. So I quit my job at the bank and became a doctoral student, encouraged by Yaacov Bar Siman Tov and supervised by Alfred Tovias and Emanuel Adler. Ever since, my fascination with European integration in general and with monetary integration in particular grew as my knowledge expanded.

When the euro was launched in 1999, I had a feeling of "mission accomplished." What more could we say and write about European monetary integration, which seemed to have arrived at its final destination after thirty years? However, as the expansion of the European Union to the east loomed, the potential membership of the transition countries in Economic and Monetary Union (EMU) seemed like the next intriguing issue. It was then that I came across Bayoumi and Eichengreen's (1997) paper in *European Economic Review*. I once again realized that observed policies, even currency unions, may not necessarily be consistent with economic and political realities, and that membership in the euro zone (the European Union's currency union) could be questionable not only for the transition countries, but also for countries already participating in it. I wanted to know how sustainable EMU is, and I have been seeking that answer ever since.

My intention in this book is to put a political *and* economic price tag on a currency union in general and on EMU in particular, and to suggest institutional reforms that would lower this price. My analysis encompasses all European Union (EU) member states and candidate countries, and even countries from the EU's neighborhood, taking account of both pre-euro data and endogenous post-euro effects. I assume in this presentation that the reader is acquainted with simple statistical analysis as taught in standard undergraduate courses on research methods in the social sciences; nevertheless, the presentation of equations and mathematical expressions is kept to a minimum, with more detailed technical explanations provided in boxes throughout the book. All of the implications arising from calculations and statistical analyses are spelled out, so the reader can just skip the tables and equations without losing the main themes.

* * *

There are many people whose help contributed to this book and to whom I am indebted. I first worked on the project while I was a postdoctoral fellow at the Davis Institute for International Relations, the Hebrew University of Jerusalem. The support of the Konrad Adenauer Foundation and the Helmut Kohl Institute for European Studies at the Hebrew University at that time is acknowledged. In particular, I would like to thank Shlomo Avineri for giving me the opportunity to participate in the Kohl Institute's activities. I am also greatly indebted to Nathan Sussman, who saw endless versions of the project's early results and guided me through its initial econometric steps.

The book would never have materialized without Jeffrey Frieden's friendly approach, his patience with my ignorance, and his illuminating comments and references. Jeff's work inspired my research agenda to a great extent. I would like to thank Alex Cukierman for his advice on collecting and analyzing the statutes of European central banks and for encouraging me to develop the project and present its results. I was also fortunate to receive encouragement from Benjamin Cohen as well as thoughtful comments that shaped much of the methodological discussion presented in Chapter 2.

Leo Leiderman enabled me to present my work to distinguished audiences at Tel Aviv University's School of Economics and the Israel Economics Association. Erik Jones offered useful suggestions in the preparation of the book proposal. Amy Verdun provided helpful comments and hosted me as a visiting fellow at the EU Centre of the University of Victoria, where parts of the manuscript were written. Chapter 8 developed from a Jean Monnet Transnational Regional Research Project coordinated by the European Documentation and Research Centre, University of Malta. I wish to thank Peter Xuereb for allowing me to participate in that project and for including some of my work in his edited collection, *The European Union and the Mediterranean, Volume 5*. Michael Beenstock, Yona Rubinstein, Graham Voss, and especially Saul Lach and Daniele Paserman patiently answered technical econometric questions and referred me to relevant literature.

Other people who read various drafts and made comments include David Andrews, Matthias Kaelberer, Jeffrey Kopstein, Patrick Leblond, Eytan Meyers, George Pagoulatos, Waltraud Schelkle, and two anonymous reviewers. I also wish to thank participants in seminars given at the Political

Science departments of Tel Aviv and Ben-Gurion universities, at the European Studies Program of the University of Toronto, and at the Bank of Israel's Research Department, as well as participants in the 2004 meetings of the Israeli Association for International Studies and International Studies Association and in the eighth and ninth biennial meetings of the European Union Studies Association.

Keren Raz-Netzer and Yael Proaktor provided excellent assistance in collecting data on institutional features of European democracies. Amit Granek, Shai Moses, and Nizan Feldman collected data on the countries of the European neighborhood and the United States. I thank you all. Any remaining errors are obviously mine.

Finally, I wish to commemorate our housekeeper, Nelly Perov, with whom I also shared my thoughts on the project. Nelly was an immigrant from Kazakhstan who sought a better life but was murdered by a suicide bomber on an early morning bus on her way to work. May she rest in peace.

1

The Puzzle of EMU

Ever since its inception, the process of monetary integration in post–World War II Europe was fraught with upheavals, as the member states of the European Community (EC), later the European Union (EU), progressed on the road to a single European currency. Periods of productive cooperation among the member states, stable exchange rates, and rapid progress were interrupted by periods of acrimonious intra-European relations, significant exchange rate adjustments, and stagnation in integration.[1] The process, which has been buried by its critics as many times as it has been praised by its supporters, culminated in 1999 in the establishment of Economic and Monetary Union (EMU) among the EU's member states and the launch of the single currency (the euro) currently shared by a large group of member states.

The historical record of political and economic instability in the process of European monetary integration poses some questions. Have the member states converged sufficiently to make a monetary union among them natural? Or could it be that the seeming calm recently observed in Europe's monetary affairs is as temporary as the calm of previous periods? Where did all the diversity disappear to in the 2000s? Is EMU an institutional lid on a simmering pot of diverse societies and economies locked together, in which tensions build up to erupt at a future international crisis? If so, what can be done to remedy the situation?

The main theme of this book is that EMU is indeed socially expensive for many of its actual or potential member states. The reason is that divergence in relevant economic and political idiosyncratic variables among EMU member states is still large, even when endogenous effects of currency union membership are considered.

The tranquility of the period of transition to the euro from 1997 contrasts dramatically with the previous tumultuous 1992–1996 period, which was characterized by exchange rate crises and political and financial upheavals. It also contrasts with the longer history of monetary integration in Europe. In fact, of the 30 years surveyed here (1969–1998), arguably only a total of seven and a half (during 1987–1992 and 1997–1998) were truly tranquil.[2]

1

The Snake

The roots of European monetary integration can be traced to the 1957 Treaty of Rome, which established the European Economic Community (later to become the EU), but sharing a currency among the peoples of Europe was not on the European agenda as a practical issue until the late 1960s (Tsoukalis, 1977). During the period 1946–1973, exchange rates of most countries were generally fixed versus the US dollar anyway in accordance with the Bretton Woods regime.

At the end of the 1960s, the EC had completed the establishment of its customs union and Common Agricultural Policy (CAP) and seemed prepared to face new challenges and make further progress with the process of economic and political integration. Indeed, the EC soon had to face great challenges in monetary issues. The tranquility of Bretton Woods was interrupted in Europe by the unilateral devaluation of the French franc in August 1969 following social unrest and wage increases. Another interruption came with the unilateral float of the German mark the next month and its revaluation in October following continuing trade surpluses. These developments created the impetus in December 1969 for the declaration of the six EC member states in The Hague that they were seeking a plan for the establishment of an EMU among them (Apel, 1998, 31–32).

In the early months of 1970, The Hague summit produced a flurry of plans for EMU. The Germans came up with the Schiller Plan. Belgium, Luxembourg, and the Commission of the European Communities (the Commission) submitted other plans (Ungerer, 1997, 99–106). In March 1970, the Council of Ministers set up the well-known Werner committee of experts to recommend practical steps to achieving an EMU. Named after Luxembourg's prime minister, who headed the committee, the Werner report, published in October 1970, suggested that an EMU was attainable within ten years.

According to the Werner report, in the first stage of the EMU process, exchange rate fluctuations among the EC members' currencies would be limited through a system of bilateral exchange rate commitments. In addition, a European Monetary Cooperation Fund (EMCF) would be established as a precursor to a system of European central banks, and the member states would manage their budgets according to the EC's objectives. The Werner report detailed the operation of a system of exchange rates, later known as the "Snake in the Tunnel." The Tunnel was the nickname for the fluctuation band of the members' currencies versus the US dollar, and the narrower band within it for cross exchange rates was dubbed the Snake (Apel, 1998, 32–33; and Ungerer, 1997, 113–114).

In March 1971, the Council of Ministers for Economic and Financial Affairs (ECOFIN) adopted the Werner plan, and in April 1972, the central banks of the member states launched the Snake. Under the Snake, member states were to keep their bilateral exchange rates within a ±2.25 percent band, and were committed to extend credit to each other for that purpose.

Credit for market operations designed to defend exchange rates was provided multilaterally through the Short Term Monetary Support (STMS) facility and bilaterally through the Very Short Term Facility (VSTF). Long-term (up to five years) conditional credit to overcome balance-of-payments problems was provided by the member states to each other under the Medium Term Financial Assistance (MTFA) credit facility. The newly established EMCF managed these credit facilities among the member states, and furthered the use of EC currencies in their interventions in the foreign exchange markets. The member states also decided to convene three times a year at a ministerial level to discuss and coordinate their short-term economic policies, as well as to adopt appropriate Council guidelines (Apel, 1998, 34–35).

However, the UK, Denmark, and Ireland left the Snake as early as June 1972. The UK was suffering industrial strife, and its government felt it could not keep the Snake's commitments. The Irish government, in turn, was not confident enough to break its currency union with the UK. Denmark went off the Snake temporarily because it preferred to weather its referendum on EC membership without the burden of exchange rate discipline, but returned in October. In February 1973, Italy left the Snake because its large public deficits and the practice of printing money to pay for these deficits were inconsistent with defending its exchange rates within the Snake. Between March and November of that year, Denmark and the Netherlands realigned their currencies by 5 percent against the other participating currencies, and Germany realigned its currency by more than 8 percent.[3] The Werner plan was in effect abandoned when, in December 1973, ECOFIN failed to proceed to its second stage, and a month later France left the Snake as well.

By this time, the Snake evolved into a club of a few small states orbiting the German economy. This club included Norway and Sweden, which were not EC member states but were associated with the Snake. Whereas exchange rates among the participating currencies were maintained within the Snake's fluctuation margins, and no realignments occurred during the next three years, exchange rates involving nonparticipating currencies fluctuated considerably. In addition, during 1970–1973, many countries extended their exchange controls in an attempt to stabilize their exchange rates. In fact, some of these controls were mandated by a Council resolution (Tsoukalis, 1977, 121–136). Divergence among EC member states was also evident in inflation rates and economic growth rates.

An important factor explaining the divergence in economic performance was the uneven way in which the oil shock of the 1970s affected

European countries. Important policy differences also arose from partisan agendas and institutional factors. Germany was bound by its constitution to follow macroeconomic policies centered on credibility, low inflation, and central bank independence, whereas most of the other EC member states followed Keynesian demand-side policies focused on full employment. The German central bank (the Bundesbank) had objected to any fixing of the German mark's parities as early as the mid-1950s, lest this would allow imported inflation to affect the German economy. The Bundesbank never liked the Bretton Woods regime and did not welcome the Snake either (Emminger, 1977, 41; Sherman, 1990, 40–41). The Bundesbank had its opponents in Germany, and yet its authority and opinion were widely accepted and appreciated (Kennedy, 1991, 30–55). Neither the German exporting industries nor the German ministry of foreign affairs seriously challenged the Bundesbank (Ludlow, 1982, 5).

In contrast, the governments of Italy and Ireland, and above all the government of the UK, in the 1960s and 1970s were pursuing policies of "cheap money." The UK political economy was characterized by assertive labor unions and government policies inspired by neo-Keynesian ideas. Thus, the response to inflation was further raises in wages rather than in interest rates. The three policy alternatives facing European countries were to follow German macroeconomic policies, to stay formally in the Snake while devaluing at will, or to leave the Snake. This policy dilemma characterized all subsequent attempts at monetary integration in Europe until the launch of the single currency in 1999.

Cabinet stability was another cause of divergence among the member states. Policy shifts in the wake of cabinet changes brought France back into the Snake in July 1975 and then out of it again in March 1976. Traditionally, the French central bank pursued policies that were designed to enable the French government to pursue its interventionist policies. There were quantitative credit quotas for different sectors of the economy and segmentation of the French money market. Real interest rates were often negative. France had no overriding commitment to price stability, and no central bank independence (Goodman, 1992, 103–111).

However, after the collapse of the Bretton Woods regime, the value of the French franc did become a concern for French right-wing leaders, and official interest rates rose (Loriaux, 1991, 33–45). These leaders seemed to be willing to absorb "stability" and the lessons of the "German way" through a currency link (Ludlow, 1982, 32). This explains the reentry of the franc to the Snake in July 1975 (Apel, 1998, 42). However, the Socialist Party, keen on neo-Keynesian ideas of money, was gaining strength early in 1976, and the French authorities preferred to float the franc again (Loriaux, 1991, 201; Sandholtz, 1993, 7).

The European Monetary System

The 1977–1978 period was characterized by competitive devaluations of the Nordic currencies, whereas Belgium and the Netherlands increasingly hardened their commitment to the peg with the German currency.[4] However, against a backdrop of deteriorating transatlantic relations in those years, France and Germany led a renewed attempt to achieve greater exchange rate stability in Europe. Such stability accompanied by a new European medium of account could lower the French and German need to hold US dollar reserves and minimize their exposure to the declining value of the dollar. It would also help both countries in their diplomatic maneuvers with the United States. Perhaps such an ambitious plan would also help to boost the more general European integration process (Ludlow, 1982).

Of course, such a move depended on the ability of these countries' leaders to face down their domestic oppositions, namely, the Bundesbank and the French left. Indeed, the domestic constellation in Germany in late 1977 and the parliamentary elections in France in March 1978 strengthened the domestic positions of both German Chancellor Helmut Schmidt and French President Valéry Giscard d'Estaing (Carr, 1985, 141; Gros and Thygesen, 1998, 36; Ludlow, 1982, 63–77). Still, a full EMU was not on the agenda.

In March 1979, the European Monetary System (EMS) was launched by all EC member states. The system was originally conceived as a multilateral regime in which all the member states would subject their macroeconomic policies to their exchange rate commitments. A divergence indicator was constructed to calculate the deviation of each member state from its central parity against a basket of EC currencies called the European Currency Unit (ECU). Quotas under the credit schemes described in the last section were extended in both their financial scope and their duration.

However, the UK would not commit to defending exchange rates, not even under the new multilateral scheme. Again, partisan stances and the durability of leadership were important factors. The Labor Party, which wanted to preserve the ability to devalue the British pound whenever this was needed to fight unemployment, buried the idea of full membership for the UK in the EMS in its conference in October 1978 (Apel, 1998, 46). Furthermore, Prime Minister James Callaghan was politically weak in the run-up to the May 1979 general elections, and he was not willing to discuss the EMS in cabinet until November 1978 (Gros and Thygesen, 1998, 53; Ludlow, 1982, 219).

Because the UK would not commit to defending exchange rates, it became technically impossible to abide by the divergence indicator as originally conceived. Stripping the ECU of its UK component would not have solved this problem because the combined weight of Germany and the Netherlands (which followed a declared policy of a near currency fix with Germany) in such an ECU would have been large enough to turn the German mark into a de facto anchor of the EMS.

Thus, the EMS ended up preserving the bilateral commitments of the Snake, now referred to as the Exchange Rate Mechanism (ERM), which enabled Germany to keep its policy autonomy (Ludlow, 1982). Faced with the same policy dilemma outlined previously, the member states chose this time to stay in and devalue when the need arose. However, realignments in the ERM were unanimously agreed upon, not unilaterally decided as in the Snake. The UK was the only EC member state not to assume exchange rate commitments, although Italy assumed the wider margin of a ±6.00 percent band.

The EMS could have been launched in December 1978 after its complicated technical issues were finalized. However, the EMS fell hostage to domestic interest groups, namely the farmers. The campaign in the first direct elections to the European Parliament produced unexpected pressure on Giscard during October and November 1978. The government was pressured to show its loyalty to the Fifth Republic and to make sure that the European Parliament's authority would not be expanded after the elections. The French farmers used this opportunity to demand the dismantling of a mechanism under which they compensated German and Dutch farmers for devaluation of the French franc. The EMS was not launched until March 1979, after the French government softened its demands (see Goodman, 1992, 125; Gros and Thygesen, 1998, 36; Ludlow, 1982, 199–205, 263).

The next four years saw an official realignment of the German currency once every eight months on average; the magnitude of these adjustments were determined by the significant differences in the rate of inflation among the member states (Cameron, 1996). In this sense the EMS really did not seem much different than the Snake. The currencies of the UK and Greece (which joined the EC in 1981 but stayed out of the ERM) were even more volatile than those of the ERM member states.

In May 1981, domestic politics once again put European monetary integration to a severe test. The winner of the presidential elections in France was the Socialist leader François Mitterrand, whose economic philosophy was completely different from that of Giscard d'Estaing. Mitterrand emphasized higher government spending and the nationalization of big firms, and he was reconsidering French participation in the ERM. Eventually, these measures brought France close to a balance-of-payments crisis and caused price inflation. In 1983, the French government famously changed its policy, emphasizing fiscal and monetary restraint and exchange rate stabilization (Cameron, 1996; Loriaux, 1991).

As Italy and other member states followed France and adopted similar policies, inflation rates converged across the continent and adjustments of central parities became fewer and smaller. Between 1983 and 1987, only four currency realignments took place, the magnitude of each being lower than international differences in inflation. In other words, the domestic political economies in the more inflationary countries were bearing the burden of disinflation with lower real wages and earnings. Official interest rates gradually replaced currency market intervention as the primary policy tool in defending the ERM, again at the expense of large segments of the domestic industry. In fact, no realignment occurred between early 1987 and late 1992, and it seemed that the EMS had turned into a German mark zone: Member states had to follow the path of German interest rates to maintain their currency link, at the expense of policy autonomy.

Market agents and academics doubted the resolve of European government to irrevocably maintain fixed exchange rates against Germany's currency because this choice was considered to be socially and politically costly for them. These doubts were reflected in higher interest rates in EU member states compared with those in Germany. However, the member states' determination to establish the EC's internal market in the 1980s lent credibility to the EMS, showing their willingness to lose some of their autonomy over economic policy for the sake of greater integration. The preamble to the Single European Act in 1987 made a direct reference to the vision of monetary union among the member states as its ultimate goal. The EMS also seemed credible against the backdrop of the end of the Cold War, Germany's unification, and the intergovernmental conferences launched in December 1990 to turn the EC into the EU and establish EMU among its member states.

On the Path to EMU

The 1990s version of EMU, like the original plan of the EMS, was supposed to make monetary cooperation in the EU more multilateral and reduce the dependency of the member states' monetary policies on Germany (Pauly, 1992, 98; Sandholtz, 1996, 94). The French became increasingly impatient with the asymmetrical nature of the EMS after their 1983 policy shift and the adoption of a strong currency policy, which ostensibly should have made the French franc as good and stable a currency as the German mark. The relaxation of capital controls as part of the implementation of the internal market, as well as liberalization and deregulation in European capital markets, made this policy dilemma—leave the ERM, follow the Bundesbank's policy, or devalue at will—ever starker. However, on the surface of things, the EMS looked calm and successful. In the early 1990s, many Europeans were convinced that the long journey for a single currency in Europe had reached its destination, that they were part of a de facto currency union, and that all that was necessary was formal recognition of the union and some institutional arrangements.

By 1992, however, the economic case for exchange rate realignment was strong. In spite of the convergence in inflation rates among the member states during the 1980s, the accumulated differences in inflation among them were substantial (Sandholtz, 1996, 88). Substantial as well were the accumulated trade deficits of member states with Germany and the Netherlands (Cameron, 1995b, 44). In addition, Germany was experiencing a postunification boom while most other member states were in a recession (Sandholtz, 1996, 90–91). This meant that in most member states the level of interest rates required to avoid realignment was much higher than the desired level for domestic policies. Relations among member states turned acrimonious over interest rates when Germany resisted immense pressure to ease them.

The EMS was also burdened in the early 1990s by the membership of countries with low macroeconomic credibility, such as Portugal and Spain (in addition to Italy), or dubious motives, such as the UK. Portugal and Spain joined the EC in 1986, but did not assume the exchange rate obligations until 1992 and 1989, respectively. The UK assumed the ERM's exchange rate obligations in October 1990. All three countries adopted the wider ±6.00 percent exchange rate bands. The British government was outspokenly hostile to EMU; it is often argued that the UK merely wanted a stronger hand in the intergovernmental conferences where EMU was being negotiated (Talani, 2000; Verdun, 1996, 78). Italy moved to the normal ±2.25 percent bands in 1990, but its ability to maintain this commitment was questionable. A sharp decline in the US dollar's value in global markets in the summer of 1992 also strengthened the German mark against its European partners.

The five-year period of exchange rate tranquility came to an abrupt end in the fall of 1992, after a referendum in Denmark rejected the Maastricht Treaty and another one in France failed to deliver a convincing endorsement. In the course of the next twelve months, five separate realignments took place, two currencies were ejected out of the ERM's fluctuation margins, and the margins were widened to ±15 percent. This crisis period demonstrated how dependent the EMS had become on the credibility of the EMU process. Once the process had been thrown in doubt, the pressure for realignment was irresistible.

However, the crisis also owed at least part of its severity to the way it was managed. ECOFIN was not convened in September 1992, and devaluation of the weak currencies was authorized by telephone, case by case. The French and German governments were determined not to allow the French franc to be devalued against the German mark. For France, the Franco-

German exchange rate had come to symbolize its partnership with Germany. If EMU was to be a multilateral symmetric regime, here was an opportunity for Germany to demonstrate that it could temporarily sacrifice domestic policy goals to help a well-disciplined France under attack by speculators. There were, of course, no compelling economic reasons to devalue the French franc, but speculation on ERM exchange rates was a one-way bet, and market agents with very little to lose were armed with greater resources than central banks could muster to defend the parities.

In March 1993, domestic politics struck again. Just as the markets were starting to calm down, a cabinet change occurred in France. Some members of the new cabinet infuriated German policymakers by suggesting that the French franc was poised to replace the German mark as the new nominal anchor in Europe. To drive the message home, they lowered French interest rates to below German levels. German goodwill was practically the only protection that France had from the wrath of speculators. Thus, these comments by the new cabinet members were either a folly reflecting the short-sightedness of some French policymakers or a deliberate attempt to break up the EMS by members of the center-right government that challenged its German leadership (Cameron, 1995a, 140). The speculators stormed the French franc, and France was left to deal with them in isolation.

To avoid the immense political damage to European integration that would most likely have resulted from devaluation of the franc, and also to make it more difficult for speculators to gamble against fundamentally stable currencies, ECOFIN decided in the early hours of August 1, 1993, to widen the fluctuation margins as mentioned above. This was interpreted by many as the end of the EMU project because it supposedly demonstrated that EU member states were not natural partners for a currency union after all, or that they lacked the political resolve to fully cooperate on monetary issues. On the technical level, maintaining stable exchange rates within the ERM's narrow fluctuation margins for at least two years was enshrined in the Maastricht Treaty as one of the economic qualification criteria for eventually joining the single currency.

European leaders picked up the pieces and followed the Maastricht blueprint for EMU as planned. The Maastricht Treaty was ratified by the parliaments of the member states, with a rerun of the Danish referendum yielding an endorsement. The European Monetary Institute was established in January 1994 as a precursor to the European Central Bank (ECB), and much technical progress was made during the rest of the decade, such as formulating common monetary policy targets and tools, determining codes for statistical reporting, dealing with various legal issues arising from a common European currency, and even agreeing on the new currency's name.

During the three and a half years between August 1993 and the

European Council in Dublin in December 1996, the only official devaluation involved the Portuguese and Spanish currencies in March 1995. Austria, Finland, and Sweden joined the EU that year, but only Austria immediately assumed the ERM's obligations. Finland waited until the fall of 1996, and Sweden has preferred to stay out of the exchange rate mechanism ever since. Italy reentered the fluctuation margins a month after Finland did.

After the 1993 widening of the ERM's official fluctuation margins, exchange rates were, in practice, supposed to stay within the now-informal ±2.25 percent band as much as possible to satisfy the Maastricht qualification criteria, and use the ±15 percent official margins only occasionally. In fact, during roughly 600 of the days between August 1, 1993 and December 31, 1996 (or half of that period), daily average exchange rates for the currencies of Denmark, France, Ireland, and Spain were outside that unofficial band against the German mark.[5] In that same period, the Portuguese currency strayed from the narrow band during more than 700 days, and even the Belgian franc spent 121 days on the wrong side of its margins.

Given the wide official margins, however, these oscillations could hardly be blamed on speculators. It is more likely that the wider margins were used to pursue diverging macroeconomic policies (Youngs, 1999, 303). European governments simply "took a break" from the EMS and German monetary policy dictates between the prior crisis years and the time the future narrow margins would have to be observed again ahead of the launch of the currency union, scheduled to occur in January 1999.

Magically, all of the member states participating in the exchange rate mechanism except Ireland managed to keep their exchange rates against the German mark within the narrow band for all of 1997 and 1998.[6] Governments were no doubt trying harder to maintain their exchange rate commitments in order to qualify for membership in the currency union. Their efforts were made easier because Germany's boom was cooling and the rest of the continent was recovering from recession. Interest rates had ceased to be so contentious in Europe.

In 1999, the EU's currency union, henceforth referred to as the euro zone, was indeed finally launched. The euro zone consists of EU member states that (1) have adopted the single currency as their currency as part of stage III of EMU (and therefore observe irrevocably fixed exchange rates among them) and (2) are committed to full capital mobility among them. The ECB was established, and one monetary policy has since prevailed among the euro zone member states, although the euro itself did not become a reality in everyone's lives until its notes and coins entered circulation in 2002.

Initially, the euro zone consisted of eleven member states. The UK and

Denmark used special opt-out clauses that they had negotiated to stay out of this currency union, although Denmark did join ERM II—the new fluctuation margins set as a "waiting room" for interested outsiders.[7] Sweden stayed out without an opt-out clause by not volunteering to introduce its currency to ERM II, in which a two-year membership is again a prerequisite to join the euro zone. Greece became the twelfth member state of the euro zone in 2001, when it was considered to have fulfilled the economic qualification criteria, including the two-year stint in ERM II.[8] Estonia, Lithuania, and Slovenia joined ERM II in June 2004, shortly after acceding to the EU, in their attempt to become full members of the euro zone in January 2007. Cyprus, Latvia, and Malta joined ERM II in May 2005 and plan to adopt the euro in January 2008. The other four new EU member states have so far chosen to abstain from ERM II.

Taking Stock: EMU and the SGP

The European Council in Dublin in December 1996 cleared an important obstacle to EMU when it reached an agreement on the Stability and Growth Pact (SGP). The Maastricht Treaty had already defined public deficits of member states beyond 3 percent of GDP as excessive, but did not specify the sanctions to be applied on deviant countries. In an attempt to placate the concerns of German voters, the German government demanded that offending countries be subject to automatic and large fines. However, the French government resisted the automation of the excessive budget procedure and the German government had to compromise. In the end, the SGP specified a schedule of hefty fines, but these fines are subject to approval by ECOFIN.

This point became crucial in recent years, as the public deficits in a number of leading member states chronically exceeded the SGP's limits. Since 2002, France and (ironically) Germany have run excessive public deficits, and repeated attempts by the Commission to issue reprimands and levy fines have failed due to ECOFIN's reluctance to endorse the Commission's proposals. In July 2004, the European Court of Justice in essence refused to interfere in this dispute between the Commission and ECOFIN, leaving the SGP and the excessive budget procedure vulnerable to political maneuvers in ECOFIN. In March 2005, the European Council further loosened the member states' commitments by allowing various exceptions to the 3 percent deficit limit, including recessions as well as spending on education, research, defense, and foreign aid. By then, five of the member states of the single currency had breached that limit.

As argued in Chapter 2, public deficits are substitutes for devaluation of exchange rates, providing short-term stimulus to slow-growth economies ridden with employment problems. In this sense, the crisis of the SGP is the equivalent of a realignment of currencies. Without an international redistribution mechanism in Europe, it is doubtful whether EU member states can forgo fiscal autonomy in addition to monetary autonomy and exchange rate manipulation as redistributive tools. For this reason, many economists welcome what they see as the demise of the SGP. Nevertheless, as the terms of the SGP were in practice being watered down, they were simultaneously being written into the EU's new Constitutional Treaty.

The story of European monetary integration that has been briefly described in this chapter highlights the determination of policymakers and leaders in Europe to pursue this path regardless of the difficulties posed by political and economic diversity among EU member states. In the face of political disagreement and market turmoil, the answer has often been more European institutions. The Snake was a response to the collapse of the Bretton Woods system of exchange rates, and the EMS was a response to the failure of exchange rate stabilization in the Snake. EMU was a response to inadequate macroeconomic policy coordination in the EMS, the SGP was a response to the Maastricht Treaty's toothless approach to fiscal issues, and the Constitutional Treaty is fortifying the failed SGP.

Even though political and economic diversity has arguably moderated over the years, however, it always had to be adjusted for at some point—either continuously (as in 1993–1996), incrementally (as in the years prior to 1987), or abruptly (as in 1992–1993). Institutions could not stop such adjustments from eventually taking place. The tranquility of the transition to the euro starting in 1997 contrasts dramatically with the longer history of monetary integration in Europe and gives rise to the puzzle as detailed at the beginning of this chapter: Have the member states indeed converged sufficiently to make a monetary union among them natural?

This book is motivated by the concern that EMU might be undone at some point in the future if its burden to society, which arises from its members' diversity, is ignored. A burdensome currency union can be sustainable, as explained in the next chapter, but it would depend on strong structural and institutional factors for its survival. As the failure of the SGP and the politics of appointing the ECB's president demonstrate, EMU's institutions might be weakened by political manipulation. Moreover, the sustainability of the single currency has not yet been tested by a political crisis among its major member states. Past experience suggests that crises expose the diversity among member states and the weakness of monetary institutions in Europe. On top of all this, diversity in the euro zone is expected to grow in the next decade as it expands to include the new central and eastern European EU member states. Thus, economic and political diversity among the member states of the euro zone should be a cause for concern to anyone who believes that EMU is an important part of the economic and political order in Europe.

Plan of the Book

Chapter 2 discusses the methodology of the book, the concept of the adjustment burden, and the book's technical design. Chapter 3 describes the policies and the actual behavior of market exchange rates, budget deficits, and real interest rates among twenty-six EU member states and candidate countries during 1992–1998. These are the major adjustment mechanisms normally available to policymakers but constrained in EMU.

Chapter 4 analyzes three economic determinants of the burden of membership in the euro zone (openness, business cycle correlation, and inflation rate disparities). The chapter develops proxies for measuring these determinants, describes their patterns among the sample countries during the sample period, and develops models for explaining them with idiosyncratic and institutional instruments. Chapters 5 and 6 do much the same type of analysis on the domestic democratic politics of exchange rates for a number of variables suggested by the literature. These include partisanship, institutions, political business cycle correlation, and cabinet duration.

Chapter 7 uses econometric methods to estimate the relationships between the variables developed in Chapters 4, 5, and 6, on the one hand, and alternative measures of EMU's adjustment burden as discussed in Chapter 3, on the other hand. Chapter 7 then uses these results to forecast the adjustment burden between each pair of sample countries. These forecasts, which consider endogenous economic effects of currency unions and the most recent available (mostly 2004) data, are interpreted as indicating the costs of EMU for these country pairs. The major EU member states are compared to find which of them is potentially the cheapest anchor for the euro zone. Suggestions are made with respect to helpful adjustments in political and economic institutions in those member states with a relatively high forecast in order to ease their adjustment to the single currency.

Chapter 8 broadens the sample to include the EU neighborhood countries in North Africa, the Middle East, and the Commonwealth of Independent States (CIS), as well as the European Free Trade Association (EFTA) countries—for a total of forty-four countries. It attempts to find how costly adopting the euro would be to these countries compared with adopting the US dollar. Basically, Chapter 8 follows the same methodology employed in Chapter 7. However, many of these added countries are not democratic. Therefore, the analysis in Chapter 8 measures the effect of autocracy and regime duration on the adjustment burden. Forecasts of this burden are made for each country for selected subperiods during the period 1975–2004, showing whether that country gravitates with time economically and politically to the euro or to the dollar. The ninth chapter summarizes the book, underscores its conclusions, and places them in the current European and international context.

Notes

1. Unless otherwise specified, the term "exchange rate" refers in this book to the nominal exchange rate.

2. This chapter offers a brief description of the process. For the full story, see Apel (1998); Dyson and Featherstone (1999); Gros and Thygesen (1998); Ungerer (1997); and Vanthoor (1996).

3. Realignment is a revaluation of the official exchange rate that serves as the center of the fluctuation margins.

4. A competitive devaluation is a policy that attempts to manipulate the exchange rate in order to improve the competitiveness of the local industry. In making the foreign currency more expensive and the local currency cheap, it spurs demand for its import substitutes and for its exports.

5. Official parities are taken from Deutsche Bundesbank, 2004.

6. To be precise, Finland and Portugal strayed for 46 and 38 days, respectively, during that period.

7. The new fluctuation margins, with the same width as the old ones, apply only to exchange rates against the euro, not to bilateral exchange rates.

8. Public accounts that served as a basis for admitting Greece are under retrospective inspection by the Commission these days, after serious doubts were raised regarding the accounting methods used at the time.

2

Research Design

What factors caused the founding of EMU? What factors affect the sustainability of EMU? These are two distinct yet related questions. Many factors that cause a currency union to form can be expected to play a persistent role in its sustainability after its establishment. However, once the currency union is in place, some factors may lose their importance. Other factors may become more important, and endogenous dynamics generated by the union may affect its sustainability.

The sustainability of EMU is interpreted as its ability to survive in terms of preserving or expanding membership in the euro zone (Cohen, 2000). Other aspects of its survival, such as observance of its principles and norms (Krasner, 1983), are regarded as being reflected in the ability to maintain fixed exchange rates among its member states under full capital mobility. Floating the currency or limiting capital flows isolates national policies from each other and reduces the dependency on other agreed rules (Cohen, 1993). In other words, the sustainability of EMU is judged by the ability of its member states to observe two rules simultaneously: fixed exchange rates and capital mobility.

Borrowing from Frieden and Jones (1998), the sustainability of EMU can be understood to depend on variables in three levels of analysis: EU, national, and domestic. At the EU level, in the absence of a dominant state willing and able to use its influence to uphold EMU's rules and maintain its membership, Cohen (2000, 1998) argued that solidarity among the member states is critical to EMU's sustainability. Solidarity could be reflected in an effective system for sharing the national burdens of adjustment to the single currency, such as fiscal transfers to depressed member states and regions.

In addition, EMU is embedded in the greater institutional and ideational structure of the EU, which raises exit costs even when other factors turn the cost-benefit analysis against staying in. EMU allows a greater variety of issue linkages (Martin, 1993), essential for intergovernmental bargains (Moravcsik, 1998). Neo-functionalists argue that trade integration among the EU member states created spillover for monetary integration (Andrews, 1994; Cameron, 1997). McNamara (1998) explained EMU in terms of a continental ideological shift away from the Keynesian paradigm, and Verdun (1996, 1999) related it to the work of transnational epistemic communities.

At the national level of analysis, the classic optimum currency areas theory argues that currency unions enhance trade and income by reducing the exchange rate trade barrier at the expense of independent macroeconomic policies. Currency unions would be efficient among major trade partners with coordinated business cycles, open economies, flexible prices, high labor mobility, and financial market integration (the so-called optimum currency area criteria). The new optimum currency area theory argues that fixing a weak currency to a strong currency also benefits the credibility and success of disinflation policies.[1]

In the early 1990s, some economists used optimum currency area theory to argue that monetary union among EU member states was undesirable (Eichengreen and Frieden, 1994). Later, however, it was argued that some optimum currency area criteria could be satisfied endogenously once a currency union was established (Frankel and Rose, 1998, 2002). Optimum currency area theory was also used for studies of potential membership of central and eastern European countries in the euro zone (Bénassy-Quéré and Lahrèche-Révil, 2000).

At the domestic level of the political economy of EMU, variations in the abilities of EU member states to fix their exchange rates since the early 1970s were explained in terms of balance of power among competing domestic interest groups (Heisenberg, 1999; Milner, 1995), as right-wing agendas (Alesina and Roubini, 1994; Garett, 1995), as a reflection of institutional features of the member states (Walsh, 2000, 2001) and in terms of the political business cycle (Alesina and Roubini, 1997).

A comprehensive study of the sustainability of EMU should consider all of the above arguments and factors together, controlling for potentially interdependent relations among them. However, this formidable task is beyond the scope of this book; indeed, it was never rigorously attempted due to the irreconcilable philosophical grounds on which various theories are based and the incompatible methodologies they use.

Philosophically, a single analytical framework must be based on a coherent ontological approach. Specifically, agent-centered analysis is incompatible with structure-centered analysis. The former views individual units—be they states, political parties, or individuals—as the primary source of social order, and reduces reality to their actions (Popper, 1966, 98). According to this view, the structure is the sum of individual actions, so it can only constrain, not enable, individual action. In contrast, structure-centered analyses view individual action as a function of social order, and reduce reality to the social structure that determines and shapes individual units. The structure is seen as enabling individual action and as empowering it rather than constraining it (Hollis and Smith, 1990).

A single analytical framework must also be based on a coherent episte-mological approach. Material approaches view reality as determined by unavoidable, predictable, and purposeless forces. In contrast, idealist approaches view the social world not as the product of natural forces, but rather as made of rules and meanings that define relations between agents and give purpose and meaning to their interactions. Because individuals learn, they do not automatically repeat their behaviors, and are thus unpre-dictable (Kratochwil, 1989; Wendt, 1987, 344–349). Optimum currency area theory and political realism can safely be categorized as agent-cen-tered, material approaches. In this way, they differ, for example, from con-structivist and ideational theories.

Thus, the purpose of this book is humble. While recognizing that there is much more to EMU's sustainability than its costs, the book focuses on developing a quantitative indicator of the political and economic burden to the societies of the member states of adjusting to actual or potential mem-bership in the euro zone. Henceforth, this indicator is referred to as EMU's adjustment burden indicator. The emphasis here is not on the burden borne by a specific decisionmaker or a specific societal group, but on the sum of burdens to all actors in the society of a given country.

EMU's adjustment burden indicator should synthesize the effects of as many of the determinants of EMU's sustainability as possible. From a ratio-nalist point of view, which this book adopts, the relative importance of these determinants is reflected in the extent to which they affect the adjustment burden. EMU's adjustment burden indicator is used to support the argument of the book that EMU is socially expensive for many of its actual or potential member states. EMU's adjustment burden indicator serves two other minor purposes of this book. One is to find which EU member state is potentially the cheapest anchor for the European currency area. The other is to find whether the European currency is potentially a cheaper external anchor com-pared with the US dollar for the countries of the EU neighborhood.

Focusing on EMU's adjustment burden rather than on EMU's sustain-ability in general, the book's argument may seem somewhat narrow. Indeed, without accounting for all of the determinants of sustainability, this book cannot forecast how sustainable EMU is. However, it can forecast how much *more* sustainable EMU can become if the adjustment burden is reduced. In other words, a given costly currency union may be sustainable, yet at the margin as its burden increases it also gets less sustainable. Thus, other factors being constant, a high adjustment burden must be compensat-ed for in some manner to make it more sustainable.

Even after narrowing the analysis to rationalist theories and quantita-tive methods, analyzing currency union sustainability simultaneously with a number of political and economic theories raises issues of methodological compatibility. Optimum currency area theory is the most established approach for measuring costs associated with currency unions, so this book cannot afford to ignore its arguments. Thus, all other theoretical arguments about membership costs to be considered must be methodologically consistent with optimum currency area theory.

This methodological consistency has two dimensions: focus of analysis and subject of analysis. Classic optimum currency area analysis looks for predetermined country idiosyncrasies that enhance international trade and reduce the need for an independent monetary policy. Such circumstances make it efficient to join a currency union. By studying the reality that predates political decisions, optimum currency analysis has an ex ante focus. A logical consequence of this ex ante focus, which this book adopts, is the emphasis on explaining phenomena with idiosyncratic exogenous variables. This allows insights into causal relationships among variables (where one variable determines the other), rather than studying simultaneous relationships (where both variables determine each other).

Many political analyses, in contrast, take political decisions to join a currency union as a starting point, and focus on the way they affect the reality that follows them. Such analyses feature an ex post focus with respect to the currency union and study effects that are endogenous to it. Such a focus is also typical of studies of the endogeneity of the optimum currency area criteria, mostly focusing on the gains from currency union membership. This focus is obviously incompatible with the ex ante focus of this book.

Currency union theories also vary in their subject of analysis. Political economists can study the effects of political and economic factors on policy choices, or they can study these effects on market developments. This book adopts market developments as its object of analysis, in line with its purpose and with the optimum currency area approach—a choice that once again narrows the range of compatible political approaches.

Given these methodological considerations, this book attempts to integrate the optimum currency area approach with compatible theories of the domestic politics of exchange rates to support its argument. Other approaches in the study of EMU are incompatible in their underlying philosophy, focus, or subject of analysis. In relying on the theory of optimum currency areas, however, this book does not adopt its interest in describing the conditions under which a currency union is efficient. Nor does it explore in full whether EMU is an optimum currency area or whether it has the potential to improve the welfare of society in Europe and beyond. In particular, the center of discussion here is less on the benefits of EMU and mostly on its costs.

The reason for this is that many of the benefits of EMU are political and unquantifiable. Optimum currency area theory does argue that currency unions encourage trade and thus growth. However, estimated in the case of EMU at a mere 0.4 percent of the member states' gross national product (Commission of the European Communities, 1990), this effect is clearly not the main motive of EMU. Methodologically, economic gains are ultimately measured in terms of national product, whereas the quantifiable political-economic costs of EMU are measured in other terms, as Chapter 3 suggests. Thus, a combined quantitative political-economic cost-benefit analysis of EMU is impossible. A study of EMU's economic benefits deserves a separate thorough analysis.

Four dependent variables related to exchange rate variation are suggested in the next chapter as the book's subject of analysis. Before the launch of the euro, these variables reflected (at least to a certain extent) market reactions to economic shocks and policy decisions. Pure market-driven variables are difficult to come by because politically driven factors are always at play. The next section of this chapter discusses this dilemma. Ever since the launch of the euro in 1999, the locking of exchange rates, and the formulation of a common monetary policy among the participating states, the actual values of these four dependent variables have been restricted. However, forecasts of their values for the post-lock period represent the burden of adjustment to membership in the euro zone.

Forecasts of these dependent variables are based on the values of independent variables suggested by optimum currency area theory and theories of the domestic politics of exchange rates. The relationships among these variables are estimated based on records predating the launch of the euro. Once these relationships are estimated, and assuming that they are unchanged by the formation of the euro zone, values of the independent variables for the post-lock period can be substituted in the equation to find the potential values of the dependent variables—the values they are expected to have had since 1999 had they been free to adjust to economic and political shocks and developments.

Admittedly, any assessment of a currency union is incomplete without considering its endogenous effects (Tsoukalis, 2000) because the very establishment of a currency union may affect economic and political variables, reducing or enhancing the adjustment burden. A lack of account of endogenous effects is no doubt a shortcoming of the ex ante approach, and this study makes certain adjustments in an attempt to compensate for it. Specifically, some of the more well-known endogenous effects of currency union are estimated separately, taking a currency union as an ex ante given. These endogenous effects are factored into the assessment of EMU's adjustment burden.

The Adjustment Burden

Different countries and regions may have different macroeconomic experiences at any given point in time. Whereas some economies experience slow or even negative growth, others can enjoy rapid growth. Some of this variation in economic conditions can be cyclical, resulting from the business cycle, which within a period of a few years can toss economies from recession to economic expansion and back. If business cycles became desynchronized between two economies, these economies would diverge in terms of such variables as their rates of growth, employment, and inflation.

Yet another source of different macroeconomic experiences across countries involves long-term trends of economic activity. Investment in capital and infrastructure, large-scale emigration, or high but sustainable fertility rates each provide an underlying basis for lasting growth. Such conditions often depend on institutional and political variables, such as political stability; rule of law; transparent decisionmaking, and the freedom to speak, organize, own property, and choose one's occupation. These variables differ across countries, and so do their long-term economic trends.

Bilateral macroeconomic diversity calls for adjustment between the two economies concerned (Masson and Taylor, 1993). Adjustment is defined in this book as the realignment of economic variables in response to economic and political bilateral diversity, whether as a result of many individual decisions (as in the market), or as a result of government policies. Indeed, this adjustment can take place through a number of mechanisms (Mundell, 1961).

One simple adjustment mechanism is the exchange rate. A country suffering adverse economic conditions can devalue its currency against the rest of the world, or see its currency depreciated by market forces. Depreciation of currency helps the local industry gain competitiveness, encourages foreign investment, and thus stimulates the economy out of its predicament. Similarly, a booming economy would see its currency revalued against the rest of the world by the market, and see its economic activity slowed down. As a result, currencies of booming economies appreciate against currencies of stagnant economies if markets are allowed to determine exchange rates or if policymakers carry out this exchange rate adjustment.

Another adjustment mechanism to bilateral diversity that can result from market activity is price and wage adjustment. Recession and unemployment put pressure on producers to cut prices and on workers to accept wage cuts. Lower prices and wages, in turn, can improve industrial competitiveness and encourage foreign investment just like depreciation of the currency. Conversely, higher prices and wages as a result of an economic boom correspond to currency appreciation. This is the famous "automatic adjustment mechanism" of the nineteenth century's gold standard (Eichengreen and Flandreau, 1997).

A third adjustment mechanism is labor and capital mobility. When unemployment of factors of production is high, workers can find jobs abroad if allowed, and unemployed capital can be exported as well. By the same token, rapid growth may produce labor and capital shortages and attract foreign workers and capital. Alternatively, cheap asset prices during a recession can attract foreign capital, as suggested above. The effectiveness of this adjustment mechanism depends on the extent of labor mobility (Bertola, 1989; Erickson, 1995) and financial market integration (Sorensen and Yosha, 1997). Mundell (1961) took the case further to argue that, on grounds of efficiency, a separate currency should be established for each region within which free factor mobility exists, ignoring political borders.

In addition to these market-driven adjustment mechanisms are the non-market adjustment mechanisms that can be applied by the government. Specifically, adjustment can take place through fiscal and monetary policies. For example, the burden of a recession can be eased by increasing public deficits, as spending rises to compensate disadvantaged sectors in spite of lower tax revenues. Likewise, a recession can be relieved by lower real interest rates, as the central bank reduces the nominal interest rate relative to inflation. In a boom, government revenues rise and can turn a deficit into a surplus, and the central bank can raise real interest rates.

Such measures can provide a temporary stimulus to the economy if the authorities enjoy a good reputation, reflected in low public debt levels and a history of low inflation. In contrast, under high levels of debt and inflation, the public may expect that a rise in interest rates and/or inflation is imminent, and the above measures would not provide stimulus because they would be offset by the public's behavior.

If adjustment between diverging economies does not take place through any of the above market- or government-driven mechanisms, some form of disequilibrium results in one or both of these countries. In a recession-hit economy, such disequilibrium can manifest in depressed economic activity and prolonged unemployment. In a booming economy, disequilibrium can take the form of higher price inflation or asset-price bubbles.

Among member states of a currency union, exchange rates are irrevocably fixed and a common monetary policy prevails. Thus, price and wage flexibility and capital and labor mobility remain the only available market-driven adjustment mechanisms, and the fiscal tool remains the only non-market adjustment mechanism. A high level of fiscal integration among the members of the currency union can ease the negative effects of an asymmetric shock. A common budget would allow transfers from members whose economies were positively affected by an external shock to those who were negatively affected by it. However, it is assumed throughout this book that no EU common budget can be utilized to compensate disadvantaged sectors on any significant scale, and that any fiscal adjustment must be carried out on a national basis.

For example, an increase in energy prices would compromise the competitiveness of energy-intensive low-technology manufactured goods, but would have little effect on the production of human-capital-intensive high-technology goods. Therefore, economies specializing in low-tech manufactured goods would suffer an adverse shock to their income, whereas economies specializing in high-tech goods would not. Such a circumstance is often referred to as an asymmetric shock.

Outside a currency union, the recession-hit low-tech economy can devalue its currency or have it depreciated by market forces. However, for the booming high-tech economy, devaluation would result in inflationary pressures. Thus, if the two economies are members in a currency union, at least one of them cannot rely on exchange rates to adjust for the asymmetric economic shock (De Grauwe, 1994). Other things being constant, without an exchange rate adjustment, unemployment in the low-tech country is expected to be higher and growth slower than if the currency link were broken. If wages came down in the low-tech economy, production costs would subside and industrial competitiveness would be restored. Alternatively, unemployed workers could emigrate to the booming high-tech economy.

Market-driven adjustment mechanisms, which make sense from a liberal economic point of view, can be socially and politically costly from a mercantilist perspective or from the perspective of domestic vested interests. From a mercantilist perspective, migration is a loss of factors of production and represents relocation of production that weakens the state by reducing its economic base. Similarly, the state might view capital flows on a significant scale as undesired or at least suspicious. In sum, capital outflows represent relocation of production, whereas capital inflows are accompanied by foreign ownership and control of factors of production. In addition, migration and immigration might challenge established perceptions of collective identity and change the ethnic composition of the population.

At the domestic level, a number of important political economic cleavages exist. As a general rule, because a currency union encourages and even depends on mobility of factors of production among the member states, the less mobile factors or sectors are at a disadvantage when it comes to bargaining over their terms of trade, whether bargaining takes place at the individual level, as in a perfect market, or through collective bargaining.

Among the more explored divisions are those between labor and capital and between skilled and unskilled labor. If, for human and technological reasons, labor is less mobile than capital and unskilled labor tends to be less mobile than skilled labor, there is a greater chance that adjustment to economic and political shocks would be borne mostly by labor, especially unskilled labor. In other words, the unskilled would see their wages cut by more than the national average or they would experience greater unemployment.

Societal divisions can also follow specific industrial branches. For example, adjustment may occur mostly in industries that cater to local customers rather than in the more mobile multinational corporations. Similarly, small and medium enterprises may be affected by adjustment differently than large companies. Domestic economic divisions may also have a spatial dimension. Adjustment may have an uneven effect on different regions and towns, depending on the industries they host. Indeed, many of these considerations are argued to have motivated the decision on the Structural Funds and the Cohesion Fund at the 1992 European Council in Edinburgh. These funds are supposed to help the poorer EU member states adjust to EMU (Martin, 1993).

Various societal groups are affected in different ways, not only by the very existence of a currency peg and the adjustments it requires, but also by the specific mechanism through which adjustment to economic and political developments takes place. If wage cuts in a certain sector of the economy produce a different income distribution than depreciation, they may be resisted or supported by different societal groups. Similarly, when wage cuts are pitted against unemployment, the question is who might be unemployed as a result of the adverse economic shock, and whose wage would alternatively be cut. If different groups of workers are involved in each case, the precise mechanism of adjustment would be subject to a political struggle or bargain between them. Labor flows could also set different groups of workers in opposition if the locals view the newcomers as unwelcome competition in the labor market.

Arguably, EMU's adjustment burden indicator should reflect this domestic diversity. However, this would require precise data on production, employment, wages, and returns on capital, which is generally not available at subnational levels of aggregation. Some macroeconomic regional data are available for the major EU member states but not for many of the small and new member states. Other data, such as exchange rates and interest rates, are by definition nonexistent at the subnational level of analysis because each country is a currency union in its own right.

Similarly, because each country is a political union of its regions and sectors, some data on political institutions and the electoral cycle may be unavailable or irrelevant at a subnational level of aggregation. In a nonfederal political system, there is only one (national) government, legislature, electoral law, and electoral calendar and cycle. On a practical side, decisions to join the euro zone or withdraw from it are still taken at a national level and can be expected to continue to be taken at that level in the foreseeable future. Thus, EMU's adjustment burden indicators are aggregated, calculated, and analyzed in this book at a national level.

The next chapter develops and describes four dependent variables that form the book's subjects of analysis, based on optimum currency area theory insights. These dependent variables are alternative measures of EMU's adjustment burden indicator. However, before discussing these variables, the technical design of this study must be laid out.

Technical Design

Existing quantitative studies of the political and economic pressures facing EMU are lacking by covering only some of the current EU member states and candidates.[2] In addition, many studies fail to distinguish causal relationships from simultaneous ones. This is a serious problem because separating effects that run in different causal directions is essential for identifying their true magnitude.

Optimum currency area studies tend to investigate only one or two criteria. Few of them seriously consider the endogeneity of business cycle correlation, and thus, tend to overplay the divergence among the member states. With a few exceptions all of them lack a methodology that can determine the relative importance of the different optimum currency area criteria and arrive at an objective and conclusive balance of their effect on the sustainability of EMU.[3] Optimum currency area studies also ignore political variables that affect the sustainability of EMU. By the same token few if any of the studies of the domestic politics of exchange rates systematically control for optimum currency area criteria, nor indeed were they ever applied to the study of the sustainability of EMU.

This book contributes to the debate on the sustainability of EMU in a number of ways. To begin with, it includes wider country and criteria coverage than available quantitative studies do. There are twenty-six countries in the sample: Bulgaria, Romania, and all current EU member states except for Luxembourg. These countries are all either current EU member states or candidate countries with near-term prospects for becoming EU member states. The twenty-six countries in the cross-sectional dataset make for 325 dyadic observations. In Chapter 8, the sample is expanded to forty-four countries (making 946 dyads) by including three nonmember European countries, thirteen of the EU's neighborhood countries, Russia, and the United States. These countries, although they are neither EU member states nor candidate countries, may wish to unilaterally adopt the euro in the future as part of their integration with the EU's internal market.

Luxembourg is not included in the sample because it has shared a monetary union and a customs union with Belgium for many years, and therefore has no exchange rate data. Although Estonia had adopted a currency board against the German mark during the entire sample period, its market exchange rate against the mark was in practice not absolutely fixed and was actually more volatile than that of Austria and the Netherlands, as shown in Chapter 3.

Observations in the dataset that this book uses consist of proxy values calculated over a sample period, mostly in the form of a period average or periodical standard deviation. Thus, this is a cross-sectional dataset. Unless otherwise specified, raw data are taken from the International Monetary

Fund (IMF)'s databases *Direction of Trade Statistics* and *International Financial Statistics*. The choice of 1992–1998 as the sample period is constrained by the availability and the relevance of pre-1992 data for the new EU member states (indeed, some of these countries did not exist earlier), and by the availability of post-1998 data for euro-bloc member states (i.e., no exchange rate variability occurred once the euro was launched).

Arguably, the proximity of the sample period to the launching of the single currency poses data credibility problems. Certain economic variables, such as inflation and especially public deficits, might have been the subject of government manipulation in the last year, designed to fulfill the Maastricht Treaty criteria. However, because EU member states are based on market economies, most of the variables that this book considers were beyond the legal or practical ability of their governments to significantly manipulate (Sadeh, 2005).

The reason for choosing a cross-sectional dataset rather than a pooled time-series cross-sectional dataset is that almost all of the variables in this book (certainly the political ones) are fairly constant over the sample period. In addition, some variables are measured as a periodical standard deviation (and thus their variance during the sample period is being considered). These would have to be estimated at a higher frequency to build a time series, for example, using monthly or weekly data to produce annual observations. Some of the data, such as production, are unavailable at such high frequencies, and this would introduce a lot of "noise" into the data—variance that is unrelated to the long-term variables of interest to this study.

As stated previously, this book uses a dyadic dataset. Clearly, a currency union is more than the sum of the bilateral relations between its member states, and its sustainability does not depend only on these bilateral relations. Rather, EMU's rules are written (and at times broken) as part of a European multilateral process. By using a dyadic dataset, this book does not argue that multilateral dynamics are not important. However, for the membership of a given country in a currency union to be sustained, all of its bilateral currency links with other member states must be sustained as well. Thus, if the sustainability of EMU is understood in terms of preserving or expanding its membership, each dyad is important.

Another, more important concern with regard to a dyadic dataset might be that dyads of small countries are unimportant because these countries' conditions are determined by their interactions with the large countries. For example, exchange rates essentially do not reflect structural differences between the political economies of small countries because currency markets do not operate equally across all currency dyads. Rather, according to this argument, currency markets tend to follow a pattern of a few hubs and many spokes, with minor currencies trading mostly into major currencies rather than among themselves. In other words, exchange rates are a function of triangular trading: The exchange rate between currency a and currency b and the exchange rate between currency a and currency c must be compatible with the exchange rate between currency b and currency c. If a is a major currency and b and c are minor currencies, then the b/c exchange rate is supposedly determined by the other two rates. Thus, dyadic observations of exchange rate variation across currencies of minor countries might seem unimportant.

Likewise, bilateral variation in fiscal and monetary policies can be argued to be the coincidental result of national policies that are often formulated with little regard to specific bilateral relations. So it would seem that many dyadic observations merely reflect these national choices rather than some bilateral reality and thus, again, are not important.

The argument about exchange rate variation seems especially compelling for financially driven currency trade (Krugman, 1991). For example, speculative trade designed to improve portfolio positions indeed involves mostly the major reserve currencies in addition to somewhat milder activity between the majors and the minors. This part of exchange rate variation may be only weakly related to fundamental variables, as just explained, and reflects mostly simultaneous relationships among variables.

However, another part of exchange rate variation is not spurious, but rather reflects structural differences between the political economies of small as well as large countries. For example, to the extent that currency transactions are conducted to underwrite trade in goods and services, the small scale of currency flows between small countries mirrors the small scale of trade between them. Similarly, hyperinflation resulting from political instability in a small country would be a decisive factor in determining its exchange rate with the currency of a small and stable country, whatever the exchange rates with the major currencies. Such exchange rate variation reflects causal relationships among variables.

Thus, even though exchange rates do form triangles among themselves, it is not clear in advance which of the sides of the triangle determines the others. There is no reason to presuppose that one exchange rate is completely determined by the others and has no causal effects on them. As for fiscal and monetary policy variation, bilateral economic and political relations do affect, to varying degrees, the macroeconomic situation in a given country and thus are partly responsible for the fiscal or monetary stance adopted. In other words, just as a recession in a major trade partner would greatly affect a country's business cycle, a recession in a minor trade partner would affect its business cycle too, even if on a smaller scale. All dyads convey some information on exogenous variables that determine EMU's adjustment burden.

The challenge is to clear out simultaneous relationships from causal ones. It is important to find a relationship between each of the variables proposed in this study and objective bilateral realities. Estimating such a relationship would enable forecasting their potential values, distilling the variables, and removing their simultaneous or otherwise irrelevant components. Only the potential values of these variables can truly indicate EMU's adjustment burden. This process is carried out in Chapter 7.

Indeed, the econometric method this book employs to estimate causal relationships between variables is another of its contributions to the debate on the sustainability of EMU. This econometric method is that of instrumental variables (IV) estimation within a generalized method of moments (GMM) framework. The features and advantages of this method are described in Chapter 7.

Even with this econometric method, the fact remains that all dyads are weighted equally in the estimation, whereas in practice they probably are not equal in determining the burden of adjustment. A possible remedy would be to focus on the influence of a core country such as Germany or some European average that excludes the observation country. However, this solution has the opposite disadvantage of assuming that the weight of all other dyads is zero. In truth, there is no simple way to tell the exact relative weight of each dyad. Assuming an equal weight to all observations is a simple and practical way out of this tangle.

Another way in which this book is meant to contribute to the debate on the sustainability of EMU is by considering endogenous optimum currency area criteria, especially the endogenous business cycle correlation, as explained in Chapter 4. Finally, this book is also innovative in analyzing economic and political variables in a single framework.

Notes

1. On the classic and new optimum currency area theory, see Gros and Thygesen (1998) and Tavlas (1993).

2. See Chapters 4–6 for references.

3. Exceptions include Artis and Zhang (2001), Bayoumi and Eichengreen (1997), and Bénassy-Quéré and Lahrèche-Révil (2000).

3

Adjustment Mechanisms

As explained in Chapter 2, this book develops a quantitative indicator of EMU's political and economic adjustment burden to the societies of the member states, used to support the argument put forth that EMU is socially expensive for many of its actual or potential member states. This chapter develops and describes the four dependent variables that form the book's subjects of analysis, based on the insights of optimum currency area theory. The analysis of these variables in Chapter 7 serves as a basis for constructing variants of EMU's adjustment burden indicator.

The four dependent variables are:

- ERV, exchange rate variation
- $RERV$, real exchange rate variation
- $ADJUSTMENT$, a weighted average of ERV, variation in fiscal policies, and variation in monetary policies
- $RADJUSTMENT$, an adjustment index similar to $ADJUSTMENT$ that uses $RERV$ instead of ERV

In accordance with this book's focus of analysis, the ideal variable would measure pure market activity, which responds to political and economic actions but is not politically manipulated in itself. However, in reality, such conditions rarely apply and the above less-than-perfect variables must be used.

In order to keep the book's promise of a wide country coverage, the dependent variables should also be calculated based on data representing all twenty-six sample countries. Some data are not available for all of these countries, however, and again a compromise is inevitable. Thus, none of the proposed dependent variables is perfect. Rather, a trade-off exists among their advantages and disadvantages.

Presenting the entire dataset of 325 observations would be very cumbersome; therefore, as a general rule, dyadic data are presented against the four major EU member states (Germany, France, Italy, and the UK), assuming that the membership of at least one of them is necessary for EMU's sustainability on political grounds. Wherever the dyadic data is a linear combination of national data, for simplicity, the latter is described rather than the former. In describing the data, the current euro zone member states are repeatedly distinguished, as are often the ex-Communist countries. The latter are referred to as transition economies when dealing with economic variables, or transition countries when dealing with political variables. The following sections detail the method of calculating these variables, discuss their advantages and disadvantages, and describe the data.

Exchange Rate Variation

The first dependent variable suggested as the subject of analysis of this book is the variation of nominal market exchange rates. For each pair of countries, percent changes are calculated between each two successive quarterly averaged nominal exchange rates (based on the *rf* series in the IMF's International Financial Statistics database). Exchange rate variation is then calculated as the standard deviation among the twenty-eight quarterly percent changes during the sample period. Thus, ERV is expressed in percentage points.

ERV values range from a low of 0.07 percent in the German-Austrian case to a high of 37.81 percent in the Bulgarian-Lithuanian case (see Table 8.2 on page 144). Its mean and standard error values are, respectively, 7.01 and 8.29 percent. Table 3.1 details ERV levels for all countries with regard to the four major EU economies and sorts them accordingly. The current euro zone countries are printed in bold type.

Table 3.1 reveals that as far as actual nominal exchange rate variation against France and Germany is concerned, Austria, Belgium, Estonia, France, Germany, and the Netherlands formed a core in the 1990s with the standard deviation among them not exceeding 1 percent. Cyprus's ERV values against France and Germany were lower than those of many current euro zone member states, whereas Italy and Finland were doing worse at the time than many of the recent accession countries such as the Czech Republic, Hungary, Malta, and Slovakia. If the record of pre-1999 nominal exchange rate variation is anything to go by, the memberships of Finland and Italy in the euro zone seem unwarranted.

Sweden and the UK experienced higher nominal exchange rate variation against France and Germany than any of the current euro zone member states did at the time. Although this is compatible with the decisions of these two countries so far not to join the euro zone, Denmark's same decision is clearly not vindicated by the above findings. Lithuania, Romania, and above all Bulgaria were far from any peg to the core currencies, to the Italian lira, or to the British pound. Italy and the UK had on average higher

Table 3.1   Nominal Exchange Rate Variation *(ERV)*, 1992–1998

France		Germany		Italy		UK	
Denmark	0.72	**Austria**	0.07	Malta	2.55	Malta	2.29
Belgium	0.72	**Netherlands**	0.10	Sweden	2.98	Slovakia	2.90
Netherlands	0.90	Estonia	0.18	UK	3.15	Cyprus	3.14
Germany	0.93	**Belgium**	0.85	**Greece**	3.16	**Italy**	3.15
Austria	0.94	**France**	0.93	**Spain**	3.17	**Greece**	3.47
Estonia	0.96	Denmark	1.06	Cyprus	3.19	**Ireland**	3.69
Cyprus	0.97	Cyprus	1.32	**Portugal**	3.29	**Spain**	3.69
Portugal	1.47	**Portugal**	2.06	Slovakia	3.43	**Finland**	3.76
Greece	1.94	**Greece**	2.17	Czech Rep.	3.44	Czech Rep.	3.78
Ireland	2.05	Czech Rep.	2.20	**Ireland**	3.53	**Portugal**	3.84
Malta	2.16	Malta	2.35	**France**	3.62	**France**	3.93
Spain	2.23	**Ireland**	2.45	**Finland**	3.80	Hungary	4.08
Czech Rep.	2.30	**Spain**	2.63	**Germany**	4.03	Sweden	4.11
Slovakia	2.37	Slovakia	2.82	**Belgium**	4.03	**Germany**	4.16
Hungary	2.91	Hungary	3.14	Denmark	4.04	**Austria**	4.18
Poland	3.53	Slovenia	3.56	**Austria**	4.05	**Netherlands**	4.18
Italy	3.62	**Finland**	3.69	**Netherlands**	4.05	Denmark	4.20
Finland	3.62	Poland	3.70	Estonia	4.28	**Belgium**	4.24
Slovenia	3.79	**Italy**	4.03	Hungary	4.36	Estonia	4.34
UK	3.93	UK	4.16	Poland	4.49	Poland	4.54
Sweden	4.00	Sweden	4.34	Slovenia	4.78	Slovenia	4.90
Latvia	7.07	Latvia	7.19	Latvia	7.43	Latvia	6.09
Romania	14.13	Romania	14.16	Lithuania	13.59	Lithuania	13.04
Lithuania	15.39	Lithuania	15.37	Romania	14.56	Romania	14.90
Bulgaria	30.86	Bulgaria	30.77	Bulgaria	31.85	Bulgaria	32.85
Average	4.37		4.43		5.57		5.67
Euro zone average	1.84		1.90		3.67		3.84
Non–euro zone average	6.34		6.42		7.21		7.51
ERV							
Average[a]	4.11		4.24		5.46		5.67
Euro zone average	1.84		1.90		3.67		3.84
Non–euro zone average[a]	6.17		6.37		7.09		7.68
RERV							
Average[a]	3.13		3.33		5.06		5.12
Euro zone average	1.88		2.06		4.09		4.22
Non–euro zone average[a]	4.27		4.48		5.94		5.93

Notes: ERV is the standard deviation of quarterly percent change in the bilateral nominal exchange rate during the sample period. RERV is the standard deviation of quarterly percent change in the bilateral real exchange rate during the sample period (see next section). Averages are simple and not weighted.

a. Excludes the three Baltic countries and Slovenia.

ERV values than France and Germany, especially with respect to the current euro zone member states.

A number of technical alternative methods exist for calculating a proxy for exchange rate variation. One alternative is to use higher or lower frequency data instead of quarterly data. The shortcoming of annual frequency data is a shortage in data during the sample period chosen in this book. Between 1992 and 1998, only seven annual observations occurred, and these do not provide a large enough base for calculating a reliable standard deviation.

In contrast, although useful for time series analysis by providing a wealth of data, higher frequency data (daily, weekly, or monthly exchange rate averages) are unnecessary for the cross-sectional dataset used in this book and furthermore have two disadvantages. The first and simple one is that such data are unavailable for the three Baltic countries and Slovenia. Thus, using these data would compromise the book's aspiration to presenting country coverage as wide as possible.

Another methodological problem is that high-frequency exchange rate data reflect much "noise," or short-term maneuvers in the foreign exchange market that may have little to do with the sustainability of EMU. Such factors could include day-trading and speculative trading in currencies, psychologically driven trade, and computerized trading. All of these maneuvers in the foreign exchange market do not represent fundamental economic and political factors, and they disappear once a currency union is formed.

In addition, short-term exchange rate variation might be misleading as a dependent variable from which an indicator of EMU's adjustment burden could be developed because of government manipulation. Foreign exchange reserves or interest rates can be used to cushion short-term exchange rate changes. One could try to adjust for such manipulation, but this is fraught with difficulties.

Adjusting for changes in foreign exchange reserves is especially difficult.[1] One reason for this is that changes in reserves contain transactions that are unrelated to government exchange rate policies. For a start, aid from international organizations to central and eastern European countries in the 1990s skewed changes in their reserves. In fact, all new EU member states except Cyprus and Malta got IMF money during the sample period. In addition, when capital is highly mobile, it is difficult for governments to manipulate exchange rates by buying and selling foreign exchange. Thus, in practice, changes in foreign exchange reserves might not, after all, reflect government policies.

Indeed, evidence suggests that most governments prefer interest rate adjustments over foreign exchange reserve adjustments as tools for exchange rate manipulation (Calvo and Reinhart, 2001). The use of interest rates to affect short-term exchange rates is, again, a reason not to use high-frequency data as an indication of EMU's adjustment burden. Admittedly, interest rates are also used to affect exchange rates in the medium and long term. Thus, this chapter later develops an alternative measure of the extent of adjustment that considers monetary policy.

Some scholars prefer to disregard actual exchange rates and instead analyze exchange rate policies, in line with the ex post approach mentioned in Chapter 2. These scholars often use a variant of a logit model, which estimates the likelihood of a decision to fix the exchange rate, given the fulfillment of a set of criteria. Most logit models are used to study Latin American countries (Edwards, 1996; Klein and Marion, 1997), but a few analyze developed countries, including some EU member states (Bernhard and Leblang, 1999; Hallerberg, 2002). The dependent variable in these studies is either binary (e.g., to fix or not to fix) or consists of a few categories of exchange rate regimes, from a free float to a complete peg (Frieden et al., 2001).

Besides the methodological inappropriateness of their ex post approach to this book, logit models have an additional disadvantage of being based on judgmental categorization of exchange rate arrangements. These arrangements convey less information about underlying economic determinants than actual exchange rate behavior (Bayoumi and Eichengreen, 1997; Calvo and Reinhart, 2001).

For example, when using a logit model, a country would be considered to be continuously on a peg even if parity realignment or short flotation intervals take place. Similarly, a country would be considered to be continuously observing fluctuation margins regardless of the extent of exchange rate variation within them. More generally, in the short term, a peg may disguise economic and political imbalances that are bound to destabilize the exchange rate at a later date.

Table 3.2 sorts the sample countries according to the variety of exchange rate policies that they adopted during the sample period, using the IMF's classification. Countries are listed alphabetically under each heading. The current euro zone member states are printed in bold type.

A simple comparison between exchange rate policies of different countries as presented in Table 3.2 and the actual variation of their exchange rates as presented in Table 3.1 is difficult because many countries changed their policies during the sample period. However, indices can be constructed to reflect the time spent by each country in applying each exchange rate policy, coding a maximum of 1 for countries that maintained the policy during the entire sample period to a minimum of 0 for those that did not maintain it at all. Equation (3.1) in Table 3.3 estimates the relationship between exchange rate policies and actual nominal exchange rate variation.

MARGINS, PEG, and BOARD are exchange rate policy indices for, respectively, fluctuation margins (mostly the ERM), conventional pegged arrangements (mostly new EU member states), and currency boards. Each is the bilateral average of national index values.[2] Equation (3.1) shows that all policies aiming to restrict exchange rate variation in 1990s Europe were indeed associated with lower exchange rate variation. However, a counter-

Table 3.2   Exchange Rate Policies, 1992–1998

Free or managed float	Fluctuation margins
Bulgaria until 7/97	**Austria** since 1/95 (ERM)
Czech Republic since 5/97	**Belgium** (ERM)
Finland between 9/92 and 10/96	Cyprus since 6/92 (to ECU)
Greece until 3/98	Czech Republic between 2/96 and 5/97 (to basket)
Italy between 9/92 and 11/96	Denmark (ERM)
Latvia between 7/92 and 2/94[a]	**Finland** since 10/96 (ERM)
Lithuania between 5/92 and 4/94[a]	**France** (ERM)
Romania	**Germany** (ERM)
Slovakia since 9/98	**Greece** since 3/98 (ERM)
Slovenia	**Ireland** (ERM)
Sweden since 11/92	**Italy** until 9/92 and since 11/96 (ERM)
UK since 9/92	**Netherlands** (ERM)
	Portugal (ERM)
Conventional pegged arrangements	Slovakia between 1/96 and 9/98 (to basket)
Austria until 12/94 (to ECU)	**Spain** (ERM)
Cyprus until 6/92 (to basket)	Sweden until 11/92 (to ECU)
Czech Republic between 1/93 and 2/96[a] (to basket)	UK until 9/92 (ERM)
Finland until 9/92 (to ECU)	
Hungary until 3/95 (to basket)	
Latvia since 2/94 (to SDR)	
Malta (to basket)	
Slovakia between 1/93 and 12/95[a] (to basket)	
	Currency boards
Crawling pegs and fluctuation margins	Bulgaria (to Germany) since 7/97
Hungary since 3/95 (to basket)	Estonia (to Germany) since 7/92[a]
Poland (to basket)	Lithuania (to United States) since 4/94

Notes: Entries apply for the entire sample period wherever dates (in month/year format) are not given. ECU is the European Currency Unit. ERM is the Exchange Rate Mechanism. SDR are Special Drawing Rights. Basket refers to baskets of currencies, other than the ECU or the SDR. Classification of policies is based on International Monetary Fund, *Annual Report on Exchange Arrangements and Exchange Restrictions.*
    a. No national currency in previous periods.

intuitive link emerges between the extent of formal restriction declared and the extent of actual exchange rate variation. Fluctuation margins were associated with a decline of 88 percent in nominal exchange rate variation, and conventional pegged arrangements were associated with a 78 percent decline. Currency boards, which represent the most restrictive obligation of the three, were associated with a mere 45 percent decline in exchange rate variation, and this effect is not very statistically significant.[3]

The effectiveness of currency boards in stabilizing currencies might be understated in Equation (3.1) because it averages the experience of only three countries, two of which spent part of the sample period in a float with significant exchange rate adjustments. Although the proxy for currency boards codes for this, it still singles out countries with an unstable history, which is reflected in their exchange rate variation. Nevertheless, Equation

Table 3.3   Exchange Rate Policies and Adjustment Indicators

Equation number:	(3.1)	(3.2)	(3.3)	(3.4) ln.	(3.5) ln.	(3.6) ln.
Dependent variable:	ln.*ERV*	ln.*RERV*	ln.*ERV*	*ADJUSTMENT*	*ADJUSTMENT*	*RADJUSTMENT*
CONSTANT	1.99***	−2.16***	−1.83***	−1.17***	−0.91***	−1.50***
	(0.13)	(0.09)	(0.14)	(0.09)	(0.13)	(0.14)
MARGINS (−)	−2.11***	−1.88***	−2.31***	−1.48***	−1.83***	−1.24***
	(0.18)	(0.12)	(0.19)	(0.12)	(0.15)	(0.21)
PEG (−)	−1.50***	−1.56***	−2.07***	−0.83***	−1.12***	−1.40***
	(0.23)	(0.17)	(0.25)	(0.17)	(0.23)	(0.31)
BOARD (−)	−0.61			0.87***		
	(0.51)			(0.22)		
Number of observations	325	231	231	325	231	231
R^2	0.33	0.53	0.43	0.42	0.38	0.15
Sum of squared residuals (SSR)	224	57.0	128	111	94.7	170
F-statistic	52.0***	128***	87.3***	78.0***	71.4***	20.5***

Notes: Equations are ordinary least squares equations. Column entries are parameter estimates, and standard error values are indicated in parentheses. Estimates are corrected with White heteroskedasticity-consistent standard errors and covariance. All equations return highly robust *F* tests. Variables underscored with a dotted line are calculated as bilateral averages of national values. The "ln" prefix denotes a logarithmic transformation of the variable (see Box 3.1) * $.05 < p \leq .10$. ** $.01 < p \leq .05$. *** $p \leq .01$. The signs in parentheses by the names of the instruments indicate their expected relationship with the dependent variables.

(3.1) supports the view that exchange rate policies, although generally related to actual exchange rate variation, are not an accurate indication of its extent.

A final technical concern is that dyadic exchange rate variation values do not represent independent observations, a critical condition for regression analysis, because, assuming efficient foreign exchange markets, any exchange rate is the product of two other exchange rates. For example, the French-British rate is the product of the French-German rate and the German-British rate. Thus, the information contained in the variation of one exchange rate can be extracted from the variation of two other exchange rates.

However, because the variation of a product is not a linear combination of the variations of its factors, dyadic observations of exchange rate variation are not linearly related to one another. This is especially true when variation is measured, as *ERV* is, over the percent change in exchange rates, rather than over exchange rate levels, and when regression analysis in Chapter 7 considers the logarithmic transformation of this variation (Bayoumi and Eichengreen, 1997, 764, footnote 7). Only when two currencies are perfectly fixed against each other would they have identical exchange rate variation against a third currency. The sample contains no

---

Box 3.1   Why Use Logarithmic Transformations in Regression Analysis?

Throughout this book, natural logarithmic transformations of variables are often used to estimate relationships among them because estimating relationships between variables that are measured with different units might result in meaningless coefficients. It is often much more useful to measure coefficients in terms of percent change. This not only makes coefficients more meaningful, it also allows comparisons among coefficients of different variables, whether in a single equation or across different equations. Measuring coefficients in percent change is possible when relationships are estimated between logarithmic transformations of variables rather than between the variables themselves.

When the dependent variable is measured in the logarithmic transformation of its absolute units, and the independent variable is measured in its absolute units, a rise of one unit in the independent variable multiplies the dependent variable by a factor equal to the exponential transformation (the opposite of the logarithmic transformation) of the estimated coefficient. For example, a coefficient of 0.5 for a natural logarithmic transformation of an independent variable implies a factor of 1.65, or a rise of 65 percent in the absolute value of the dependent variable as a result of a rise of one absolute unit in the independent variable. This method is referred to as a semi-logarithmic transformation, and is useful mostly when the independent variable ranges between 0 and 1.

When both the dependent and the independent variables are measured in the logarithmic transformation of their absolute units (a full logarithmic transformation), the estimated coefficient reflects the percent change in the dependent variable as a result of a 1 percent rise in the independent variable. For example, a coefficient of 0.5 implies a rise of 0.5 percent in the dependent variables in response to a 1 percent rise in the independent variable.

---

such currencies, so it is safe from a technical point of view to use it for regression analysis.[4]

Nominal exchange rate variation is a market development that reacts to economic shocks as well as to policy decisions (Bayoumi and Eichengreen, 1997). Certainly, its simplicity is its advantage as a dependent variable from which an indicator for EMU's adjustment burden could be developed. However, the extent to which nominal exchange rate variation can reliably reflect the magnitude of adjustment among countries depends on the responsiveness of other mechanisms of adjustment to economic and political shocks.

Indeed, it is often argued that among EU member states, prices and especially wages are "sticky" rather than flexible, and labor flows are small. Labor markets are heavily regulated in many countries, with state agencies, legislation, unionization, and collective bargaining constraining market activity. Such regulation causes wages to respond only partially to economic and political developments, often with a lag. Labor flows within each economy as well as between them are similarly inflexible (Gros, 1996).

Capital flows, although formally free and definitely more flexible than labor flows, are argued to be inhibited by the segmentation of European financial markets. The single European market in financial services is yet uncompleted. Banks still charge high commissions for cross-border transactions, stock exchanges are slow to consolidate on a continental basis, and foreign investment in local banks is sometimes blocked by the authorities.

Real Exchange Rate Variation

An alternative to ERV as a dependent variable from which an indicator of EMU's adjustment burden could be developed is the real exchange rate variation (RERV), which is calculated similarly but uses real rather than nominal exchange rate data (see Box 3.2). Unfortunately, real exchange rate data provided by the IMF and the EU are incomplete for the purposes of this book. The IMF's real effective exchange rate (REER) data are unavailable for the three Baltic countries and Slovenia, whereas Eurostat's REER41CPI series is available for all sample countries but not prior to 1994, when major exchange rate adjustments occurred.[5] The IMF data are preferred because it seems better to lose four sample countries than to draw conclusions based on only mid- and late-1990s data. Thus, wherever real exchange rate data are used, the sample consists of only 231 dyadic observations (henceforth, this sample is referred to as the restricted sample).

For the sake of brevity, individual RERV values are not detailed. Instead, Table 8.2 on page 144 provides some descriptive statistics, and the bottom rows in Table 3.1 compare RERV average values with ERV average values recalculated without the three Baltic countries and Slovenia. The bottom rows in Table 3.1 show that there was very little difference in the variation of nominal and real exchange rates between each of the four major EU member states, on the one hand, and other current euro zone member states, on the other hand. However, in dyads involving sample countries that are not euro zone member states, nominal exchange rate variation tended to significantly exceed real exchange rate variation.

Equation (3.2) in Table 3.3 shows that fluctuation margins and conventional pegged arrangements were associated with lower real exchange rate variation in 1990s Europe compared with other exchange rate policies.

Box 3.2   What Is the Real Exchange Rate?

Real exchange rates are calculated as an index of the nominal exchange rate of the currency, adjusted for price level changes in both countries, such that a rise in the index represents an appreciation of the currency. Thus, a rise in the amount of foreign currency traded against one unit of local currency (the nominal exchange rate), a rise in domestic prices of traded goods, or a decline in foreign prices all cause an appreciation of the real exchange rate. Opposite developments represent real exchange rate depreciation. The real exchange rate is a more precise measure of the terms of trade facing competing industries than is the nominal exchange rate.

Equation (3.3) is run for comparison on nominal exchange rate variation without the three Baltic countries and Slovenia. The index that codes for currency boards is dropped as well for this equation because in the restricted sample it relates only to Bulgaria and only for part of the sample period. The coefficients in the two equations are not identical but are relatively similar. Again, exponential transformations of coefficients show that conventional pegged arrangements were associated with an 87 percent decline in nominal exchange rate variation and a 79 percent decline in real exchange rate variation. The figures for fluctuation margins are 90 and 85 percent, respectively. This is evidence that price adjustment played a minor, although not negligible, role between countries that adopted these policies.

A simple explanation of the results presented in this section is that among most EU member states in the 1990s, the adjustment to economic and political developments tended to be carried out mostly through changes in nominal exchange rates rather than through changes in prices and labor costs, as suggested above. In contrast, many transition and Southern European economies experienced relatively higher inflation, which caused an appreciation of real exchange rates. The depreciating nominal exchange rates in those countries restored competitiveness to local industries. Thus, part of the variation in nominal exchange rates merely reflects adjustment for high inflation in southern and eastern European economies. The experience of European countries with price inflation in the 1990s is discussed more extensively in Chapter 4.

The comparison between nominal and real exchange rate variation in 1990s Europe suggests that perhaps nominal exchange rate variation is not inferior to real exchange rate variation as a dependent variable, as long as bilateral differences in price inflation are controlled for. Furthermore, nominal exchange rate variation has the advantage of drawing on a larger sample and better country coverage, which is one of the ways in which this book seeks to contribute to the literature on EMU.

However, even if market-driven adjustment mechanisms are not significantly at play among European countries, nominal exchange rate variation does not yet measure the full extent of adjustment taking place in response to economic and political shocks. In addition to the exchange rate policies detailed so far in this chapter, governments may also use fiscal and monetary tools as alternative adjustment mechanisms to exchange rate variation.

Considering Fiscal and Monetary Policies

The third proposed dependent variable from which an indicator for EMU's adjustment burden could be developed is *ADJUSTMENT*, a weighted average of exchange rate variation, variation in fiscal policies, and variation in monetary policies. *ERV* values are taken for exchange rate variation. For the variation in fiscal policies, however, annual bilateral differences in public balances are calculated, each balance measured as a percentage of gross domestic product (GDP). Then the standard deviation of these differences is calculated (henceforth called *FISCAL*). Data of annual public balances is taken from the IMF's *Government Finance Statistics Yearbook* and aggregates all levels of government.

Similarly, variation in monetary policies is measured as the standard deviation over the sample period of quarterly bilateral differences in real interest rates. Real interest rates are calculated as the difference between nominal interest rates on key short-term central bank policy tools and the rate of consumer price inflation.

A standard deviation is calculated for each of these three index components over its 325 dyadic values. For each dyadic observation, the value of each of these three index components is then divided by its standard deviation, and these three ratios are summed. *ADJUSTMENT* is the product of this sum and *ERV*'s standard deviation. This calculation makes *ERV* and *ADJUSTMENT* values comparable.[6] Thus, *ADJUSTMENT*, which is a broad index of adjustment, is the sum of the standardized values of its components, expressed in percent change of exchange rates.

ADJUSTMENT values range from a low of 2.60 percent in the Danish-French case to a high of 124.86 percent in the Bulgarian-Slovakian case (see Table 8.2 on page 144). Its mean and standard error values are, respectively, 22.03 and 23.80 percent. The average *ADJUSTMENT* value is three times as high as the average *ERV* value, reflecting the extent of adjustment taking place beyond exchange rate variation. Table 3.4 details *ADJUSTMENT* levels for all countries with regard to the four major EU economies, and sorts them accordingly. The current euro zone countries are printed in bold type.

Table 3.4 reveals that the rankings of the different countries against France and Germany according to their *ADJUSTMENT* levels are generally similar to their rankings according to *ERV* levels. Estonia was an exception, showing much higher bilateral variation when fiscal and monetary polices are considered than mere exchange rate variation suggests. This seems reasonable, given Estonia's special effort to maintain exchange rate stability against the German mark. Spain and the UK also change their ranking significantly against France and Germany from *ERV* to *ADJUSTMENT*, but in the other direction. In Spain and the UK, much of the bilateral variation against France and Germany in the 1990s was indeed in the form of exchange rate adjustment.

Changes in country rankings among dyads involving Italy or the UK

Table 3.4   Broad Adjustment Indicator Levels (*ADJUSTMENT*), 1992–1998

France		Germany		Italy		UK	
Denmark	2.6	**Netherlands**	3.4	**Ireland**	7.1	**Spain**	5.5
Austria	4.0	Denmark	4.0	**Spain**	7.2	**France**	6.6
Germany	4.1	**France**	4.1	UK	7.4	**Ireland**	7.1
Netherlands	4.2	**Belgium**	4.4	**Belgium**	8.2	**Greece**	7.3
Spain	4.8	**Austria**	4.4	**Austria**	8.3	**Italy**	7.4
Ireland	5.1	**Ireland**	5.4	Denmark	8.5	Denmark	7.5
Portugal	5.5	Czech Rep.	7.2	**Finland**	9.0	**Austria**	7.7
Belgium	5.7	**Portugal**	7.3	**France**	9.2	**Portugal**	7.9
Greece	6.3	Cyprus	7.6	**Portugal**	9.6	**Germany**	8.9
UK	6.6	Poland	7.8	**Germany**	9.8	**Belgium**	9.3
Czech Rep.	8.0	**Spain**	7.8	**Greece**	10.0	**Netherlands**	10.0
Cyprus	9.0	**Greece**	8.4	**Netherlands**	10.7	**Finland**	11.1
Italy	9.2	UK	8.9	Poland	12.7	Poland	12.1
Poland	9.3	**Italy**	9.8	Latvia	12.9	Latvia	13.0
Malta	11.8	Malta	10.0	Czech Rep.	13.1	Malta	13.1
Hungary	11.9	Slovakia	11.3	Hungary	13.5	Czech Rep.	13.1
Finland	12.2	Hungary	12.3	Sweden	13.8	Slovakia	13.4
Slovakia	12.9	**Finland**	12.9	Cyprus	14.0	Cyprus	13.6
Slovenia	14.0	Slovenia	13.2	Slovakia	14.5	Sweden	13.6
Latvia	14.4	Latvia	16.0	Malta	15.0	Hungary	14.0
Sweden	15.8	Sweden	17.8	Slovenia	19.0	Slovenia	17.9
Estonia	18.3	Estonia	18.2	Estonia	25.0	Estonia	22.2
Lithuania	33.7	Lithuania	33.4	Lithuania	29.1	Lithuania	28.3
Romania	38.8	Romania	36.2	Romania	38.8	Romania	40.0
Bulgaria	95.8	Bulgaria	94.3	Bulgaria	93.1	Bulgaria	95.1
Average	14.6		14.6		16.8		16.2
Euro zone average	6.1		6.8		8.9		8.1
Non–euro zone average	20.2		19.9		22.0		22.6

Notes: ADJUSTMENT is the sum of the standardized values of bilateral variations in exchange rates, fiscal, and monetary policies during the sample period, expressed as a percent change of exchange rates. Averages are simple and not weighted.

are more frequent than changes in country rankings among dyads involving France or Germany. Cyprus, Malta, and Slovakia experienced mild exchange rate adjustments against Italy and the UK compared with the full extent of bilateral variation suggested by *ADJUSTMENT*. In contrast, Austria, Belgium, Denmark, Latvia, and Poland experienced relatively great exchange rate variation against Italy and the UK compared with variation in fiscal and monetary policies.

No group of countries forms an obvious core in Table 3.4, but Finland and Italy seem as relatively distant from any such core as they appear according to exchange rate variation in Table 3.1. Euro zone member states were fiscally and monetarily more synchronized than nonmembers in the 1990s, and Lithuania, Romania, and Bulgaria appear again in Table 3.4 as outliers. Interestingly, the gap between Italy and the UK, on the one hand, and France and Germany, on the other, in terms of average *ADJUSTMENT* values is much smaller than in terms of average *ERV* values. In other words, France, Germany, and the small western European countries are more diverse and less symmetric in their bilateral relations than exchange rate variation suggests.

Equation (3.4) in Table 3.3 shows that the extent of adjustment in dyads involving countries that adopted fluctuation margins or conventional pegged arrangements was again lower than in dyads that did not involve these countries. The coefficients are robust but smaller than those for Equation (3.1). This can be interpreted to reflect the greater success of exchange rate policies in limiting exchange rate variation, rather than in limiting bilateral variation in fiscal and monetary policies. In fact, none of the equations in Table 3.3 suggests a particular direction of causality, so it may very well be that the above exchange rate policies were adopted by countries that ex ante had a lower need for adjustment between them.

Interestingly, currency boards are robustly associated with 139 percent greater adjustment when fiscal and monetary policies are considered. Although, again, this figure might overstate the true adjustment in countries under a currency board (see the discussion above regarding Equation (3.1), it is still far from the estimated negative effect on nominal exchange rate variation. This difference reflects on the extent of adjustment that was taking place through fiscal and monetary polices in 1990s Europe.

Equation (3.5) compares the relationship of *ADJUSTMENT* to exchange rate policies with the relationships of *ERV* and *RERV* to exchange rate policies, using the restricted sample. Coefficients remain robust but are smaller than in Equations (3.1) and (3.2), an expected result if fiscal and monetary policies are indeed used as channels of adjustment. Judging by the differences between the coefficients in Equations (3.3) and (3.5), these channels were much more actively used among countries adopting conventional pegged arrangements than among those adopting fluctuation margins (mostly ERM member states).

Compared with *ERV* and *RERV*, *ADJUSTMENT* has the advantage of covering a wider spectrum of adjustment mechanisms. As argued previously, exchange rate variation might be misleading as a measure of the bilateral adjustment if fiscal and monetary policies are pursued extensively. *ADJUSTMENT* also has some disadvantages, however. The first is that it is less centered than *ERV* and *RERV* on market developments as a subject of analysis, in accordance with this book's methodological choice. The fiscal and monetary stances as recorded here result in part from market activity. For example, enhanced economic activity automatically reduces a deficit, and higher inflation reduces the real interest rate. Thus, the fiscal and monetary stances may undershoot or overshoot their targets and do not amount to pure decision variables in the way that exchange rate policies do. They are, however, policy tools, and therefore part of *ADJUSTMENT* does measure policy choices.

Another problem concerns public balances data, one of *ADJUSTMENT*'s components. As mentioned in Chapter 2, some governments might have manipulated reports on public deficits in the last year of the sample period in order to fulfill the Maastricht fiscal criterion. On the technical side, annual fiscal data are used instead of quarterly data, which would have been better from a statistical point of view, as explained in the technical discussion on *ERV* at the beginning of this chapter. Unfortunately, quarterly fiscal data are unavailable. Finally, missing data relating to the early 1990s for some eastern European countries might be distorting *ADJUSTMENT*. Thus, *ADJUSTMENT* is not obviously better than *ERV* or *RERV* as an indicator of EMU's adjustment burden after all.

Because the book's subject of analysis is market development, neither of *ADJUSTMENT*'s fiscal and monetary components in itself can serve as a dependent variable. Nevertheless, correlation in fiscal policies among EU member states is a contentious issue and deserves further discussion. Table 3.5 details *FISCAL*, the nonstandardized fiscal component of *ADJUSTMENT*, for all countries with regard to the four major EU economies and sorts them accordingly. The current euro zone countries are printed in bold type. *FISCAL* values range from a low of 0.50 percent of GDP in the Austrian-Latvian case to a high of 28.10 percent in the Bulgarian-Slovakian case. Its mean and standard error values are, respectively, 4.53 and 3.98 percent (see Table 8.2 on page 144).

Euro zone member states show a slight tendency for greater synchronization of their fiscal positions compared with non–euro zone countries. Poland's shadowing of the German fiscal position might be overstated, given that its public debt data are missing the important pre-1994 adjustment years. Similar data problems apply to Latvia and Slovakia. In contrast, Sweden's fiscal positions were exceptionally unsynchronized with other western European economies. There is very little difference between the four major EU countries in terms of average *FISCAL* values. In other words,

Table 3.5   Bilateral Variation of Fiscal Policies (FISCAL), 1992–1998

France		Germany		Italy		UK	
Denmark	0.76	Poland	0.53	Latvia	0.73	**Spain**	0.57
UK	1.00	Denmark	1.07	**Ireland**	1.61	**France**	1.00
Spain	1.02	**Ireland**	1.13	**Spain**	1.74	**Greece**	1.15
Poland	1.21	**France**	1.27	**Belgium**	1.74	Denmark	1.22
Ireland	1.25	**Netherlands**	1.31	UK	1.80	**Portugal**	1.29
Germany	1.27	**Belgium**	1.51	Denmark	1.80	**Ireland**	1.38
Greece	1.27	Slovenia	1.58	**Austria**	1.84	Latvia	1.46
Austria	1.31	Czech Rep.	1.79	**Finland**	2.26	**Austria**	1.53
Portugal	1.44	**Portugal**	1.87	**France**	2.40	**Italy**	1.80
Netherlands	1.51	**Austria**	1.96	Poland	2.41	**Germany**	2.07
Latvia	1.62	UK	2.07	**Germany**	2.49	**Belgium**	2.21
Slovenia	1.81	**Spain**	2.26	**Greece**	2.50	Poland	2.26
Czech Rep.	2.18	Latvia	2.34	**Portugal**	2.54	**Netherlands**	2.49
Belgium	2.30	**Greece**	2.35	**Netherlands**	2.93	Slovenia	3.22
Italy	2.40	**Italy**	2.49	Hungary	3.70	**Finland**	3.29
Cyprus	3.19	Cyprus	2.57	Slovenia	3.75	Czech Rep.	3.94
Hungary	3.56	Slovakia	2.99	Czech Rep.	4.11	Slovakia	4.00
Slovakia	3.83	Malta	3.43	Slovakia	4.20	Hungary	4.09
Finland	3.91	Romania	3.64	Cyprus	4.63	Sweden	4.26
Malta	4.23	Hungary	3.79	Romania	4.70	Cyprus	4.56
Romania	4.88	**Finland**	4.26	Lithuania	4.88	Lithuania	4.76
Sweden	5.30	Estonia	5.99	Sweden	4.91	Malta	4.98
Estonia	5.62	Lithuania	6.07	Malta	5.66	Romania	5.11
Lithuania	6.16	Sweden	6.18	Estonia	7.32	Estonia	6.01
Bulgaria	16.24	Bulgaria	15.58	Bulgaria	14.47	Bulgaria	14.93
Average	3.17		3.20		3.64		3.34
Euro zone average	1.77		2.04		2.20		1.71
Non–euro zone average	4.11		3.98		4.60		4.63

Notes: FISCAL is the standard deviation of annual bilateral differences in public balances during the sample period, expressed in percent of GDP. Averages are simple and not weighted.

all four have a similar tendency to use the fiscal mechanism of adjustment. This finding contrasts with France and Germany's more stable profiles in Tables 3.1 and 3.4.

If member states are not to exceed public deficits of 3 percent, as required by the Maastricht Treaty and the SGP, and assuming that surpluses are rare and at best governments achieve a balance in their books, then bilateral differences in deficits should range between –3 and +3 percent. If these bilateral differences distribute normally around the midpoint of this range and exceed it only 4.6 percent of the time, then the standard deviation of bilateral differences in deficits (*FISCAL*) would be 1.5 percent in each dyad.[7] Thus, dyads with an implied *FISCAL* score that exceeds this threshold have a statistical tendency to breach their commitments under the SGP.

Table 3.5 seems to show a mixed picture. The performance of most of the dyads involving euro zone member states was compatible with the EU's restrictions on public deficits during the sample period. The exceptions, again, were Finland and Italy, with Belgium falling outside the 1.5 percent threshold against France, and Portugal, Austria, Greece, and Spain failing that threshold against Germany. However, the 1.5 percent threshold is a necessary but not a sufficient condition to indicate a statistical tendency for compliance with the rules of the SGP. In other words, it is clear that dyads with a higher score include at least one country with a statistical tendency to flout the rules, but dyads that satisfy that threshold may still be breaking the rules if they do so in tandem.

The fourth indicator proposed for EMU's burden of adjustment is RAD-JUSTMENT, an adjustment index that is calculated similarly to ADJUSTMENT but uses real exchange rate variation (RERV) instead of nominal exchange rate variation (ERV). RADJUSTMENT values range from a low of 0.32 percent of GDP in the Austrian-German case to a high of 68.45 percent in the Bulgarian-UK case. Its mean and standard error values are, respectively, 14.62 and 14.39 percent. Individual RADJUSTMENT values are not reported here for the sake of conciseness. This variable has the advantage of being the most comprehensive of all dependent variables suggested in this chapter in terms of the adjustment mechanisms it covers, but it also has many of the disadvantages of those variables discussed above.

Equation (3.6) in Table 3.3 estimates the relationship between the extent of adjustment and exchange rate policy choices, this time using RAD-JUSTMENT as an indicator of adjustment. Fluctuation margins return a smaller coefficient than in any of the other equations in the table, suggesting again some role for prices in effecting adjustment. However, the proxy for conventional pegged arrangements returns a larger coefficient in Equation (3.6) than in Equation (3.5), pointing to a tendency of changes in domestic prices to offset rather than compound adjustments in fiscal and monetary policies.

Actual and Potential Indicator Values

As stated throughout this chapter, none of the four dependent variables suggested as a basis for developing EMU's adjustment burden indicator is perfect. One shortcoming is that none of them considers labor and capital flows. The reason for this is that data on capital flows are problematic because they introduce much "noise," as discussed earlier in this chapter. In other words, many of the financial transactions represent short-term asset portfolio adjustments rather than real investments.

In addition, reliable data on bilateral labor flows among all sample countries is unavailable. Even available data, mostly among the major western European countries, understates the true level of immigration due to the large scale of illegal immigration to Europe, estimated in the hundreds of thousands annually. Most of the illegal immigrants originate outside of Europe, and thus may not seem to be relevant to the purpose of this book. However, the engagement of these immigrants in the economies of EU member states and their migration among them (or their substitution for native workers that migrate) makes them a potentially important factor in measuring the extent of adjustment to asymmetric shocks.

The following three chapters discuss the independent variables that explain the dependent variables suggested in this chapter.

Notes

1. For example, Bayoumi and Eichengreen's (1998) attempt to adjust exchange rate variation for changes in foreign exchange reserves yields results with low significance.

2. In the cases of Bulgaria-Germany and Estonia-Germany, the dyadic score of BOARD is 0.5 higher to distinguish it from other dyads involving Bulgaria and Estonia. For example, the Estonian-German dyad scores 1, rather than 0.5, which is the average of 1 for Estonia and 0 for Germany.

3. These numbers are derived as exponential transformations of the coefficients shown in Table 3.3 for Equation 3.1. For example, in the case of MARGINS the exponential transformation of –2.11 is 0.12, which reflects a 0.88 (88 percent) drop in ERV ($1 - 0.12 = 0.88$).

4. See also the discussion in the previous chapter on the usefulness of dyadic observations.

5. Eurostat's data is available online at http://epp.eurostat.cec.int.

6. This index is inspired by foreign exchange market pressure indices developed Eichengreen et al. (1995) and Leblang (2003, 545).

7. In a normal distribution, only 4.55 percent of observations fall beyond two standard deviations on either side of the mean.

4

The Economic Costs of EMU

As Mundell (1961) has argued and as explained in Chapter 2, country pairs with diverse macroeconomic conditions are pressured into an adjustment between each of them through any of a number of mechanisms. This chapter focuses on economic determinants of the extent of adjustment to membership in the euro zone. It develops proxies for measuring these determinants, describes their patterns among the twenty-six sample countries during 1992–1998, and presents the book's hypotheses about their relationships with the extent of adjustment. The three adjustment determinants analyzed in this chapter are business cycle correlation, economic openness, and inflation rate disparities. With the exception of the latter, the theoretical arguments behind these variables draw on the theory of optimum currency areas.

This chapter also discusses models for explaining the determinants of adjustment with idiosyncratic and institutional instruments. To avoid confusion with the main hypotheses of the book, theoretical arguments about instruments are referred to as expected relationships rather than hypothesized ones.

Business Cycle Correlation and Trade

The first economic determinant of adjustment to be studied is business cycle correlation. As explained in Chapter 2, the less correlated the business cycles are between countries, the greater the need to resort to adjustment between them. In the absence of a currency union, when one country is in recession and another is in a boom, some combination of exchange rate and price adjustment, factor flows, and fiscal and monetary policy variation would occur between them.

> **Hypothesis 1:** *The less correlated the business cycle is between European partners, the greater the adjustment between them.*

CYC is a measure of business cycle correlation between any two countries. It is the standard deviation of the difference in their detrended quarterly industrial growth rates during the sample period. Either GDP or employment growth rates are used for countries with unavailable quarterly industrial production data. The Hodrick-Prescott filter is used for detrending of data for long-term technological and demographic processes. Thus, *CYC* measures only the cyclical component of bilateral macroeconomic variation. Because high values of *CYC* represent low business cycle correlation, it is hypothesized to be positively associated with the four measures of the extent of bilateral adjustment developed in Chapter 3.

CYC values range from a low of 1.07 percent in the French-German case to a high of 25.49 percent in the Austrian-Bulgarian case (see Table 8.2 on page 144). Its mean and standard error values are, respectively, 6.01 and 3.46 percent. Table 4.1 details *CYC* values for all countries with regard to the four major EU economies and sorts them accordingly. The current euro zone member states are printed in bold type.

Table 4.1 reveals that for business cycle correlation, Finland, France, Germany, and Spain formed a core in 1990s Europe. Greece's relatively high correlation with France, Germany, and the UK, and Austria's and Belgium's relatively low correlation with the four major economies are less expected. Not surprisingly, the business cycles in the transition economies tended to be less correlated with those in the four major economies than were cycles in the other sample countries. Slovenia performed better than the other transition economies in this respect, and Bulgaria, Lithuania, and Poland performed the worst.

Another interesting finding is that the business cycles in the five non-transition non-euro economies were more correlated with cycles in the four major economies than were cycles in the current euro zone member states. Among the four majors, Italy's business cycle was a bit less correlated on average with the other sample countries, but none of the four had a significant advantage over the other as a potential anchor for the euro zone. Thus, the pattern of business cycle correlation seems to be only partly compatible with the evidence on adjustment levels reported in Chapter 3. A more decisive judgment on this is delivered in Chapter 7.

What causes business cycles to diverge among economies? One important factor, according to the classic optimum currency area theory, is the degree of specialization in their output (Tavlas, 1993). The more specialized production is, the more exposed the economy is to global variations in prices. In the extreme situation, production is concentrated in one sector. A rise in the global price of that good lifts the country's GDP, and a slump in global markets for that good causes a recession. This is the experience, for example, of oil countries or agricultural countries that specialize in a certain crop. In contrast, countries with diversified economies (as is the case for

Table 4.1   Business Cycle Correlation *(cyc)*

France		Germany		Italy		UK	
Germany	1.1	**France**	1.1	Malta	1.9	Malta	1.6
Spain	1.6	**Spain**	1.2	Netherlands	2.1	Netherlands	1.7
Finland	1.6	**Finland**	1.7	UK	2.1	France	2.0
Greece	2.0	Sweden	1.8	**Germany**	2.2	**Italy**	2.1
Netherlands	2.0	Denmark	1.9	**Spain**	2.2	**Finland**	2.2
UK	2.0	**Netherlands**	2.1	France	2.4	**Greece**	2.2
Sweden	2.1	**Greece**	2.1	Sweden	2.5	**Germany**	2.2
Denmark	2.3	**Italy**	2.2	Denmark	2.5	Sweden	2.4
Italy	2.4	UK	2.2	**Finland**	2.6	Denmark	2.5
Portugal	2.7	Malta	2.6	**Greece**	2.7	**Spain**	2.6
Malta	2.7	**Portugal**	3.1	**Portugal**	3.4	**Portugal**	3.3
Austria	3.3	**Austria**	3.3	**Ireland**	3.8	Slovenia	3.7
Slovenia	3.6	Slovenia	3.6	Slovakia	3.9	Slovakia	4.0
Ireland	3.8	**Ireland**	3.7	Slovenia	4.0	**Austria**	4.2
Cyprus	4.0	Cyprus	3.9	**Austria**	4.2	**Belgium**	4.2
Belgium	4.2	**Belgium**	4.2	**Belgium**	4.3	**Ireland**	4.6
Latvia	4.5	Latvia	4.3	Cyprus	4.4	Cyprus	4.6
Slovakia	4.5	Slovakia	4.3	Latvia	5.3	Latvia	5.8
Hungary	5.5	Hungary	5.6	Czech Rep.	5.6	Hungary	5.8
Estonia	5.9	Czech Rep.	5.8	Hungary	5.9	Czech Rep.	6.0
Czech Rep.	6.0	Estonia	6.1	Romania	6.0	Estonia	6.1
Romania	7.0	Romania	6.6	Estonia	6.6	Romania	6.2
Bulgaria	10.3	Bulgaria	10.4	Bulgaria	11.1	Bulgaria	10.9
Lithuania	10.4	Lithuania	10.4	Lithuania	11.3	Lithuania	11.1
Poland	12.2	Poland	12.7	Poland	12.1	Poland	11.2
Average	4.3		4.3		4.6		4.5
Euro zone average	2.5		2.5		3.0		2.9
Transition economies	7.7		7.7		8.0		7.9
Other five sample economies	1.2		1.0		1.1		0.8

Note: Entries represent the standard deviation of the difference in detrended quarterly industrial production growth rates in each dyad. Entries' units are percentage points of growth rate.

most European countries) that do not rely for their income on the production of a specific good enjoy lower volatilities in their incomes. Such countries tend to experience greater business cycle correlations among them.

Industrial concentration can be measured with an index that calculates for each sample country the sum of squares of the shares of its industrial branches in total industrial output. This index ranges potentially between a maximum of 1 (when all production is concentrated in one branch) and a minimum equal to the inverted number of branches (when production is evenly distributed among the branches). Calculations are based on 1995 data (or later data, if 1995 data are unavailable) from the UN *International Yearbook of Industrial Statistics*, aggregated into twenty-three branches (thus, the minimum value is 1/23 = 0.043). Among the sample countries, Malta had the highest score (0.246) in 1995, Italy had the lowest (0.067), and the mean and standard deviation were, respectively, 0.113 and 0.047. Transition economies and the current euro zone member states did not differ much in terms of industrial concentration, with an average of 0.117 and 0.104, respectively. Thus, superficially, industrial concentration does not seem to explain business cycle correlation patterns in 1990s Europe.

Another important factor that should affect business cycle correlation is the similarity in specialization of output between the two countries. The closer the distribution of output across sectors in the two economies, the more symmetrically would global shocks affect them. In the extreme case that both countries feature an identical bundle of production, changing global supply and demand need not cause adjustment between them. If the members are similarly structured, they would be evenly affected by a given shock.

Industrial similarity can be measured with the Finger-Kreinin index, which, in each dyad and for each of the twenty-three industrial branches, selects the lower of the two national shares and then sums these minimum shares. This industrial similarity index (*INDSIM*) potentially scores a maximum of 1 for complete similarity and 0 for complete dissimilarity. *INDSIM* ranges in the sample from a low of 0.25 in the Belgian-Maltese case to a high of 0.88 in the Austro-Czech case (see Table 8.2 on page 144). Its mean and standard error values are 0.64 and 0.12, respectively.

Table 4.2 shows *INDSIM* values between each country and each of the four major EU economies. Compared with Germany, Italy, and the UK, France had, on average, lower industrial similarity with the sample countries. Surprisingly, according to Table 4.2, the current euro zone member states and the transition economies did not differ much in terms of their industrial similarity to the four major economies. On average, the other five sample (nontransition, non–euro zone) economies were less similar to the four major economies than were the current euro zone member states. Thus, industrial similarity may not provide a good explanation for business cycle correlation.

Equation (4.1) in Table 4.3 summarizes the discussion so far by estimating the relationship between *CYC* and its potential determinants. Industrial concentration returns a positive coefficient, as expected. According to Equation (4.1), a rise of 1 percent (not a percentage point) in the average level of industrial concentration between the partner countries was associated in the 1990s with a corresponding deterioration of 0.76 percent in business cycle correlation. However, industrial similarity returns a positive coefficient too, in contrast to the expected relationship discussed above.

Two main concerns exist regarding the usefulness of the industrial concentration and similarity indices in explaining business cycle correlation. One is their sensitivity to the level of industrial aggregation used, which is arbitrary. Generally, the more specific the level of aggregation becomes, the lower industrial concentration and similarity tend to be. Another, more seri-

Table 4.2   Industrial Similarity Index *(INDSIM)*, **1992–1998**

France		Germany		Italy		UK	
Germany	0.81	UK	0.85	Germany	0.83	Germany	0.85
UK	0.80	Italy	0.83	Poland	0.82	Spain	0.83
Spain	0.75	France	0.81	UK	0.81	Hungary	0.82
Italy	0.74	Spain	0.81	Hungary	0.81	Italy	0.81
Hungary	0.73	Czech Rep.	0.79	Romania	0.79	Poland	0.81
Sweden	0.70	Hungary	0.78	Portugal	0.79	France	0.80
Slovenia	0.70	Sweden	0.78	Slovakia	0.79	Austria	0.78
Austria	0.69	Austria	0.75	Spain	0.79	Slovakia	0.77
Poland	0.68	Poland	0.75	Austria	0.78	Czech Rep.	0.77
Czech Rep.	0.68	Denmark	0.75	Czech Rep.	0.77	Denmark	0.77
Slovakia	0.68	Slovenia	0.73	Greece	0.76	Portugal	0.75
Portugal	0.63	Slovakia	0.72	Bulgaria	0.76	Sweden	0.74
Bulgaria	0.63	Bulgaria	0.68	Denmark	0.74	Bulgaria	0.73
Romania	0.63	Portugal	0.68	France	0.74	Romania	0.72
Denmark	0.61	Romania	0.68	Slovenia	0.71	Netherlands	0.70
Finland	0.59	Finland	0.66	Sweden	0.70	Slovenia	0.70
Greece	0.59	Greece	0.64	Finland	0.68	Greece	0.70
Netherlands	0.59	Netherlands	0.64	Lithuania	0.65	Finland	0.69
Ireland	0.52	Cyprus	0.55	Estonia	0.63	Ireland	0.64
Belgium	0.51	Ireland	0.54	Netherlands	0.61	Estonia	0.60
Lithuania	0.49	Estonia	0.54	Cyprus	0.60	Cyprus	0.60
Estonia	0.47	Lithuania	0.53	Latvia	0.55	Lithuania	0.59
Cyprus	0.47	Malta	0.48	Ireland	0.52	Latvia	0.55
Latvia	0.42	Latvia	0.47	Malta	0.49	Malta	0.47
Malta	0.36	Belgium	0.45	Belgium	0.45	Belgium	0.46
Average	0.62		0.67		0.70		0.71
Euro zone average	0.64		0.68		0.70		0.73
Transition economies	0.65		0.70		0.76		0.74
Other 5 sample economies	0.51		0.62		0.60		0.56

Note: Entries represent an index of bilateral similarity in industrial output composition based on a twenty-three-branch breakdown.

ous concern is the simultaneity of industrial concentration and similarity with other variables. In other words, the relative size of various sectors in the economy is not an idiosyncratic feature of a country, but rather a dynamic variable that responds to developments in exchange rates, prices, government policies, labor flows, and other factors.

In particular, industrial concentration and similarity may be responding to trade patterns. According to the endogenous optimum currency area theory, business cycles tend to become more correlated if enough intra-industry trade (i.e., trade motivated by economics of scale) develops between the partners as a result of their currency union (Artis and Zhang, 1995; Frankel and Rose, 1998). However, if intra-European trade is mostly inter-industry trade (i.e., traditional specialization-based trade), the member states would become more specialized in their production as a result of a currency union

Table 4.3   Ordinary Least Squares Equations of Business Cycle Correlation *(cyc)*

Equation number:	(4.1)	(4.2)
CONSTANT	−0.88**	−2.80***
	(0.36)	(0.06)
ln.*INDCONC* (+)	0.76***	
	(0.14)	
ln.*INDSIM* (−)	0.88***	
	(0.18)	
fit.ln.*TRADE* (+/−)		0.13***
		(0.04)
fit.ln.*TRADE/TRANSPOSE* (−)		−0.39***
		(0.04)
Number of observations	325	325
Sum of Squared Residuals (SSR)	97.8	64.5
R^2	0.07	0.39
t-statistic for sum of coefficients of fit.ln.*TRADE* and fit.ln. *TRADE/TRANSPOSE*		367***
F-statistic	12.4***	102***

Notes: Estimates are corrected with White heteroskedasticity-consistent standard errors and covariance. Standard error values are indicated in parentheses. ** $.01 < p \leq .05$. *** $p \leq .01$. The signs by the names of the independent variables indicate their expected relationship with the dependent variable. Variables underscored with a dotted line are calculated as bilateral averages of national values.

among them. This would both raise their industrial concentration levels and cause them to be less similar in the composition of their outputs. Thus, business cycles would become less correlated (De Grauwe and Aksoy, 1999; Krugman, 1991).

Table 4.4 presents bilateral trade ratios (henceforth *TRADE*). These are averages of national ratios of bilateral trade volume (exports plus imports) to GDP, the ratios being expressed in percentage points. Bilateral trade volumes and GDPs (both in current US dollars) are averages of annual data during the sample period (Sadeh, 2005).

TRADE values reached highs of 18–20 percent in obvious cases, such as Italian-Maltese, Czech-Slovak, Estonian-Finnish, and Irish-British trade, but in most cases were lower than 1 percent. Table 4.4 reveals that as far as trade patterns are concerned, there was again no obvious core in 1990s Europe. Different countries concentrated their trade on different major economies. However, the four bottom rows of the table show that Germany was the greatest trader among the major economies, with an average *TRADE* value of 7.5 percent. German trade was, on average, more important to the trading partners when conducted with transition economies than when conducted with euro zone member states (Sadeh, 2005). However, the opposite is true when it comes to French, Italian, and UK trade. Thus, it is unclear

Table 4.4 Bilateral Trade Ratios *(TRADE)*, 1992–1998

France		Germany		Italy		UK	
Belgium	12.0	Czech Rep.	14.4	Malta	22.0	**Ireland**	17.9
Malta	8.4	**Belgium**	13.9	Slovenia	8.4	Malta	8.0
Germany	5.7	**Netherlands**	12.9	**Germany**	5.1	**Belgium**	6.2
Netherlands	5.1	Slovenia	12.7	**France**	4.2	**Netherlands**	5.9
Spain	4.7	**Austria**	12.2	Romania	3.8	**Germany**	4.4
Italy	4.2	Slovakia	11.7	**Belgium**	3.6	**France**	3.7
Slovenia	4.2	Hungary	11.4	Bulgaria	3.4	Cyprus	3.6
Ireland	4.1	Poland	8.6	Slovakia	2.9	Sweden	3.3
Portugal	3.7	Malta	8.3	Hungary	2.9	**Finland**	2.7
UK	3.7	Lithuania	7.6	**Netherlands**	2.9	Latvia	2.6
Sweden	1.8	Latvia	6.5	**Austria**	2.7	**Portugal**	2.5
Denmark	1.6	**Ireland**	6.3	**Greece**	2.7	Denmark	2.4
Romania	1.5	Denmark	6.0	**Spain**	2.6	**Italy**	2.2
Czech Rep.	1.5	**France**	5.7	Cyprus	2.3	**Spain**	2.2
Bulgaria	1.5	Bulgaria	5.2	UK	2.2	Lithuania	1.8
Hungary	1.5	**Italy**	5.1	**Portugal**	2.1	Estonia	1.7
Austria	1.4	Estonia	5.1	Poland	2.1	Czech Rep.	1.4
Slovakia	1.4	Sweden	4.8	Czech Rep.	2.1	Poland	1.3
Poland	1.4	**Portugal**	4.7	**Ireland**	1.9	Bulgaria	1.2
Finland	1.3	Romania	4.4	Lithuania	1.4	Hungary	1.2
Greece	1.3	UK	4.4	Sweden	1.2	Slovenia	1.1
Lithuania	1.2	**Finland**	3.9	Denmark	1.2	**Greece**	1.0
Cyprus	1.2	**Spain**	3.4	Estonia	1.0	**Austria**	1.0
Latvia	0.8	Cyprus	3.2	**Finland**	1.0	Romania	0.8
Estonia	0.7	**Greece**	2.8	Latvia	1.0	Slovakia	0.7
Average	3.1		7.5		3.5		3.2
Euro zone average	4.4		7.1		2.9		4.5
Transition economies	1.0		9.6		1.2		0.5
Other five sample countries	4.6		4.1		9.5		6.5

Note: For each dyad, the trade ratio is calculated as the simple average of their ratios of bilateral trade volume (exports plus imports) to GDP, the ratios being expressed in percentage points.

from Table 4.4 whether trade can provide a better explanation of business cycle correlation than can industrial concentration and similarity.

Because *TRADE* is a simultaneous variable, it, too, cannot serve as an instrument for business cycle correlation. However, idiosyncratic determinants of *TRADE* could serve as indirect instruments for *CYC*. The most simple and common model used in economics literature for estimating trade is the Gravity Equation, in which distance, income, and population are the independent variables. Its main advantage, from this book's point of view, is its use of idiosyncratic exogenous variables to explain bilateral trade. In its classic form, this equation explains trade flows in dollar or volume terms (Frankel, 1997; Frankel and Rose, 2002). However, trade is relevant as an explanatory variable of business cycle correlation only as a proportion to GDP. Equation (4.3) is a variant of the gravity equation that drops irrelevant independent variables, such as GDP (here in the denominator of the dependent variable), population (which is often associated with trade flows, but not trade ratios), and per capita income (a potentially simultaneous variable). The equation is corrected with White heteroskedasticity-consistent standard errors and covariance and shows standard errors in parentheses. The "ln" prefix denotes a logarithmic transformation of the variable. Statistics related to Equation (4.3) are indicated below the equation.

(4.3) $\ln.TRADE$ $= 10.9 - 1.29 \times \ln.DISTANCE + 0.73 \times LANGUAGE$
                          (0.73) (0.10)   (0.37)

$+ 1.28 \times FREETRADE + 0.18 \times ADJACENCY$
(0.12)   (0.22)

$- 0.98 \times LANDLOCKED$
(0.23)

$R^2 = 0.51$; 325 dyadic observations; Sum of Squared Residuals = 345; F-statistic = 67.0; $p = 0.0500$ for coefficient of $LANGUAGE$; $p = 0.3948$ for coefficient of $ADJACENCY$; $p < 0.0001$ for all other estimated coefficients.

In Equation (4.3), $DISTANCE$ is the distance between the capitals of the two states. As a natural trade barrier, it is expected to have a negative coefficient. The bilateral trade ratio is estimated to have decreased by 1.29 percent for every 1 percent increase in the distance between the partners. $LANGUAGE$ is an index of the similarity of mother-tongue spoken languages between the two countries, with a maximum value of 1 representing perfect similarity (only the same language is spoken in both countries), and a minimum value of 0 for total dissimilarity (no one in either of the countries is a native speaker of any of the languages spoken in the other). Specifically, for each pair of countries, the number of people speaking each language in one country is multiplied by the number of people speaking it in the other country. The sum of these products is divided by the product of the two countries' populations. Thus, $LANGUAGE$ is the chance that two randomly selected people, one from each country, would speak the same language. Linguistic composition data are based on Gordon (2005).

$LANGUAGE$ ranges in the sample from a low of 0 in fifty-one dyads to a high of 0.88 in the Ireland-UK case (see Table 8.2 on page 144). EU member states had a slight advantage in language similarity over the transition economies, with $LANGUAGE$ averaging 0.06 among dyads of EU countries, and 0.04 among dyads involving only transition economies. Its mean and standard error values are 0.02 and 0.10, respectively. Languages are another trade barrier, so $LANGUAGE$ is expected to be positively associated with trade. $LANGUAGE$'s coefficient means that bilateral trade was greater in

1990s Europe relative to GDP by a factor of 2.1 between countries with perfect language similarity, compared with countries with absolutely no similarity.

FREETRADE is a proxy for the complex system of trade agreements in 1990s Europe that were notified to the World Trade Organization (WTO) and that are considered as free trade areas within the meaning of Article XXIV of the General Agreement on Tariffs and Trade (GATT). Some of these agreements were already fully implemented in 1992, whereas others were not completed until after 1998 (a free trade area is defined here as fully implemented once its transition period for removing tariffs is over). At the center of the system stood the EU's customs union, which had been fully implemented since the late 1960s. Austria, Finland, and Sweden, which joined the EU in 1995, had fully implemented their free trade areas with the EU during the 1980s. In contrast, Portugal and Spain did not complete their transition periods following their accession to the EU until the end of 1993.

The main free trade agreements still in their transition periods in 1990s Europe were the Europe agreements between the EU and each of the ten transition economies in the sample. The first Europe agreements to enter into force (March 1992) were with Czechoslovakia, Hungary, and Poland. These were referred to as the Visegrad countries after their joint declaration in February 1991 in that Hungarian town. The last Europe agreement to enter into force (January 1997) was with Slovenia. The transition periods of these agreements ended between January 1999 and the accession of May 2004. Generally, the larger the country the longer the transition period. Estonia was the only country to have no transition period in its Europe agreement.

In addition, during the sample period, the EU had customs unions in their transition periods with Cyprus and Malta. Cyprus's agreement first came into force in 1973. However, military conflict delayed the implementation of this agreement, which did not start in practice until 1988. The transition period was to end by 2002, but duties on trade were abolished and the EU's common customs tariff was adopted by 1998. Malta's agreement first came into force in 1971, but Malta did not seriously eliminate duties on EC goods until October 1999. By January 2003, a free trade area was fully operational between Malta and the EU, but the customs union was not completed until Malta became an EU member state in 2004.

A number of free trade area agreements were signed among non-EU member states during the 1990s. The one with the widest membership—the Central European Free Trade Agreement (CEFTA)—eventually included all transition economies in the sample except the Baltic countries. It was established in December 1992 by the Visegrad countries. Bulgaria was the last country to join it, in January 1999. The Czech Republic and Slovakia, both member states of CEFTA, maintained a customs union between them ever since Czechoslovakia was split in 1993. The Baltic three—Estonia, Latvia, and Lithuania—established the Baltic Free Trade Agreement (BAFTA), which came into immediate and full effect in April 1994. Other bilateral free trade agreements involved a Baltic country on the one side and some CEFTA country on the other.

FREETRADE is an index scoring 1 for the 58 pairs of countries between which one of the above free trade areas was fully implemented during 1992–1994, 0 for the 158 dyads with no free trade area at all, and a value between 0 and 1 for partially implemented free trade areas. Partial scores are derived assuming a linear rate of tariff reductions from the date of entry into force of the agreement to the end of the transition period. The coding does not distinguish between free trade areas and customs unions. For each dyad, *FREETRADE* is the average of the scores of each of the three years.

The focus on the first three sample years is intended to avoid measuring a possibly simultaneous relationship between trade agreements and trade. Obviously, the gains from an agreement that removes trade barriers are higher the more extensive existing trade is. Thus, existing trade between countries can motivate as well as be the result of free trade agreements. In Europe, trade agreements are embedded in a comprehensive political order, a political vision, and geostrategic considerations. Whatever the EU represents to its member states, most of its member states and citizens would probably agree that it is more than just a trade organization. Thus, it can be forcefully argued that existing intra-European trade is a result of the EU's trade agreement much more than its motive.

To be on the safe side, and to reduce the possibility for simultaneity between *FREETRADE* and *TRADE*, the former is calculated over the 1992–1994 subperiod, whereas the latter is calculated over the entire sample period. It would seem difficult to argue that trade in later years caused agreements that preceded it. *FREETRADE*'s coefficient in Equation (4.3) means that a free trade area expanded bilateral trade relative to GDP by a factor of roughly 3.6 when fully implemented. This factor increases to 4.9 when Equation (4.3) is run with a *FREETRADE* variable that is calculated over the entire sample period.

ADJACENCY is a dummy variable coding 1 for dyads of adjacent countries, and 0 otherwise. *ADJACENCY*'s coefficient means that bilateral trade is greater relative to GDP by a factor of roughly 1.2 (i.e., 20 percent higher) between adjacent countries. The rationale behind this effect is that adjacent countries enjoy border trade, which is motivated by proximity of individual partners.

LANDLOCKED is another dummy variable coding 1 for dyads of two land-locked countries, 0.5 for dyads with only one landlocked country, and 0 otherwise. There are four landlocked countries in the sample (Austria, Czech Republic, Hungary, and Slovakia). When exponentially transformed *LAND-LOCKED*'s coefficient means that relative to GDP, trade between two landlocked countries was only a bit more than a third of trade between two non-landlocked countries. The rationale here is that although goods can be shipped by trucks and aircraft, the cheapest transportation method remains the seaborne one. Thus, lack of access to the sea is akin to a trade barrier.

Because trade can enhance or impede business cycle correlation, it is important to find a variable that explains the type of trade that develops—whether it is intra- or inter-industry trade. One such variable could be the extent of integration with the EU's internal market. EU member states share a customs union. However, the internal market goes much beyond this customs union in integrating the member states' economies. Ever since the reforms initiated by the Single European Act in the late 1980s, EU member states have adopted common legislation on almost any issue that affects the flow of goods, services, labor, and capital (the Four Freedoms) among them. From consumer protection, to common standards, environment, public procurement, and corporate law, the internal market forges an increasingly unified economy, in which economies of scale can be reaped. Thus, it is expected that business cycle correlation is greater among integrated members of the EU's internal market.

The main vehicle to advance the internal market is EU legislation. Most internal market laws take the form of either regulations or directives. Regulations automatically supersede national laws, but directives require national legislation to become effective in each member state, and the member states' progress in this matter differs. Thus, the rate of transposition of internal market directives into national legislation (the ratio between directives transposed in a given country and total number of relevant directives) is a proxy for the extent of EU member states' progress in integrating with the internal market. The number of outstanding directives to be transposed increases with time as the EU's Commission succeeds in pushing more legislation through the Council of Ministers. Thus, the rate of transposition fluctuates, rising in the wake of major transposition drives in the member states or declining when they are behind schedule.

TRANSPOSE is the bilateral average of the national rates of transposition of the EU's internal market directives. More specifically, it considers measures transposed, nonapplicable, or derogated in each member state's case as of 1995 as reported by the Commission in its *Single Market Scoreboard*. (See the list of databases presented at the beginning of the bibliography for references to datasets throughout the book). Nonmember states as of mid-1995 are assumed to have transposed no directives. This assumption might not be accurate because some of the nonmembers were starting to align their political economies with EU legislation ahead of their accession negotiations. However, there is no available information on progress achieved by 1995, and any such progress was probably not very advanced. The highest transposition rate was achieved by Denmark (0.953), and the lowest among EU member states was by Austria (0.869).

Equation (4.2) in Table 4.3 estimates the relationship between business cycle correlation and fitted values of bilateral trade: fit.ln.*TRADE* is the fitted value of ln.*TRADE* based on Equation (4.3), and fit.ln.*TRADE/TRANSPOSE* is the product of this fitted value and *TRANSPOSE*. The positive coefficient of fit.ln.*TRADE* confirms that trade tended to reduce business cycle correlation for nonmembers of the internal market, presumably as a result of being specialization-based. The negative coefficient of fit.ln.*TRADE/TRANSPOSE* means that membership in the internal market was associated with a tendency of trade for greater cycle correlation. According to Equation (4.2), at the margin a 1 percent increase in the bilateral trade ratio between two perfectly transposing EU member states was associated with a 0.261 (= 0.381 – 0.120) percent improvement in business cycle correlation. The break-even point between the two trends is at a *TRANSPOSE* value of 0.315 (= 0.120/0.381).

However, the difficulty with using the rate of transposition of internal market directives as an instrument for business cycle correlation is that it may very well be endogenous to other instruments and variables. In other words, countries may respond to the extent of trade and the type of trade that develops among them by being more enthusiastic about implementing the internal market or, to the contrary, by attempting to block further economic integration. Witness, for example, the failure of the EU's Council of Ministers to adopt the services directives proposed by the Commission in March 2005. This failure was widely explained as a response on the part of national governments to vocally expressed anxieties over potential job losses as a result of the accession of central and eastern European countries in 2004. Thus, whereas distance, language similarity, free trade areas, adjacency, and sea access, are all suggested as instruments for business cycle correlation, the level of integration with the internal market is not.

As explained previously, the endogenous theory of optimum currency areas argues that currency unions enhance trade, which may then affect business cycle correlation either positively or negatively. The underlying proposition in both cases is that a currency union enhances trade because it eliminates exchange rate variation and thus removes a trade barrier between the partners. This proposition, compelling as it is theoretically, has been the subject of a long and inconclusive debate. It is very difficult to prove empirically that exchange rate volatility is a trade barrier (Edison and Melvin, 1990; Kenen and Rodrik, 1986). Indeed, world trade has expanded ever faster since the breakdown of the Bretton Woods system of fixed exchange rates and subsequent floating of exchange rates. However, recent work seems to suggest that currency unions do have a clear positive effect on trade (Frankel and Rose, 2002; Rose, 2000, 2001). Chapter 7 considers this possible endogenous effect of exchange rate variation on business cycle correlation.

Openness

The more open an economy is to international trade and investments, the less potent is its exchange rate as a policy tool (McKinnon, 1963). An open economy is characterized by a dominant tradable goods sector compared with the nontradable goods sector. Tradable goods are goods that can be exchanged internationally. Traditionally, this has referred to merchandise, and services have been regarded as nontradable. However, in recent decades this distinction has been challenged by the spectacular growth in international trade in services, such as tourism, transportation, and finance. Today the term "nontradable" products refers mostly to services that cannot be provided to customers abroad, nor to foreign customers visiting the provider's home country. These are services that are tailored to the local population, such as community services, security, K–12 education, and various other government services. Nontradables could also include restricted merchandise, such as arms and military or dual-use technology, and endangered species.

The exchange rate affects the terms of trade between the tradable and nontradable sectors. For example, devaluation or depreciation of the currency increases profitability in the tradable goods sector and—given the labor and capital constraint of the economy—causes reallocation of resources from the nontradable goods sector to the tradable goods sector. The smaller the nontradable goods sector, the more difficult it becomes to satisfy demand by producers of tradable goods for suitable workers and capital. In the extreme case, in which all the goods produced in the economy are tradable, there are no further factors of production available for the tradable goods sector, and depreciation of the currency would only serve to increase inflation while having no effect on real variables such as employment and growth. Thus, the greater the share of the tradable goods sector in the economy, the less effective would an independent exchange rate policy be in managing the business cycle and the greater its effect on price inflation.

Another motivation for exchange rate stabilization in a highly open economy is the reduction in transaction costs. If exchange rate variation is a trade barrier, then the greater the trade the more beneficial exchange rate stabilization is expected to be. Consumption in small open economies is also especially vulnerable to trade barriers such as exchange rate variation (Alesina and Barro, 2002). Thus, if policymakers are motivated by the welfare of the economy, they would pursue price stabilization, avoid manipulating the exchange rate, and do their best to avoid market-driven exchange rate adjustments.

Of course, openness does not reduce the extent of adjustment required between two countries in the wake of asymmetric shocks. If anything, highly open economies are ever more exposed to external shocks and resort to greater adjustments. In fact, countries often respond to globalization and increased openness with greater fiscal cushioning (Rodrik, 1998). In the absence of a currency union, greater short-term financial market activity in open economies may also offset government exchange rate stabilization policies, increasing daily and weekly exchange rate variation. However, in the long term, government policies to stabilize exchange rates should be dominant, reducing quarterly or annual exchange rate variation.

Hypothesis 2: *The greater the openness,*
the smaller the nominal exchange rate variation
but the greater the overall extent of adjustment
between European economies.

The most accurate measure of a country's openness would be the relative size of its tradable goods sector. However, data on the size of the tradable goods sector are not available for all countries; furthermore, these data are subject to varying definitions. Therefore, the most common measure of openness is the ratio between a country's trade and its GDP. This measure does not capture the true level of openness because global conditions affect prices and volume of domestically traded goods as well as exported and imported goods. For example, a rise in the global price of an exported good forces domestic consumers to pay the higher price or see local producers divert their sales to foreign markets. Measuring openness with the ratio between a country's trade and its GDP, however, has the advantage of simplicity and availability of data.

Thus, for each country, OPENNESS is the sum of exports and imports of goods and services divided by GDP, averaged over the sample period. The most open economy in the sample is Malta, which in the 1990s had an openness ratio of 192 percent of GDP (see Table 4.5). The least open countries were Greece (Sadeh, 2005) and Italy with 43 percent, followed closely by France and Spain. The average OPENNESS value is 88 percent and its standard deviation is 40 percent. Among the current euro zone member states, the average openness ratio in the 1990s was 73 percent, and among the ten transition economies in the sample, it was 101 percent. Among the four major EU economies, the UK is the most open (55 percent). Thus, it seems that openness is not a strong predictor of decisions to join the euro zone or to adopt a currency board. Whether it is helpful in assessing EMU's adjustment burden remains to be seen in Chapter 7.

Of course, the level of openness is at least partly simultaneous with exchange rate variation and other measures of the extent of adjustment

Table 4.5   Openness and Country Size

	OPENNESS	*AREA*
Malta	192	0.3
Estonia	151	45
Belgium	137	31
Ireland	135	70
Slovakia[a]	129	49
Slovenia	115	20
Latvia	114	65
Lithuania	113	65
Czech Republic[a]	112	79
Bulgaria	100	111
Netherlands	100	42
Cyprus	99	6
Austria	79	84
Sweden	71	450
Hungary	68	93
Denmark	66	43
Finland	64	337
Portugal	62	92
Romania	60	238
UK	55	245
Germany	50	357
Poland	49	313
Spain	48	505
France	45	547
Greece	43	132
Italy	43	301
Average	88	166
Euro zone average	73	227
Transition economies	101	108
Other five sample countries	97	149

Notes: OPENNESS is the sum of exports and imports of goods and services divided by GDP, and averaged over the sample period. AREA is the size of a country's territory in thousands of square kilometers.

a. Country did not exist in 1992.

because it reflects policies as well as idiosyncratic country features. Opening up to global markets is a matter of economic strategy, often reflecting an attempt to improve the competitiveness of the local industry by subjecting it to global competition. This no doubt was and still is the strategy of all EU member states, not just the transition economies. However, the disadvantage of openness, as explained previously, is the exposure of the economy to greater volatility in global markets. This might mitigate policymakers' enthusiasm for openness. Still, policy variables such as WTO membership and various economic liberalization measures are not exogenous to other variables in this study. Rather, they depend much on idiosyncratic features that, to begin with, make openness a potentially successful and appealing strategy.

What might such idiosyncratic features be? Openness is most common-ly explained by country size. The argument is that small economies are more reliant than large economies on foreign specialists for many goods. Within a small territory there is less chance than in a large territory to find an abundance of natural resources. Economies with small territories also record more border trade than larger ones in relation to their size. In con-trast, in large territories the nearest border may be very distant. Thus, GDP and territorial size could both theoretically serve as instruments of open-ness.

However, GDP data might again be simultaneous with other variables in this study. Just like industrial concentration and similarity, the composi-tion of the national output is affected by trade patterns, and given the rela-tive prices between various products this changes the measured value of output—GDP. Data adjusted for Purchasing Power Parity (PPP), which enables international and intertemporal comparisons, can improve the credi-bility of this potential instrument, but it remains sensitive to those relative prices. Thus, territorial size is the preferred instrument for openness, and is expected to be negatively associated with it.

AREA is the size of a country's territory in thousands of square kilome-ters (sq km). The most spacious country in the sample is France (547,000 sq km), followed closely by Spain (see Table 4.5). The country with the small-est territory is Malta (300 sq km). The sample average is 166,000 and its standard deviation is 164,000 sq km. Among the current euro zone member states, the average territorial size is 227,000 sq km, and among the ten tran-sition economies in the sample, it is 108,000 sq km. These patterns seem compatible with openness patterns analyzed above. In other words, small countries tend to be more open than large countries.

This conclusion is strengthened by Equation (4.4). For simplicity, this equation is based on national rather than dyadic observations. A rise of 1 percent in the territorial size of a country was found to be associated with a decline of 0.21 percent (not percentage points) in its openness ratio during the sample period. For example, a large country twice the size of a small country (and thus 100 percent larger) tended to have four-fifths of the small country's openness ratio (or a 21 percent lower ratio). The equation is cor-rected with White heteroskedasticity-consistent standard errors and covari-ance and shows standard errors in parentheses. The "ln" prefix denotes a logarithmic transformation of the variable.

(4.4) $\ln.OPENNESS = 5.32 - 0.21 \times \ln.AREA$
$$(0.18)\ (0.04)$$

$R^2 = 0.56$; 26 national observations; Sum of Squared Residuals = 2.13; F-statistic = 31.1; $p < 0.0001$ for all estimated coefficients.

Inflation and Disinflation

Countries with different rates of price inflation are pressured to adjust their exchange rates, whether by administrative decisions or by the markets. If the exchange rate between countries with different rates of inflation remains fixed, the high-inflation country experiences revaluation of its real exchange rate. This revaluation makes it more difficult for its industry to compete with foreign producers. In contrast, the low-inflation country experiences real depreciation to the advantage of its industry. Therefore, over time the bilateral trade balance would deteriorate from the point of view of the country with the higher rate of inflation and improve for the country with the lower rate of inflation.

Adjusting the exchange rate could balance the trade account. Slow foreign exchange earnings by exporters in the high-inflation country would make foreign exchange gain value there and raise its price. Thus, market activity would cause a nominal depreciation of the exchange rate. Conversely, an abundance of foreign exchange in the low-inflation country would cause it to lose value against the local currency and bring about a revaluation of the exchange rate. These developments in the nominal exchange rate can balance the effect of inflation on industrial competitiveness and maintain a stable real exchange rate and a balanced trade account.

At least this is the argument of the PPP theorem: market exchange rates should adjust to equalize prices of similar goods across economies. In reality, considerable lags often occur in the external adjustments brought about by the exchange rates (Krugman, 1991). This is true especially if national rates of inflation are of a similar order of magnitude. Exchange rates are affected by market agents' expectations regarding prospects for investments and growth, and developments in the trade balance can affect these expectations in many ways.

For example, a trade deficit can be interpreted as a reflection of rapid growth and a resulting dependency on imported inputs. In this sense, the trade deficit resembles a loan to finance growth. Market agents may very well believe in the growing economy's prospects and be willing to extend such loans. The inflow of investment funds would thus balance the shortage of foreign exchange earnings and prevent exchange rate adjustment. The subjectivity of expectations about future growth may further weaken the relationship between bilateral disparities in inflation and nominal exchange rate adjustments. Sometimes market agents are overoptimistic and willing to extend loans to deficit countries, and sometimes they are too cautious. Nevertheless, as bilateral disparities in inflation grow, so does the potential for eventual exchange rate adjustments.

Hypothesis 3: *Greater bilateral disparity in rates of price inflation increases adjustment between European countries.*

In contrast to this classic analysis of the effect of inflation on exchange rates, the "new optimum currency area" theory argues that fixing a weak, high-inflation currency to a strong, low-inflation currency generates endogenous effects that bring about a convergence in national rates of inflation both directly and indirectly. Under fixed exchange rates, external prices affect the general local price level through the share of imports in the consumption basket and in production inputs. The inability to devalue its currency means that the inflationary country enjoys lower levels of inflation. This is the direct effect.

Hypothesis 4: *Greater nominal exchange rate variation increases bilateral disparity in rates of price inflation between European countries.*

In addition, fixing the exchange rate with a strong currency benefits the credibility of disinflation policies of the weak currency's authorities (Giavazzi and Pagano, 1988). This indirect effect is supposed to make disinflation easier by rapidly reducing inflationary expectations (Sandholtz, 1993). The reason for this is that fixing exchange rate parities quickly exposes any cheating (Fratianni and Von Hagen, 1993).

However, fixed nominal exchange rates come at the expense of the high-inflation country's industry, as previously explained. Thus, the high-inflation country might lobby against this policy. In addition, depending on the relative size of the two economies, the low-inflation country might suffer a rise in inflation as a result of the fix. Thus, the fix has political opponents. In addition, governments with a reputation for breaking promises might find that declaring a peg is not enough to win the trust of investors. Thus, a fixed exchange rate depends on certain conditions to achieve credibility, such as institutional features that ensure the irrevocability of the fix. Preferably, these should take the form of a unilateral currency board or a multilateral currency union, enshrined in a constitutional commitment. However, such policies are simultaneous with political factors, as explained in Chapter 5, and therefore cannot be used as instruments for inflation or exchange rate variation.

A fixed exchange rate is not the only way to try to earn greater monetary credibility. Independent domestic monetary institutions can provide an alternative to external anchors in enhancing credibility (Sandholtz, 1993). This independent-institution approach presumes that politicians in democratic governments are shortsighted, focusing on electoral cycles and vulnerable to interest groups. In contrast, independent central banks are staffed with disinterested economists guided by the teachings of their discipline. Because inflation is a redistributive mechanism, benefiting certain sectors at the expense of others and at the price of future potentially painful adjustments, this approach is more typical of economies with low central bank independence. Thus, a currency is strong according to this approach when its monetary authorities are independent from the government (Cukierman, 1992). When a country opts to fix its exchange rate with a strong currency, its monetary authorities earn indirect independence from their own government and "borrow" credibility from the strong currency's authorities.

What factors affect the success of each of these two disinflation strategies? Broz (2002) and Keefer and Stasavage (2002) argue that the credibility of government policy depends on its transparency (the public's ability to monitor it), but is hampered by a proliferation of selfish veto players in the domestic political system. An independent central bank can provide credibility when there are many veto players, but does not in itself make policy more transparent. Conversely, a fixed exchange rate provides transparency (either the peg is maintained or it collapses), compensating for a lack of it in public decisionmaking, but is undermined when there are many veto players, which destabilize cabinets and long-term commitments (see Chapters 5 and 6).

Thus, when it is more difficult for the public to observe policymakers' actions, a fixed exchange rate is more effective than a free float in reducing inflationary expectations. However, greater central bank independence will not be effective in reducing inflation in this case because subtle and less visible ways exist for the government to pressure the bank. When there are multiple veto players in government, granting central bank independence would be effective as an anti-inflationary device, but a fixed exchange rate would not be more effective than a free float as an anti-inflationary device (Lohmann, 1998). At the extreme, when there is one veto player, it is likely to dictate monetary policy, even if the central bank is nominally independent.

For member states of EMU (and indeed, of the EU in general) the dilemma between fixed exchange rates and an independent central bank is resolved. Legal central bank independence is mandatory. All (except the UK) must reform their central bank laws to conform to the ECB's statute, which grants it a high level of independence. By both raising the level of central bank independence in EMU member states and harmonizing it among them, EMU has an endogenous effect of reducing the potential for disparity in the rate of price inflation among its members.

In accordance with the above discussion, inflation can be instrumented with an index of central bank independence. A number of such indices have been proposed by different scholars, mostly focusing on the extent of independence granted by law (Armingeon et al., 2004). For example, Alesina's (1988) index considers the extent to which the central bank has final authority over monetary policy and government direct or indirect representation on its governing board. Eijffinger and De Haan (1996) use a similar index with a somewhat different coding method.

Grilli et al. (1991) focus on appointment procedures for board members, the length of their office terms, the existence of a statutory requirement to pursue monetary stability, and the extent to which the central bank is free from government influence in implementing monetary policy. Cukierman (1992) aggregates sixteen legal features of central-bank legislation grouped into four categories. These are (1) the appointment, dismissal, and legal office term of the governor of the central bank; (2) the procedures for resolution of conflicts between the government and the central bank; (3) the relative importance of price stability among other possible policy objectives; and (4) the firmness of restrictions on the ability of the government to borrow from the central bank. Cukierman's method yields the most nuanced and detailed index and is chosen here for constructing a central bank independence index.

Table 4.6 lists average annual central bank independence (CBI) values for each sample country according to Cukierman's (1992) method. A value of 0 corresponds to complete control of the bank by the government, and a value of 1 represents total independence of the bank from the government. Values are based on the legal text that applied in each year. Reforms to central bank laws are considered only since the first full year in which they were in force (these values are underscored in the table). Entries for the ten transition economies in the sample are taken from Cukierman et al. (2002). Entries for other countries are based on Cukierman (1992), adjusted for reforms in the late 1980s and 1990s.

Table 4.6 reveals that the German Bundesbank was, on average, the most independent central bank in Europe during the sample period, and Romania's bank was the least. Among the current euro zone member states (indicated by bold type in the table), Italy's central bank was the least independent in 1992–1998. The current euro zone member states tended in the 1990s to feature more independent central banks than did the other sample countries. However, this was not the case before the enforcement of Article 101 of the Maastricht Treaty and Council Regulation (EC) No 3603/93 of December 13, 1993, which prohibited central banks from extending credit to governments.

Even after 1993, reforms in would-be members of the euro zone were postponed for as long as possible. In 1998, on the eve of the launch of the euro, the average *CBI* score among the current euro zone member states was 0.82. In 1999, following the launch of the euro and the entry into force of further reforms, this average score jumped to 0.92 (not shown in the table), thus strengthening the impression that many countries were reluctant to

Table 4.6   Central Bank Independence *(CBI)*, Price Decontrol *(CLI)*, and Inflation *(CPI)*, 1992–1998

	1992	1993	1994	1995	1996	1997	1998	*CBI*	*CLI*	*CPI*
Austria	0.67	0.67	0.67	<u>0.81</u>	0.81	0.81	0.81	0.75	7.0	2
Belgium	0.32	0.32	<u>0.76</u>	0.76	0.76	0.76	0.76	0.63	7.0	2
Bulgaria	0.55	0.55	0.55	0.55	0.55	0.55	<u>0.86</u>	0.59	3.6	130
Cyprus	0.53	0.53	0.53	0.53	0.53	0.53	0.53	0.53	7.0	4
Czech Rep.[a]	n.a.	0.73	0.73	0.73	0.73	0.73	0.73	0.73	4.6	9
Denmark	0.50	0.50	<u>0.70</u>	0.70	0.70	0.70	0.70	0.64	7.0	2
Estonia	n.a.	0.00	<u>0.78</u>	0.78	0.78	0.78	0.78	0.65	3.9	32
Finland	0.32	0.32	<u>0.27</u>	<u>0.70</u>	0.70	0.70	<u>0.86</u>	0.55	7.0	1
France	0.24	0.24	<u>0.90</u>	0.90	0.90	0.90	0.90	0.71	7.0	2
Germany	0.69	0.69	<u>0.89</u>	0.89	0.89	0.89	0.89	0.83	7.0	3
Greece	0.56	0.56	<u>0.79</u>	0.79	0.79	0.79	0.79	0.72	7.0	10
Hungary	0.67	0.67	0.67	0.67	0.67	0.67	0.67	0.67	5.0	21
Ireland	0.44	0.44	<u>0.77</u>	0.77	0.77	0.77	0.77	0.68	7.0	2
Italy	0.25	0.25	<u>0.65</u>	0.65	0.65	0.65	0.65	0.54	7.0	4
Latvia	0.00	<u>0.49</u>	0.49	0.49	0.49	0.49	0.49	0.42	3.3	49
Lithuania	n.a.	0.28	0.28	0.28	0.28	<u>0.78</u>	0.78	0.45	3.6	61
Malta	0.46	0.46	0.46	<u>0.53</u>	0.53	0.53	0.53	0.50	7.0	3
Netherlands	0.42	0.42	<u>0.74</u>	0.74	0.74	0.74	0.74	0.65	7.0	2
Poland	0.46	0.46	0.46	0.46	0.46	0.46	<u>0.89</u>	0.52	5.0	27
Portugal	0.32	0.32	<u>0.65</u>	0.65	<u>0.90</u>	0.90	<u>0.89</u>	0.66	7.0	5
Romania	0.34	0.34	0.34	0.34	0.34	0.34	0.34	0.34	3.0	112
Slovakia[a]	n.a.	0.62	0.62	0.62	0.62	0.62	0.62	0.62	4.3	11
Slovenia	0.63	0.63	0.63	0.63	0.63	0.63	0.63	0.63	5.0	29
Spain	0.45	0.45	<u>0.66</u>	<u>0.92</u>	0.92	0.92	0.92	0.75	7.0	4
Sweden	0.29	0.29	0.29	<u>0.63</u>	0.63	0.63	0.63	0.49	7.0	2
UK	0.27	0.27	<u>0.65</u>	0.65	0.65	0.65	0.65	0.54	7.0	3
Average	0.43	0.44	0.61	0.66	0.67	0.69	0.72	0.61	5.9	20
Euro zone average	0.43	0.43	0.71	0.78	0.80	0.80	0.82	0.68	7.0	3
Transition economies	0.43	0.45	0.56	0.56	0.56	0.61	0.68	0.56	4.2	48
Other 5 sample countries	0.41	0.41	0.53	0.61	0.61	0.61	0.61	0.54	7.0	3

Notes: Annual columns display an index rising with legal central bank independence. Entries of first full year following reform of central bank laws are underscored. *CBI* is the simple period average for each country. *CLI* is the period average of a cumulative index rising with the progress of price decontrol. *CPI* is the average annual rate of consumer price inflation for the sample period. n.a. – Data unavailable.

a. Country did not exist in 1992.

make their central banks more independent and did so only when forced by the timetable of EMU. This was especially the case with Austria, Belgium, Greece, Ireland, Italy, and the Netherlands.

Countries that were not planning to join the third stage of EMU and adopt the euro in 1999 were clearly in an even lesser hurry to reform their central banks' statutes. Sweden and the UK (which under the special opt-out protocol it negotiated was not obliged to reform its central bank's law) followed the practice of the above six countries. However, Denmark basically had not reformed its laws since 1969.[1] Among the transition economies, the average *CBI* score did not reach 0.81 until 2003, when Maastricht-compatible reforms came into force in Estonia, Hungary, and Slovenia. The leading countries in this group were Bulgaria, Latvia, and Poland, which carried out Maastricht-compatible reforms in the late 1990s. In contrast, the Czech Republic, Lithuania, and Slovakia waited until they joined the EU in 2004. Romania changed its laws in 2004 as well.

However, central bank independence is not the only institutional factor affecting the rate of inflation. Cukierman et al. (2002) suggested that the process of decontrol of domestic prices in the 1990s produced sizeable non-monetary jumps in the rate of inflation for many transition economies as prices of domestic goods were allowed to adjust toward market values. *CLI* (price decontrol in Table 4.6) attempts to capture this effect. It is an index of the average cumulative effect of domestic price liberalization in the transition economies. The state of liberalization is graded in each country and year (starting in 1989) on a scale from 0 (full control) to 1 (full liberalization). Cumulative values are then calculated for each country and year, adding up the previous years' liberalization grades. *CLI* is the simple 1992–1998 average of these cumulative values.

Liberalization grades for the ten transition economies are taken from Cukierman et al. (2002) and are based on de Melo et al. (1996). As long-standing market economies, the other sixteen countries in the sample are assumed to have had the highest liberalization grades each year. Each of these countries had a cumulative liberalization value of 10 in 1998, and a *CLI* value of 7.0. In contrast, the transition economies had an average *CLI* value of 4.2 (see Table 4.6).

Table 4.6 also presents period average consumer price inflation (*CPI*) levels for each country. These are calculated as the seventh root (or sixth where applicable) of the compounded cumulative inflation rate over the sample period. Finland enjoyed the lowest average rate of inflation, in spite of its central bank's relative dependence on the government. In contrast, Bulgaria experienced the highest average rate of inflation. Clearly, all transition economies were characterized by high rates of inflation. Thus, the relationship between central bank legal independence and the rate of inflation seems weak.

In contrast, inflation emerges as a powerful explanation of actual exchange rate variation, as expected: Countries with low inflation tended to experience low adjustment among them. However, Italy and the UK experienced higher exchange rate variation and adjustment against France and Germany than their rates of inflation would suggest (see Tables 3.1 and 3.3). Among the four major EU economies, France experienced the lowest rate of inflation and Italy experienced the highest rate. Thus, as far as inflation is concerned, France had a slight advantage as an anchor for the euro zone.

Table 4.7 studies the relationship between *CBI*, *CLI*, and inflation more rigorously. Again, for simplicity, the equations in this table are based on national rather than dyadic observations. The depended variable is the national transformed rate of inflation (D), which is a nonlinear transformation of the rate of consumer price inflation suggested by Cukierman et al. (2002). This transformation is designed to reduce the weight of observations with three-digit inflation rates. Equation (4.5) is based on the specification employed by Cukierman et al. (2002). Equation (4.6) is similar to Equation (4.5) but without CLI.

The negative coefficients of CBI in both equations support the argument that independent central banks achieved lower levels of inflation in 1990s Europe. The negative coefficient of CLI in Equation (4.6) is in line with the argument that as liberalization proceeded, the decontrol shocks receded and inflation was brought down. Clearly, Equation (4.6) has better explanatory power than Equation (4.5), but CBI's significance is weakened, probably as a result of a multicolinear relationship between CBI and CLI ($r = 0.44$). These findings support the expectation that central bank political independence from the government is a good instrument for inflation. Accordingly, bilateral disparity of the extent of central bank independence is expected to make national rates of inflation less similar. However, in order to avoid overidentification of variables in the second-step equation, CLI is not used in Chapter 7 to instrument bilateral inflation disparity.

A possible concern that should be addressed here is that CBI and inflation might be simultaneous, with the level of inflation not only being affected by, but also affecting the level of independence of central banks from

Table 4.7   Ordinary Least Squares Equations of the Transformed Rate of Inflation (D)

Equation number:	(4.5)	(4.6)
CONSTANT	0.78***	0.56***
	(0.09)	(0.16)
CBI (−)	−0.20	−0.71***
	(0.15)	(0.23)
CLI (−)	−0.09***	
	(0.02)	
Number of observations	26	26
Sum of Squared Residuals	0.13	0.48
R^2	0.80	0.26
F-statistic	46.4***	8.29***

Notes: $D = (CPI/100)/(1 + CPI/100)$. Estimates are corrected with White heteroskedasticity-consistent standard errors and covariance. Standard error values are indicated in parentheses. The signs by the names of the independent variables indicate their expected relationship with the dependent variable. * $.05 < p \leq .10$. ** $.01 < p \leq .05$. *** $p \leq 0.01$. Variables underscored with a dotted line are calculated as bilateral averages of national values.

governments. However, such simultaneity is unlikely for a number of reasons. To begin with, it would seem unreasonable to conclude from CBI's negative coefficients that in 1990s Europe higher rates of inflation led to a desire for greater political control over central banks. This would only make sense if inflation originated in incompetent central bankers rather than in political pressures.

More important, reforms in central bank laws in 1990s Europe were motivated by a desire of EU member states to signal their continued commitment to price stability and to the goal of EMU as prescribed in the Maastricht Treaty. EMU was supposed to be part of the new post–Cold War European political order. Similarly, reforms in the transition economies were greatly influenced by their strategic choice for EU membership, for which central bank independence is a prerequisite. Such long-term political considerations can be argued to have dominated more immediate macroeconomic policy considerations. This impression is strengthened by the evidence presented earlier on the progress of central bank reforms in European countries. In other words, the level of inflation was more likely a derivative of the level of central bank independence, which in turn reflected high politics, than a cause of high politics.

Arguably, a more general political trend that can be referred to as the "triumph of neo-liberalism" in the 1980s and 1990s can explain both the drive for greater central bank independence and lower levels of inflation in European countries as well as in many of the world's countries during the sample period. Although this ideological factor should optimally be controlled for in Table 4.7, this is very difficult in practice. The J tests in Chapter 7 provide further quantitative evidence of the weak simultaneity, if any, between central bank independence and inflation.

Note

1. Denmark's central bank independence scores in Table 4-6 account for the judgment of the European Monetary Institute (1998, 15), which confirmed that "The statute of the Danmarks Nationalbank does not contain incompatibilities in the area of central bank independence. The legal integration of the Bank in the ESCB does not need to be provided for and other legislation does not need to be adapted as long as Denmark does not adopt the single currency." This judgment is at odds with the conclusion of Cukierman et al. (1992), which graded Denmark in the 1980s at 0.41. Adjusting for Council Regulation (EC) No 3603/93, this score rises to 0.61—still far from the levels reached by reforms in euro zone member states.

5

The Political Costs of EMU

Chapter 4 studied economic determinants of adjustment to membership in the euro zone. This chapter focuses on political determinants of the extent of this adjustment. It develops proxies for measuring these political determinants, describes their patterns in European countries, and discusses possible simultaneous relationships with which they are involved. These variables, which include interest groups, partisanship, institutions, cabinet duration, and the political business cycle, are mostly suggested by the literature on the domestic democratic politics of exchange rates.

Admittedly, exchange rate variation is only one among a few mechanisms of adjustment, as discussed in Chapter 2; by focusing on the politics of exchange rates, the discussion may seem to be too narrow. As this chapter argues, however, some domestic political factors have the capacity to affect other mechanisms of adjustment, such as fiscal and monetary policies, as well.

Another potential concern about the usefulness of the theory of domestic politics of exchange rates for the purpose of this book is its methodological consistency with optimum currency area theory as discussed in Chapter 2. In particular, with a few exceptions (Bernhard and Leblang, 2002a; Leblang and Bernhard, 2000), the subject of analysis of most of the domestic politics literature is policy rather than market developments. Thus, it is important to stress that the emphasis of this book is on the effects that political factors have on market developments, even if such effects materialize through policy. It is assumed that if certain political factors support a policy of stable exchange rates, these factors also support (although not necessarily ensure) actual exchange rate stability. Henceforth, the expression "policy outcomes" refers to market responses to policy.

Interest Groups

The activities of interest groups are perhaps the logical starting point for the analysis of political causes for exchange rate variation. Exchange rate policies in general, and currency unions in particular, redistribute income among interest groups. Thus, interest groups struggle to influence the choice of policy, including membership in currency unions (Milner, 1995).

In a number of publications, Frieden (1997, 1998, 2002) has argued that the division between supporters and opponents of fixed exchange rates can be predicted fairly well. On the side of the supporters, Frieden expects to find multinational corporations. Because these corporations carry out global operations, they prefer to reduce global economic segmentation, which hampers access to markets and resources. Exchange rate variation is just one among many such barriers to global economic activity.

Industries that compete mostly over the quality rather than the price of their products are also expected to favor fixed exchange rates. For such industries, any possible advantage of exchange rate manipulation is minor compared with market access considerations. This is the case of high-technology industries and many service providers, for example. Indeed, there is evidence that employers' organizations in the UK, France, and Germany were in favor of EMU for the sake of a strong currency and fewer regulations (Verdun, 1996).

In addition, any actor that in the absence of a fix expects to lose from exchange rate adjustment can be expected to favor a fix. In a country with a weak non-pegged currency, a process of continued depreciation is expected, as explained in Chapter 4, and consumers of mostly foreign goods or foreign currency–indexed goods would suffer. The same goes for borrowers in foreign currency, who thus can be expected to support a fix. Another important interest group expected to be in favor of fixed exchange rates in these circumstances is the nontradable sector because its profitability is hampered by depreciation, again as explained in Chapter 4. In contrast, in a country with a strong non-pegged currency, a process of continued appreciation is expected. Exporters, creditors to foreign customers, and anyone with foreign currency earnings is expected to support the fix.

The same logic explains which interest groups can be expected to oppose a fix. These should consist of small and medium enterprises, traditional tradable-goods industries, consumers of foreign goods, and borrowers in foreign currency in a country with a strong currency. In a country with a weak currency, exporters and creditors to foreign customers also are expected to oppose a fix. The changing balance among French and Italian political parties in the 1980s, each supported by constituencies based in such economic sectors, can explain the evolution of exchange rate policies of these countries (Frieden, 2000).

Pressure groups that are interested in influencing exchange rate policy can be identified, and not only by the direct way in which their profitability is exposed to exchange rate adjustment. For example, the British opposition to EMU can be explained by the powerful position enjoyed by the city of

London, which was concerned that EMU might give rise to a competing European financial center (Talani, 2000). This, in spite of its general support for globalization, reduced trade barriers and open markets.

In addition, a number of scholars attribute at least the early stages of European monetary integration to the need to stabilize exchange rates for the benefit of the operation of the complicated mechanism of the EC's Common Agricultural Policy (CAP). (See McNamara [1998]; Story [1988]; and Story and de Cecco [1993].) If this policy had collapsed, it might have caused serious damage to the entire EC system because the CAP was an important incentive for France's participation in the EC by buying its farmers' support (Dyson, 1994; Kaltenthaler, 2002).

Of course, other actors are involved in policymaking beyond industrial firms, banks, and labor unions, and other motives exist beyond economic profits. Sometimes struggles over monetary and exchange rate policies take place among ministries and agencies of a single government, as occurred in Germany (Heisenberg, 1999). The German chancellery and foreign ministry had been interested since the 1960s in using monetary integration as a way of improving Germany's relationship with its European neighbors. They were able to overcome the Bundesbank's and finance ministry's opposition to monetary integration whenever they could convince the German industry and banks that a foreign policy crisis had to be averted. Once the urgency abated, the Bundesbank and finance ministry always grew powerful again and shaped the final plans for the common monetary institutions (Kaltenthaler, 2002).

Whatever their motives, competing interests struggle to influence exchange rate policies and manipulate actual exchange rates. Policy outcomes are based on a balance of these competing interests' power, organizational skills, and access to policymakers. Quantitative and qualitative evidence seems to support this argument (Blomberg et al., 2004; Frieden, 2002; Frieden et al., 2001; Leblang, 2003).

For example, Cameron (1996) explained France's famous switch to a strong franc policy in the early 1980s as a balance of interests. According to this explanation, French labor was weak and divided, the export sector lacked influence and a clear voice for or against a strong currency, and the financial sector was in part publicly owned and controlled. Against this backdrop, officials at the treasury were powerful and authoritative in promoting the strong franc policies and persuading Mitterand to pursue them.

Compelling as the interest group's approach is as a theory, however, a significant methodological difficulty surrounds any attempt to test it empirically. In spite of the general ex ante focus of this approach, which regards interest groups as country idiosyncratic, there is no established way to exogenously measure the power of such groups. The proxies used by studies for the power of interest groups are most often endogenous variables, as they may determine exchange rates as much as be determined by them.

For example, the share of a sector in GDP, a common proxy for its political power, may reflect many factors, and not necessarily its power to determine national policy. Indeed, in spite of the large size of Poland's agricultural sector, its farmers could not secure the subsidies of the CAP upon its accession to the EU in 2004.

Beyond this methodological difficulty, interest group power is an elusive concept. Even without going into the famous debate in political science on the definition of power and whether it is situation specific, it is clear that the power of interest groups is not exogenous to policy, let alone quantifiable. Success at policy manipulation may reflect the power of interest groups as well as further empower them. Admittedly, some scholars attempt to resolve this problem by using lagged proxies for interest group power (Frieden et al., 2001). This technique can improve the statistical estimation and make it more reliable, but it does not solve the conceptual problem. Power and policy outcomes are simultaneous and, to a great extent, inseparable. Most of the literature on the role of interest groups in European monetary integration is descriptive and retrospective. Few studies have predictive power. As a consequence, interest groups cannot be used in this study as determinants of the extent of adjustment among member states of the euro zone.

Some argue that the influence of domestic actors on the shape of EMU has always remained limited. In the short term, each sector preferred others to pay for EMU and the reforms it entailed, but on balance public opinion remained in favor of it and there was very little discussion of its principles and details. Domestic opposition to EMU was mostly opportunistic, not ideological, and any domestic schism was overshadowed by international divisions as well as divisions within societal groups. In sum, the effects of monetary policies are too complicated for domestic actors to formulate a clear position about them, and the nature of monetary policymaking remains top-down (Youngs, 1999).

Partisanship

Partisanship is another explanatory variable of exchange rate policy outcomes. The traditional view is that right-wing parties are more inflation averse than left-wing parties, and likelier to fix exchange rates and refrain from fiscal or monetary policies that attempt to redistribute market-allocated resources (Hibbs, 1977). A contrary view is that left-wing governments have a greater need for an exchange rate peg precisely because they are suspected of focusing their macroeconomic policies on job creation rather than on disinflation, and thus suffer from lower credibility in their macroeconomic polices (Frieden, 2002). Considering these opposing views, governments dominated by left-wing parties could be either negatively or positively associated with the extent of adjustment.

The evidence suggests that, compared with right-wing governments, left-wing governments are associated with softer exchange rate commitments in the long term but stronger commitments in the short term (Alesina and Roubini, 1997; Blomberg and Hess, 1997; Frieden, 2002; Garrett, 1995; Leblang, 2002; Leblang and Bernhard, 2000). Some scholars, however, have found it difficult to make a strong empirical case in support of either of the partisan views (Bernhard and Leblang, 1999, 2002a; Eichengreen et al., 1995; Hallerberg, 2002; Lobo and Tufte, 1998). One reason why partisanship is a problematic predictor of exchange rate policies is that the socioeconomic left-right divide is not always the dominant political cleavage, making it sometimes difficult to tell right from left among political parties, thus changing the intensity of ideology's effect on policy. Ideological classification of observed governments might therefore be difficult in practice.

In addition, Bernhard et al. (2002) stress the interdependence of the choice of central bank independence and exchange rate regime: Choosing central bank independence may obviate the need for a left-wing government to seek the discipline of an exchange rate peg. It is important to add that exchange rate policies matter not only to macroeconomic policies but also to foreign policies. Thus, a bipartisan consensus may consider a certain peg to be beneficial on foreign policy grounds whatever the macroeconomic consequences. This may very well be the case of the Baltic countries and, indeed, of many other European countries in the 1990s.

Partisan differences of policy are based on worldviews that change only over very long periods. Thus, they could be regarded as exogenous to other variables in this study. Partisanship is not an idiosyncratic feature of a democratic country, however. Rather, in democratic countries the partisanship stance of the government remains a cyclical factor, even if such ideological cycles last for longer than a decade. Thus, partisanship is regarded in this study as an exogenous control variable, which can be positively or negatively associated with the extent of adjustment.

PARTY is a partisanship index. In each country, each year is coded 1 if the largest government party was a left-wing party, −1 if it was a right-wing party, or 0 otherwise (coding taken from Beck et al., 2001). *PARTY* is the bilateral average of the national codes from 1992 through 1998. Table 5.1 details annual partisanship codes and the period average for each sample country. Countries are sorted by their period average from left-wing oriented countries at the top of the table down to right-wing-oriented countries at the bottom. The current euro zone member states are printed in bold type.

Table 5.1   Partisanship Bias *(PARTY)*

	1992	1993	1994	1995	1996	1997	1998	*PARTY*
Austria	1	1	1	1	1	1	1	1.00
Slovakia[a]	n.a.	1	1	1	1	1	1	1.00
Lithuania	1	1	1	1	1	1	−1	0.71
Poland	1	−1	1	1	1	1	1	0.71
Slovenia	−1	1	1	1	1	1	1	0.71
Denmark	−1	−1	1	1	1	1	1	0.43
Finland	0	0	0	0	1	1	1	0.43
Greece	−1	−1	1	1	1	1	1	0.43
Spain	1	1	1	1	1	−1	−1	0.43
Hungary	−1	−1	−1	1	1	1	1	0.14
Netherlands	−1	−1	−1	1	1	1	1	0.14
Sweden	−1	−1	−1	1	1	1	1	0.14
France	1	1	−1	−1	−1	−1	1	−0.14
Portugal	−1	−1	−1	−1	1	1	1	−0.14
Italy	0	0	0	−1	−1	0	0	−0.29
Romania	0	0	0	0	0	−1	−1	−0.29
Latvia	n.a.	n.a.	−1	−1	0	0	0	−0.40
Bulgaria	−1	−1	−1	1	1	−1	−1	−0.43
Malta	−1	−1	−1	−1	−1	1	1	−0.43
Estonia	1	−1	−1	−1	−1	−1	−1	−0.71
UK	−1	−1	−1	−1	−1	−1	1	−0.71
Belgium	−1	−1	−1	−1	−1	−1	−1	−1.00
Cyprus	−1	−1	−1	−1	−1	−1	−1	−1.00
Czech Rep.[a]	n.a.	−1	−1	−1	−1	−1	−1	−1.00
Germany	−1	−1	−1	−1	−1	−1	−1	−1.00
Ireland	−1	−1	−1	−1	−1	−1	−1	−1.00
Average	−0.35	−0.40	−0.27	0.00	0.15	0.08	0.15	−0.09
Euro zone average	−0.40	−0.40	−0.20	−0.10	0.20	0.10	0.10	−0.10
Non–euro zone average	−0.31	−0.40	−0.32	0.07	0.12	0.06	0.19	−0.08

Notes: Annual columns display an index of partisanship. *PARTY* is the average for each year in the period 1992–1998. In each country, each year is coded 1 if the largest government party was a left-wing party, −1 if it was a right-wing party, or 0 otherwise (Beck et al., 2001).

n.a. Data unavailable.

a. Country did not exist in 1992.

The dotted line distinguishes mostly left-wing-oriented countries (above) from mostly right-wing ones (below).

Table 5.1 shows that seven countries maintained the same partisanship bias throughout the sample period, two of them to the left (Austria and Slovakia), and five to the right (Belgium, Cyprus, the Czech Republic, Germany, and Ireland). Other mostly left-wing-biased countries were Lithuania, Poland, and Slovenia; Estonia and the UK were mostly right-wing biased . Only three countries (Bulgaria, France, and Italy) experienced two swings in their partisanship bias during the sample period.

The average partisanship code for all countries and years is −0.09, which means that the continent was not dominated as a general rule by either left- or right-wing parties, although there was a light tendency to the right. The three bottom rows of Table 5.1 show that there was a pronounced right-wing bias throughout the continent during the early 1990s, but this trend reversed in the late 1990s, producing in the end a mild left-wing bias. The absence of any difference in these patterns between the current euro zone member states and the other sample countries seems to be compatible with the common wisdom that the cause of EMU was not biased to the left nor to the right.

The evidence in Table 5.1 does not reflect, of course, on specific exchange rate policies chosen during the 1990s, as revealed by the classification in Table 3.2 for the seven countries mentioned as having the strongest partisanship bias. Austria and Slovakia alternated between the conventional pegged arrangements and fluctuation margins. Belgium, Cyprus, Germany, and Ireland chose fluctuation margins essentially throughout the sample period as well, whereas the Czech Republic alternated between a float and a peg. Thus, superficially, partisanship does not seem to explain any specific exchange rate policy in 1990s Europe.

The same goes for actual nominal exchange rate variation as revealed in Table 3.1. Austria maintained low variation against France and Germany, but Slovakia, another country with a strong left-wing-biased government, experienced higher variation than the median values against these two major countries (2.63 and 2.30, respectively). Germany, a country with a strong right-wing bias in the sample period, maintained low exchange rate variation against France. So did Belgium and Cyprus against both France and Germany. The Czech Republic and Ireland, however, were closer to the median levels. The experience of all seven countries against Italy and the UK seems even less related to their partisan stances. Data presented in Table 3.3 lead to similar conclusions about the relationship between partisanship and the broader measure of adjustment.

Of course, the analysis in this section is superficial because no control is provided for other important variables and instruments. A more accurate assessment of the effects of partisanship on adjustment is performed in Chapter 7. The next three sections of this chapter discuss variables that mediate between the influence of interest groups and partisanship, on the one hand, and exchange rate policy outcomes, on the other. These variables are institutions (lines *a* and *b* in Figure 5.1), cabinet duration (lines *d* and *e*), and the political business cycle (lines *h* and *i*).

Institutions

The extent to which policymakers are sensitive to the demands of interest groups in the shaping of policy in general and exchange rate policy in partic-

Figure 5.1   The Domestic Political Economy of Exchange Rates

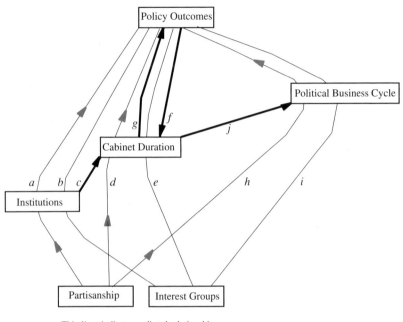

Thin lines indicate mediated relationships.
Thick lines indicate direct relationships.
Arrows indicate causal relationships.
Lines without arrows indicate simultaneous relationships.

ular depends on various institutional features of a country's political system. Domestic political institutions affect the preferences and political influence of interest groups, as well as the way they access policymakers and their ability to organize, deploy their political resources, and project their power. Institutional features of society and economy also affect the extent to which the government can successfully pursue its partisan ideology.

The literature suggests a number of institutions as being specifically relevant to making exchange rate policy. One such set of institutions relates to the labor market and determines the influence of labor unions and industry on policies. For example, corporatist systems such as those in Germany allow for representation of workers on corporate boards and enhance the power of employees in decisionmaking (Garrett, 1995).

The ownership structure of the financial sector, mass media, and industry, as well as the degree of government involvement in the economy, are all important factors. For example, domestic political institutions have been suggested to explain varying exchange rate policies since the 1970s in EU member states, against a similar backdrop of high inflation (Walsh, 2000). In countries with credit-based financial institutions, such as France, Germany, and Italy, in which firms raise capital mostly through bank loans, the industry, and the banking sectors should support a strong currency policy and membership in EMU in order to make debt repayments easier. In contrast, in the UK, where capital is raised mainly through issues of bonds and equities, there should be little support for EMU (Walsh, 2001).

In federal democracies such as Austria, Belgium (since 1991), and Germany, a significant portion of government resources is commanded by local governments. Fixing exchange rates and forgoing monetary policy as a result leaves the federal government with no macroeconomic adjustment tools. Therefore, the incentive of a federal government to fix exchange rates is weak (Hallerberg, 2002).

Policymakers in democracies based on an electoral formula of proportional representation are expected to be more responsive to pressures from interest groups than are those in democracies with a majoritarian electoral formula (Bernhard and Leblang, 1999). Democracy generally exposes policymakers to interest group pressure and engages them in redistributive policies (Alesina and Drazen, 1991; Haggard and Kaufman, 1992). In contrast, autocratic rulers are more insulated from the distributive demands of the citizenry (Leblang, 1999).

Some of the political institutions suggested so far, such as working relationships between banks and industry, are endogenous to economic and political activity and cannot be regarded as ex ante idiosyncratic country features. Therefore, these institutions are less useful for the purpose of this book. Political institutions enshrined in law, however, such as autocracy, corporatism, federalism, the electoral formula, and many others suggested in Chapter 6, can be potentially useful as instruments or as exogenous variables independently affecting the adjustment indicators. One could argue that laws are written by humans to serve their selfish interests, and therefore do not represent an exogenous objective reality. To remedy this potential problem, this book focuses as much as possible on institutions that are established by constitutions. Constitutions require special majorities to be amended and are relatively less sensitive than other forms of legislation to opportunistic behavior on the part of political-economic actors.

Cabinet Duration

The second intervening variable between interest groups and partisanship, on the one hand, and exchange rate policy outcomes, on the other, is cabinet duration (lines d and e in Figure 5.1). Low-duration cabinets are more sensitive to pressure from interest groups because the less secure are policymakers in their positions, the more immediate is their need to ensure the support of their constituents and affiliated societal groups. Lower cabinet duration is like a net with bigger holes, providing societal interests with better opportunities to influence policy, which would be less motivated by international politics or national welfare. What this means for the sustainability of a currency link is less clear, though, because low cabinet duration could affect the balance among competing interest groups in many ways, which are beyond the scope of this study.

A clearer argument can be made about the effect of cabinet duration on currency links by studying its interaction with partisanship. Frequent changes of cabinet, through elections or changing governing coalitions, accelerate partisan-motivated policy changes. Such frequent changes may theoretically be incompatible with a currency link, and for this reason, low cabinet duration can be argued to be associated with greater exchange rate variation and/or more frequent fiscal and monetary policy shifts. However, this is true only if the currency link is a partisan issue—a condition that may not have existed in 1990s Europe (see previous discussion).

Cabinet duration is also directly and simultaneously associated with exchange rate variation. One group of empirical studies emphasizes how fixed exchange rates cause greater cabinet duration, serving as focal points for policy agreement and bargaining, and helping politicians manage intraparty and intracoalition conflicts (line f in Figure 5.1). Bernhard and Leblang (2002b) argue that fixed exchange rates improve cabinet durability in open economies because openness increases intraparty conflicts and makes it more difficult to use traditional fiscal and monetary policy tools for redistributive purposes. Monetary commitments deprive policymakers of information advantages that they can use to betray their partners, and thus foster trust among them. In addition, fixed exchange rates can be a scapegoat on which unpopular policies and reforms can be blamed.

Hallerberg (2002, 791) makes a related argument—namely, that office-seeking veto players in a multiparty coalition may give up monetary autonomy because it is difficult for each of them to target the benefits of monetary policy directly to their constituencies. Similarly, Frieden (2002) argues that unstable governments tend to seek credibility through an exchange rate peg. Indeed, Bernhard and Leblang (2002b) found that during 1972–1998, fixed exchange rates improved cabinet durability in eleven of the EU member states.

Hypothesis 5: *Higher exchange rate variation reduces cabinet duration in Europe.*

Another group of empirical studies reverses the direction of causality and argues that durable cabinets are more likely to fix exchange rates. The rationale is that maintaining a fixed exchange rate may require politically difficult adjustments by abandoning redistributive policies that benefit cabinet members directly or important interest groups for the sake of uncertain gains in the more distant future (Broz, 2002; Frieden et al., 2001). Devaluation, such as budget deficits and low interest rates, represents an intertemporal transfer, so members of a short-lived cabinet have a temptation to use such tools to spend resources in the immediate term and endow subsequent cabinets with debts. Thus, the specter of cabinet dissolution enhances the cabinet's inflationary tendencies, and low cabinet duration means more active manipulation of exchange rates and fiscal and monetary policies to finance the struggle for the cabinet's survival (line *g* in Figure 5.1). Expecting this, market agents often preempt political processes and increase exchange rate variation.

Many studies have underscored the important role that cabinet duration plays in ex ante determining exchange rate variation. For example, Bernhard and Leblang (2002a) found that exchange rate risk premiums in Belgium, Britain, France, Germany, Italy, and the Netherlands (as well as Canada and Japan) between 1974 and 1995 existed more often when the government's tenure in office was insecure because economic agents found it difficult to forecast exchange rate movements. Leblang and Bernhard (2000) determined that the probability of speculative attacks on the exchange rate increased in ten of the EU member states (as well as five other countries) during 1970–1995 when the probability of a cabinet dissolution was high. (See also Bernhard and Leblang [1999, 2002b]; Edwards [1996]; Frieden [2002]; and Frieden et al. [2001].)

Hypothesis 6: *Higher cabinet duration reduces the extent of adjustment in Europe.*

In contrast, Laver and Shepsle (1996) imply that there need be no relationship between cabinet duration and exchange rate variation. Rather, they argue that policy may be consistent even when cabinets are frequently dissolved if the same party keeps returning to the same portfolio. They assume that parties support cabinets according to cabinets' policies, even if they are excluded from them, and argue that each portfolio is given to the median party on the relevant policy's ideological continuum because it holds the parliamentary balance on that topic.

These conditions, however, do not always apply in reality. Parties cannot always use their portfolios to dictate their platform to other coalition members. Issue linkages and politics of context may drive a party to compromise over its platform, for example, when a vote is declared a motion of confidence in the government. Parties often make ideological compromises for the sake of the material benefits of being in power. In addition, parties are rarely homogenous, and it often matters which faction holds the portfolio. Methodologically, ideas are not always easily placed on a continuum with a clear median, and they may be difficult to operationalize as exogenous variables for the purpose of this book.

To summarize, the lower the cabinet duration, the more difficult it becomes to maintain stable exchange rates, but the more beneficial this stability is if achieved. Low-duration cabinets find it hard to stabilize exchange rates because maintaining a fixed exchange rate may require politically difficult adjustments by abandoning redistributive policies that benefit either cabinet members directly or important interest groups for the sake of uncertain gains in the more distant future.

It is important to stress that cabinet duration is an important determinant of the adjustment burden of a currency union even after it is established. Although the exchange rate cannot be used for redistributive policies among members of a currency union, joining the union might not immunize countries with low-duration cabinets from reneging on related policy commitments in the long term (Hallerberg et al., 2002). Such cabinets might acquire (and hide) debts, avoid structural reforms designed to make prices more flexible as well as make labor and capital flows more mobile, and abuse the trust of investors for short-term gains. These policies would make the currency union costly to society even after it is established. Hypothesis 6 therefore expects cabinet duration to be negatively associated not only with nominal exchange rate variation but with all of the adjustment indicators developed in Chapter 3.

A number of definitions for cabinet duration are offered in the literature, depending on how cabinet change is defined. First is the suggestion that a cabinet changes merely when the combination of parties in the governing coalition changes, without regard to elections or other developments (Dodd, 1976, 121–123; Robertson, 1983a; Taylor and Herman, 1971). In other words, a cabinet term is considered to be uninterrupted by elections if the coalition does not change in the wake of the election. The rationale is that the importance of a government stems from its policy, always a compromise among coalition partners, and the policy compromise changes when the governing coalition changes.

Another definition recognizes cabinet change merely when the top executive is replaced, again without regard to other developments (Beck et al., 2001; Edwards, 1996; Frieden et al., 2001; Klein and Marion, 1997; Taylor and Herman, 1971). The top executive is the person with whom rests the final authority on the major issues deemed as central to the national interest. In democratic political systems, this is typically the prime minister or the president. This approach to cabinet change is especially relevant whenever formal or de facto responsibility for policy rests mostly with the top executive rather than being shared among the ministers. This is typically the case with presidential democracies. Of course, even in other circumstances, replacing the top executive is a significant development.

A third approach, inspired by the political business cycle literature, identifies cabinet change with elections, no matter the results. This approach argues that the electoral cycle determines the life expectancy of a policy, which is aimed at yielding results by the time of elections. Even when elections return the same governing coalition and top executive to power, this result cannot be taken for granted by the cabinet, which must please the voters.

A fourth definition offered is a change in cabinet status (Bernhard and Leblang, 2002b). Scholars have sorted cabinets into three major groups, representing the expected duration of cabinets: (1) *Minority governments* are governments that are not supported by the majority in the legislature but nevertheless are not brought down. Most scholars argue that these are shaky coalitions, but some argue that minority governments may endure for a lack of any other viable coalition, perhaps for ideological reasons (Laver and Shepsle, 1996; Strøm, 1984, 1990). (2) *Minimum winning coalitions* rest on the smallest majority in the legislature required for their survival. A majority of scholars consider minimum winning coalition governments, especially in the form of a one-party majority government, to be the most durable. (See, for example, Alt and King [1994]; Dodd [1976]; King et al. [1990]; Lijphart [1999, 135–139]; Robertson [1983b]; Taylor and Herman [1971]; and Warwick [1994].) (3) *Wide coalitions* are any coalitions that occupy more seats than they would as a minimum winning coalitions. Their weakness lies in the increasing difficulty of arriving at an agreed political agenda among proliferating coalition partners.

These four definitions of cabinet change are not mutually exclusive. For example, a change of coalition may involve a change of top executive and/or an election. In fact, it is conceivable that in certain countries during a given period of time, coalitions or top executives are replaced only in the wake of elections. The above definitions for cabinet change can also be combined in various ways into composite definitions. For example, Lijphart (1999, 131–134) suggests that a cabinet would be considered to have changed if the coalition changed and in addition any of the above other three events occurred (i.e., change of the top executive, elections, or change of cabinet status). Indeed, a fifth definition suggested in the literature is that a cabinet changes whenever the share of parliament seats commanded by the combined coalition parties changes (Edwards, 1996; Frieden, 2002; Frieden et al., 2001). This definition is approximately the same as defining a change of cabinet whenever either the party composition of the governing coalition changes or an election occurs.

Other, less common definitions of cabinet change include Warwick's (1979, 1994) suggestion that a cabinet should be considered to have been replaced upon any formal inauguration, even if the same coalition and ministers return to cabinet, ignoring any developments between inaugurations. Harmel and Robertson (1986) have composed an index based on the way a cabinet is replaced, which basically is a weighted combination of all of the six definitions given.

Finally, cabinet duration can be measured by the rate of portfolio reshuffles among cabinet members (Macridis, 1959; Lijphart, 1968, 72; Robertson, 1983a). Ministers with short office terms would generally not be eager to make hard choices that involve certain and immediate large costs while the future gains are either uncertain or might be reaped by their successors. Changes in portfolio allocation also disrupt the orderly functioning of the cabinet and the ability to make decisions, as each new minister takes time to study his or her new assignments.

Accordingly, a cabinet change can be defined to occur when 100 percent of its portfolios have been reshuffled, often on an incremental basis. This measure reflects the extent to which portfolios were reshuffled in the wake of elections, coalition changes, inaugurations, and changes of government status. In this way, counting portfolio reshuffles acts as a weighted index of all of these events, the weight of each being determined by the percentage of cabinet positions they affected.

As always when studying cabinet duration, some cabinets begin before the start of the sample period, and others terminate after its end. Most of the studies in comparative politics use a sample period at least two decades long and simply drop cabinets that extend beyond the sample period in either direction. This method is impossible for this book, given the short period covered. Alternatively, one could just consider the total duration of such extending cabinets on an equal basis with nonextending cabinets. The trouble here is that any meaningful explanation of cabinet duration must be based on instruments measured over the same period.

The compromise adopted is that each country's average cabinet duration is based on all cabinets during the sample period weighted by their duration rounded to months. The weight of cabinets with terms that extend beyond the sample period (either starting before 1992 or ending after 1998) is the part of their terms that fall within the sample period. For example, in Germany, cabinets were inaugurated following elections in January 1991, November 1994, October 1998, and October 2002. Thus, Germany's ELEC-TION value in months is (34 X 46 + 47 X 47 + 3 X 48) / 84 = 46.6, or 3.9 years. The weighted average plays down extending cabinets that existed for only a short part of the sample period.

In presidential democracies, the governing coalition is considered to have changed when the president is replaced. In addition, relevant elections for the purpose of measuring cabinet duration are presidential elections rather than elections to the legislature. In bicameral parliamentary democracies, the relevant elections are those to the house on whose support the cabinet depends (most often the lower house).

Transition cabinets are disregarded in the calculation of cabinet duration because they represent intervals in which the democratic game is suspended, and therefore the various arguments to be considered do not apply. The same goes for governments inaugurated in eastern Europe before the first elections. Finally, a cabinet is not considered to have changed if a transition cabinet took office between two of its terms, as long as indeed the cabinet was identical in these terms according to the definition used.

Table 5.2 reports the average duration of cabinets in years in the period 1992–1998 in the sample's twenty-six countries, in accordance with some of the more common definitions detailed above. The variables COALITION, EXECUTIVE, and ELECTION are each based on one of the first three definitions of cabinet duration offered earlier in this section, in accordance with their order of presentation. SHARE considers cabinets to change when either the coalition changes, the top executive is replaced, or both (the fifth definition). ALL considers changes of coalition, changes of the top executive, the occurrence of elections, or any combination of these (all first three definitions combined) as cabinet changes.

COALITION and EXECUTIVE suffer from a special censoring problem because some of the cabinets that took office before January 1999 are still in office now, according to the definitions used, making it impossible to measure their duration. The coalitions of Fianna Fail and the Progressive Democrats in Ireland, the Nationalist Party in Malta, and the Labor Party in the UK all remain. As for top executives, taoiseach Bertie Ahern in Ireland, prime minister Mikulas Dzurinda in Slovakia, and prime minister Tony Blair in the UK are all still in office too.

This censoring problem essentially prevents the use of COALITION and EXECUTIVE as proxies for cabinet duration when attempting to explain it with instruments. Nevertheless, these variables are still useful for presentational and illustrative purposes. Thus, Table 5.2 considers all of the nonterminated coalitions and top executives to have terminated their offices in April 2006. This makes the measure of cabinet duration in these countries speculative to a certain degree. However, in the Maltese and Slovakian cases, the weight of the nonterminated cabinets is small enough to make the figures in the table reliably representative of cabinet duration. In the Irish and British cases, there is a greater risk that COALITION and EXECUTIVE are downplaying the true level of cabinet duration.

This problem does not occur when using ELECTION as a proxy for cabinet duration because all countries have by now held elections at lease once since January 1999. The latest first post-1998 elections took place in Malta in March 2004. As a result, any composite definition of cabinet duration based on elections is also free of nonterminated cabinets. Moreover, the higher fre-

Table 5.2   Cabinet Duration, 1992–1998

Variable name:	COALITION	EXECUTIVE	ELECTION	SHARE	ALL	RESHUFFLES
Cabinet change defined by:	A change in the party composition of the coalition	A change of the top executive	An election	A change in coalition parties and/or an election	A change in parties and the top executive and/or an election	A gradual replacement of the entire college of ministers
Austria	13.1	8.3	3.5	3.5	2.8	4.7
Belgium	7.8	7.5	3.7	3.6	3.6	4.2
Bulgaria	2.4	2.4	3.0	2.4	2.4	1.5
Cyprus	4.1	9.2	5.0	4.1	4.1	2.9
Czech Rep.	3.3	5.9	3.3	3.3	3.3	2.6
Denmark	2.1	9.0	2.9	2.1	2.1	3.7
Estonia	1.5	1.9	3.4	1.5	1.3	1.5
Finland	5.2	6.1	4.0	3.3	4.0	6.0
France	3.8	3.2	3.2	2.6	2.6	1.7
Germany	7.6	15.7	3.9	3.9	3.9	3.8
Greece	8.7	5.1	3.3	3.3	2.9	2.1
Hungary	4.1	3.7	4.1	4.1	3.7	2.1
Ireland	3.9	4.1	4.4	3.1	2.7	2.4
Italy	1.7	1.6	3.1	1.5	1.5	1.2
Latvia	1.4	1.7	2.8	1.4	1.4	1.2
Lithuania	3.0	2.7	3.8	3.0	1.8	1.3
Malta	7.3	7.2	3.9	3.9	3.9	2.7
Netherlands	6.7	6.7	4.2	4.2	4.2	4.6
Poland	2.0	2.1	3.5	2.0	1.5	1.4
Portugal	6.3	8.2	4.0	4.0	4.0	4.0
Romania	1.4	2.9	3.9	1.4	1.3	1.5
Slovakia	2.8	3.2	3.4	2.8	2.8	1.5
Slovenia	2.0	7.3	4.0	2.0	2.0	2.3
Spain	4.4	10.3	3.2	3.2	3.2	3.4
Sweden	2.6	4.1	3.6	2.6	2.6	3.8
UK	15.8	7.1	4.8	4.8	4.7	2.9
Average	4.8	5.7	3.7	3.0	2.9	2.7
Euro zone average	6.5	7.3	3.7	3.4	3.3	3.6
Transition countries	2.4	3.4	3.5	2.4	2.1	1.7
Other five sample countries	6.2	6.8	4.0	3.5	3.5	3.0

Notes: Columns differ by the definition used for cabinet change as detailed in the second row. Entries are period averages, given in years and based on *Keesing's Record of World Events.*

quency of cabinet change when measured with a combination of definitions further reduces the weight of extending cabinets in the country average and minimizes the censoring problem from a practical point of view.

RESHUFFLES is the only proxy for cabinet duration in Table 5.2 that is not based on either COALITION, EXECUTIVE, or ELECTION. It is the average number of years it took for 100 percent of the cabinet's ministers to be incrementally replaced, or the inverted annual rate of cabinet reshuffles (see Box 5.1 for technical details).

Table 5.2 shows that by all measures of cabinet duration, the transition countries featured significantly fewer durable cabinets than did the other European countries in the 1990s. The exception is ELECTION, the average interval between elections, for which the averages for the transition countries is close to the averages of the other countries. In other words, elections were more or less as frequent in western Europe as they were in central Europe. In addition, by all measures there was very little difference between the experience of the current euro zone member states and the other non-transition sample countries.

Looking at the average for the entire group of twenty-six countries, cabinet reshuffles (RESHUFFLES) were the most frequent form of change in

---

Box 5.1   How Is the Inverted Rate of Cabinet Reshuffles (RESHUFFLES) Calculated?

RESHUFFLES is calculated as the number of years in the sample, divided by the sum of the weights of all cabinet reshuffles. The weight of each cabinet reshuffle during the sample period equals the number of portfolios reshuffled divided by the total number of portfolios in the cabinet. The number of portfolios reshuffled in each event is the higher of the numbers of outgoing or incoming ministers. Reshuffling of portfolios among existing cabinet members is disregarded. When a cabinet reshuffle changed the total number of portfolios in the cabinet, the higher of the two numbers is taken as the denominator. Cabinet reshuffles occurring within three months of each other are considered as one event.

For example, in the Netherlands, one minister was replaced in January 1993 and again in January 1994, keeping the number of ministers at fourteen. Each of these two events weighs 7.1 (= 1/14) percent. In May 1994 two ministers resigned and in August a new cabinet with fourteen ministers was inaugurated following elections. Three of these fourteen ministers had served in the outgoing cabinet. These developments are considered as one event weighing 78.6 (= 11/14) percent. Finally, in August 1998, another cabinet was inaugurated following fresh elections, this time with fifteen ministers of which six served in the previous cabinet. The weight of this event is 60.0 (= 9/15) percent. Thus, cabinet reshuffles in the Netherlands weighed a total of 152.8 percent, and the implied cabinet duration during the seven years (1992–1998) is 4.6 (= 7/1.528) years.

cabinets in the 1990s, replacing cabinets incrementally roughly once in every two years and eight months. Elections, taking place roughly once in every three years and eight months, were more frequent than coalition changes, meaning that they had some tendency to return incumbents to power. This is especially true with prime ministers and presidents, who were replaced almost once in every six years.

The conclusion is that if cabinet duration is indeed important for the sustainability of EMU, then EMU would be most sustainable if participating in it was the personal responsibility of top executives. EMU's sustainability would also be helped if EMU enjoyed the support of all parties, and thus was not sensitive to changes in the governing coalition, and if it were not an electoral campaign issue, and thus not sensitive to elections. This indeed seems to be a more or less correct description of the domestic politics of EMU in many EU member states in the 1990s.

A vertical view of Table 5.2 shows that coalitions were most durable in Austria and the UK and least durable in Estonia, Italy, Latvia, and Romania. Top executives were especially durable in Germany and Spain, and least durable again in Estonia, Italy, and Latvia. The electoral cycle was especially long in Cyprus and the UK and relatively short in Denmark and Latvia. Finally, a minister's post tended to be the most secure in Austria, Belgium, the Netherlands, and especially Finland. In contrast, ministers in Latvia, Lithuania, and Poland, and above all Italy could expect on average to last little more than a year in office.

Thus, if personal leadership is important for a country's membership in EMU, then Germany, and Spain seem like potentially stable member states, whereas Estonia, Italy, and Latvia are less so. However, if EMU became politically contentious and sensitive to coalition changes and elections, the distinction between compatible and incompatible member states as far as cabinet duration is concerned would change. Austria, Cyprus, and the UK would lead the parade, and Denmark and Romania would bring up the rear.

From a horizontal overview of performance according to the various measures of cabinet duration, the cabinets of Estonia, Italy, Latvia, Lithuania, Romania, and Poland were the least durable in the sample. Among pre-2004 EU member states, Denmark stands out as featuring short-lived coalitions and frequent elections, but a highly durable prime minister. Indeed, in accordance with (or at least in the spirit of) Hypothesis 6, Italy alternated during the sample period between a float and the wide margins of the Exchange Rate Mechanism (ERM), Poland chose a crawling peg, and Romania was floating for the whole period (see Table 3.2). Latvia spent much of the sample period adopting a conventional pegged arrangement, and Estonia and Lithuania adopted a currency board. Thus, the evidence is mixed.

Clearer evidence in support of Hypothesis 6 emerges from Table 3.1, which shows that among those six countries with particularly unstable cabinets, only Estonia was able to stabilize its actual nominal exchange rate variation against France and Germany, only Italy did so against the UK, and none of the other five countries were able to do so against Italy. Similarly supportive evidence is suggested in Table 3.3 with regard to the broader measure of adjustment.

In contrast, the cabinets of Germany, the Netherlands, Portugal, and the UK tended to be the most durable in the sample. This is compatible with the two former countries' choices to participate in the ERM, and especially their resolve to observe its narrow (informal) margins. However, Portugal did resort rather liberally to the wider margins of the ERM (see Chapter 1) and the UK's currency was floating for almost all of the sample period. So, again, the evidence is mixed. The same pattern of behavior is repeated in Table 3.1 with regard to actual exchange rate variation against France and Germany, but Table 3.3 shows that all four countries with particularly stable cabinets did experience relatively low adjustment among themselves. Among the four major EU countries, Germany and the UK stand out as potentially better anchors for the European currency zone than France and Italy, as far as durable cabinets are concerned.

The Political Business Cycle

The third intervening variable between interest groups and partisanship, on the one hand, and exchange rate policy outcomes, on the other, is the political business cycle, which creates opportunities for interest-group action (Blomberg et al., 2004; Leblang, 2003). Two schools—the traditional and the rational—have developed in the literature on the political business cycle. The traditional political business cycle theory assumes that the economy is described by an exploitable Phillips curve and concludes that the incumbent government stimulates the economy prior to elections in order to create jobs and get reelected (MacRae, 1977; Nordhaus, 1975). Such stimulation may take the form of public deficits, devaluation of the currency, and low interest rates.

To the extent that the public can be assumed to hold rational expectations, however, such manipulation is doomed to failure. Even workers in traditional industries, who may see devaluation as a means to secure their jobs and improve their income prospects, suffer from the inflationary effect of devaluation. This is especially true in open economies. Bargaining for a simple wage increase is a more direct and clear way to improve one's income than devaluation, which has multiple effects.

According to the rational political business cycle theory, politicians hold office in order to deliver benefits to favored interest groups (Frieden et al., 2001), or for the sake of office perks (Stein and Sterb, 1999). To get reelected, they hide these costs from the voters and avoid pre-election inflation and devaluation, which, like a tax, erode the voters' purchasing power (Alesina and Roubini, 1994).

Pre-election inflation and devaluation are avoided by accumulating debt, which is visible to the electorate only with a lag (Stein and Sterb, 1999). After the elections, the true size of the deficit is revealed, and inflation and devaluation ensue, at which time the government opts for fiscal restraint. Rogoff (1990, 27) puts it in a slightly different way, arguing that policy choices of the government prior to the elections are meant to signal its competency, and that the government has an interest to deceive the public about its competency.

Is there a political business cycle in Europe? Alesina and Roubini (1997) have studied the sensitivity of unemployment, growth, output, and inflation to changes of government and to their political orientation in eleven of the EU-15 member states (as well as seven non-EU countries) during 1960–1987. They find that elections did not have real effects. Accordingly, the dummy variable that Bernhard and Leblang (1999, 83) use for election years in twenty industrialized democracies during 1974–1995 is also statistically insignificant. Hallerberg (2002) reports similar results.

Most of the evidence points in the direction of the rational political business cycle theory. Eichengreen et al. (1995) finds that government defeats in elections increased the probability of devaluation and realignment in twenty OECD countries during 1959–1993 because it is easier for a new administration to blame devaluation and any implicit tax on its predecessors. Post-election dummies used by Alesina and Roubini (1997) show that inflation does tend to increase immediately after elections. Blomberg and Hess (1997) detect a tendency of the German mark and the British pound to appreciate in pre-election periods during 1974–1994.

It follows from both approaches to the political business cycle that unsynchronized electoral cycles in two countries (i.e., each country holding elections at a different time) lead to different fiscal positions at a given point in time. For example, when a country is one month ahead of elections, its government may wish to increase spending and the public deficit, even if covertly, while at the same time a government of another country may introduce a post-election austerity program, cutting the deficit and even entering a surplus.

However, the two approaches to the political business cycle yield two different hypotheses about the exchange rate and monetary policies pursued at a given point in the cycle. The traditional approach calls for devaluation and low interest rates ahead of elections, whereas the rational approach prescribes devaluation and inflation after elections. If two countries are similarly affected by their own political business cycles (i.e., both go through a traditional cycle or both go through a rational cycle) then it is expected that overlapping cycles in two countries would be associated with low values of the bilateral adjustment indicators. In contrast, if one country experiences a traditional political business cycle while the other experiences a rational cycle, then political business cycle correlation would be insignificantly associated with the dependent variables or even inversely associated with them.

Of course, the political business cycle in a given country is endogenous to its domestic politics, not an idiosyncratic feature of the political system. Specifically, it is much influenced by cabinet duration (line *j* in Figure 5.1). Whether elections are held next June or September is a reflection of the combined effects of cabinet duration and institutions, as analyzed in Chapter 6. The lower the cabinet duration and longevity of parliamentary coalitions, the more frequent are elections.

To a certain extent, the political business cycle is also endogenous to the economic business cycle. For example, a severe recession can bring a cabinet down ahead of scheduled elections. Or an opportunistic policymaker may want to call early elections if economic prospects are good. The former example is an extreme situation, however, and the latter depends on the ability to manipulate the electoral calendar. This ability, in turn, is explained by various institutional features, many of which are studied in Chapter 6 as determinants of cabinet duration. Thus, once cabinet duration and its determinants are controlled for, the economic business cycle is expected to have very little effect on the political cycle.

Cabinet duration affects not only the timing of elections but also the effectiveness of opportunistic policies that are inherent to the political business cycle. The reason for this is that the ability of governments to keep deceiving voters ahead of elections depends on the way that past experience influences voters' expectations. If the distant past weighs less in the formation of expectations than the recent past, then the shorter the intervals between elections and the greater the weight that the last post-election devaluation would carry. When elections become frequent, the time intervals between elections become shorter, and the incumbents find it harder to distance themselves from past deceptions.

However, in contrast to individual national political business cycles, bilateral correlation of political business cycles is to a great extent a matter of coincidence. Because it is a random variable, political business cycle correlation obviously cannot be regarded as a bilateral idiosyncratic feature. Nevertheless, it is exogenous to other variables in this study and may have its distinct effect on adjustment between countries. Thus, like partisanship, political business cycle correlation is regarded in this book as an exogenous control variable, the effect of which needs to be isolated if meaningful insights are to be drawn about the determinants of adjustment. Political business cycle correlation can be positively or negatively associated with the extent of adjustment, as suggested here.

POLICYC is the logarithmic transformation of the standard deviation of the difference in the quarterly coding of the electoral cycle during the sample period in the two countries. In each country, each quarter is coded 1 (0 being the default case) if: (1) regular or early elections took place, (2) it is one of the three quarters preceding regular elections, or (3) it is one of the quarters between early elections and the political crisis that preceded them (there were never more than two such quarters).

Regular elections are elections to the national legislature that were held at the constitutionally stipulated interval. In bicameral systems, only elections to the lower chamber of the legislature are considered. In Cyprus, presidential elections are considered instead of elections to the legislature. In France, both presidential and parliamentary elections are considered because of the special features of the French democracy (see Chapter 6). Early elections are elections to the national legislature that took place before the constitutionally stipulated quarter. A crisis is signaled by the last coalition change and/or cabinet reshuffle and/or successful no-confidence motion within the nine months before early elections.

Out of a total of fifty-five elections in the sample, twenty-five were early, and of these nine were not preceded by any apparent crisis as just defined. These nine elections are assumed to have been opportunistically rescheduled by the ruling party or major coalition partner. Because their timing was therefore controlled by the incumbent, they are coded like regular elections. In each dyadic observation, the difference between the two countries' coding is calculated for each quarter. *POLICYC* is the logarithmic transformation of the standard deviation of these differences. The lower the value of *POLICYC*, the more correlated are the electoral cycles in the two countries.

Table 5.3 presents *POLICYC* values for dyads involving the four major EU member states. The closest correlation between electoral cycles in the sample (0.19) is found in the Romanian-Slovenian case (not shown in the table). In contrast, two dyads reached a similar *POLICYC* score of 0.85, the highest score in the sample. These are France and Hungary and France and the Netherlands. The average score in the sample is 0.61 (see Table 8.2 on page 144).

Judging from the data at the bottom of Table 5.3, very little difference exists between the current euro zone member states and the transition countries in terms of the overlapping of their elections with those of each of the four major EU member states. This is in stark contrast to the tendency of euro zone countries presented in Tables 3.1 and 3.3 for lower exchange rate variation and lower adjustment in general. Thus, this evidence seems to superficially suggest that political business cycle correlation is not associated in any clear manner with the indicators of adjustment.

However, elections in France happened to be less correlated on average

Table 5.3 Political Business Cycle Correlation (*policyc*), 1992–1998

France		Germany		Italy		UK	
Ireland	0.39	Sweden	0.27	Czech Rep.	0.45	**Ireland**	0.43
Bulgaria	0.46	Slovakia	0.33	Romania	0.47	Romania	0.43
UK	0.50	Hungary	0.38	**Austria**	0.47	Bulgaria	0.47
Lithuania	0.57	**Austria**	0.42	Slovenia	0.50	Slovenia	0.47
Cyprus	0.59	**Finland**	0.43	**Portugal**	0.51	**France**	0.50
Slovenia	0.59	Denmark	0.47	UK	0.51	**Italy**	0.51
Belgium	0.60	**Netherlands**	0.47	Slovakia	0.52	Poland	0.51
Portugal	0.60	Bulgaria	0.52	Estonia	0.54	Lithuania	0.54
Romania	0.61	Malta	0.58	**Spain**	0.57	Malta	0.57
Austria	0.65	**Belgium**	0.59	**Belgium**	0.58	Estonia	0.58
Spain	0.65	**Italy**	0.63	Bulgaria	0.58	**Belgium**	0.60
Estonia	0.67	Czech Rep.	0.64	**Greece**	0.58	Cyprus	0.60
Finland	0.67	Estonia	0.64	Lithuania	0.58	**Portugal**	0.60
Poland	0.67	Latvia	0.64	Malta	0.59	**Greece**	0.61
Italy	0.70	**Portugal**	0.65	**Ireland**	0.60	Czech Rep.	0.63
Latvia	0.74	Cyprus	0.67	Cyprus	0.63	Slovakia	0.63
Greece	0.74	**Greece**	0.72	Denmark	0.63	**Austria**	0.64
Denmark	0.76	Lithuania	0.72	**Germany**	0.63	Denmark	0.66
Germany	0.76	UK	0.72	Hungary	0.63	**Finland**	0.69
Malta	0.79	**Ireland**	0.74	**Netherlands**	0.63	**Germany**	0.72
Slovakia	0.79	Poland	0.74	Sweden	0.63	Hungary	0.72
Sweden	0.80	Romania	0.74	**Finland**	0.66	**Netherlands**	0.72
Czech Rep.	0.83	**France**	0.76	Poland	0.66	**Spain**	0.72
Hungary	0.85	Slovenia	0.77	**France**	0.70	Sweden	0.72
Netherlands	0.85	**Spain**	0.77	Latvia	0.71	Latvia	0.74
Average	0.67		0.60		0.58		0.60
Euro zone average	0.66		0.62		0.59		0.61
Transition countries	0.68		0.61		0.58		0.61
Other 5 sample countries	0.69		0.55		0.56		0.56

Notes: Entries represent the standard deviation of the bilateral difference in quarterly coding for pre- or post-election periods in each two countries. Entries are in code units. Current euro zone member states are printed in bold type.

with elections in the other sample countries than were elections in the other three major EU member states. On average, France experienced lower adjustment against the other sample countries, as shown in the tables in Chapter 4. This suggests that perhaps there may be an inverted relationship between the political business cycle and adjustment: As elections in countries become less correlated there is less adjustment between them. This is possible, as previously explained, if some countries follow a traditional cycle whereas others follow a rational one.

In sum, it is difficult to tell whether political business cycle correlation has a clear effect on the extent of adjustment between countries. Chapter 7 makes a more rigorous estimation of the effects of political business cycle correlation on exchange rate variation and other adjustment mechanisms.

6

Cabinet Duration and Institutions

Cabinet duration has a simultaneous relationship with exchange rate variation, so it must be instrumented to provide a meaningful causal explanation of exchange rate variation and other measures of adjustment. In other words, part of cabinet duration reflects a country idiosyncrasy and part of it is a simultaneous ex post feature. The proper way to instrument cabinet duration is to explain it with institutional features of the country's system of government.

Institutions affect cabinet duration (see line c in Figure 5.1). Electoral laws have a strong influence on parliamentary fragmentation, which in turn affects the viability of governing coalitions. Procedures for dissolution of cabinets and parliaments could make it more difficult or easier to replace policymakers. Presidential democracies can make cabinets more durable compared with parliamentary democracies. This chapter discusses the main institutional features suggested in the literature as determinants of cabinet duration.

Data for all institutional instruments presented in this chapter are based on the written letter of the law, mostly the constitution, in order to minimize simultaneity between the instruments and cabinet duration. It is assumed that the players observe the law and that the legal framework—especially constitutional rules, which require a special majority for modifications to be introduced—does operate as a constraint on the set of the democratic game's possible outcomes (Strøm et al., 1994).

The Age of Democracy

Highly institutionalized parties contribute to cabinet duration (Brass, 1977) because they enjoy a large core of loyal voters and a stable share of the votes. Institutionalized parties also enjoy greater discipline among their representatives in parliament, as the personal turnover among these representatives is low and their dependency on the party is great. Because democracies take time to develop institutionalized parties, the age of the regime could serve as a proxy instrument for party institutionalization.

Young democracies also tend to be more corrupt than mature ones. Corrupt members of democratic and accountable cabinets are often forced to step down, so corruption is a cause of cabinet reshuffles and political crises, and thus is a politically destabilizing phenomenon. AGE is a variable equal to the number of years between 1995 (the median year of the sample period) and the year of first democratic elections with women suffrage since the most recent switch to democracy. AGE is expected to be positively associated with cabinet duration.

Table 6.1 shows that the transition countries, with an average AGE of almost four years, are much younger democracies than the euro zone countries, which average 45 years. The youngest democracy in the sample is Latvia, which had its first democratic elections in 1993, and the oldest is Finland, with 78 years. Democracy was also uninterrupted by World War II in Ireland, Sweden, and the UK.

Presidential Democracies

Cabinets are expected to be more durable in presidential democracies compared with parliamentary ones because the cabinet is staffed with the president's team, and its composition does not reflect coalition agreements and crises. A presidential cabinet can also be understood to be a one-party minimum winning coalition (Lijphart, 1999, 104–106).

Presidential democracies are distinguished from parliamentary democracies by featuring a two-tier political system in which the president is the top executive, rather than a one-tier political system based on the legislature (Power and Gasiorowski, 1997; Strøm, 2000). Lijphart (1999, 116–124) suggests that presidential democracies are characterized by: (1) direct elections to the presidency without parliamentary review, and (2) a balance of power between the president and the legislature. This balance can be maintained when, for example, the president and the legislature cannot dissolve or dismiss each other, or when both can and both stand for new elections as a result. Semi-presidential democracies are characterized by a directly elected president and a prime minister appointed by the legislature, the latter being the top executive. Thus, semi-presidential democracies are essentially parliamentary democracies.

Based on Lijphart's (1999) definitions and judgment, the only fully presidential democracy in this sample is Cyprus. In France, the president is the top executive, but a prime minister backed by the majority in the national assembly (a cohabitation government) can be more powerful than the president. Thus, according to Lijphart, France is alternating between being a presidential democracy and parliamentary one; it is a presidential democracy whenever the president and the prime minister are from the same party, and it is a parliamentary democracy otherwise.

Table 6.1 Potential Instruments of Cabinet Duration (1992–1998)—Part 1

	AGE	PRESIDENT[a]	N	FETHNICITY	FRELIGION	FLANGUAGE	MAJORITARIAN[a]	THRESHOLD[a]	(Number of seats in the legislature[a])	SEATS 100[a]
Austria	50		3.32	0.22	0.36	0.15		14.3	183	
Belgium	49		8.21	0.56	0.38	0.56		8.8	150	
Bulgaria	4		2.55	0.29	0.28	0.22		8.6	240	1
Cyprus	14	1	3.51	0.26	0.36	0.37		7.3	56	
Czech Rep.	5		4.55	0.32	0.67	0.04		5.0	200	
Denmark	50		4.70	0.06	0.10	0.05		2.0	179	
Estonia	3		4.82	0.49	0.82	0.46		7.4	101	
Finland	78		5.03	0.12	0.20	0.13		0.0	200	
France	50	0.46	3.26	0.11	0.30	0.24	1	37.5	574	1
Germany	46		3.33	0.16	0.69	0.30		25.0	656	
Greece	21·		2.29	0.04	0.04	0.12		12.2	300	
Hungary	5		3.25	0.19	0.50	0.15	0.46	23.3	386	
Ireland	74		3.32	0.02	0.16	0.17		14.9	166	
Italy	49		6.59	0.11	0.31	0.39		4.0	630	
Latvia	2		5.60	0.58	0.78	0.53		4.6	100	
Lithuania	3		3.28	0.34	0.28	0.33	1	37.5	141	
Malta	29		2.00	0.00	0.00	0.02		12.5	65	
Netherlands	49		4.79	0.30	0.70	0.18		0.7	150	1
Poland	4		5.17	0.05	0.10	0.12		5.0	460	
Portugal	19		2.38	0.02	0.11	0.02		6.5	230	
Romania	5		5.46	0.19	0.47	0.27		8.5	341	
Slovakia	5		4.06	0.25	0.59	0.28		5.0	150	
Slovenia	3		5.95	0.22	0.44	0.03		6.3	90	
Spain	18		2.73	0.10	0.42	0.43		9.7	350	
Sweden	76		3.77	0.23	0.50	0.13		6.4	349	
UK	67		2.23	0.32	0.19	0.06	1	37.5	659	
Average	29.9		4.08	0.21	0.38	0.22		11.9	273	
Euro zone average	45.3		4.20	0.17	0.34	0.25		9.6	302	
Transition countries	3.9		4.47	0.29	0.49	0.24		11.1	221	
Other five sample countries	51.2		3.08	0.15	0.22	0.13		18.3	322	

Notes: Variables in parentheses are not used as instruments for cabinet duration. Data are based on national legal text, as well as on Berglund et al. (1998); Strøm and Swindle (2002, 577); and Kurian (1998).

a. Based on the explicit letter of the law.

Also according to Lijphart (1999), the president in Finland has been even weaker than that in France ever since the 1991 reform. Other semi-presidential democracies in the sample include Austria, Ireland, Lithuania, Poland, Portugal, Romania, Slovakia, and Slovenia. In Poland and Romania, the 1990s saw fierce struggles over the division of authority between the legislatures and the presidents. Both Lech Walesa and Ion Iliesco, being the leaders of the revolutions in their respective countries, tried to assert themselves as top executives and amend the constitutions accordingly. However, in the end both had to accept a more powerful prime minister than they had wished for.

PRESIDENT is a dummy variable, coding 1 for Cyprus, 0.46 for France, and 0 otherwise. The French code represents the proportion of the sample period during which there was no cohabitation government. A cohabitation government existed in France from March 1993 to April 1995 and again from June 1997 until after the sample period ended in December 1998, so France is considered to have been a presidential democracy during 39 of the 84 sample months (or 46 percent). This solution has the disadvantage of introducing a degree of endogeneity into this variable, but coding France as either 0 or 1 would represent an even greater distortion. It is expected that PRESIDENT is positively associated with cabinet duration.

Parliamentary Fragmentation

The greater the number of parties in the legislature, the less durable the cabinet (Taylor and Herman, 1971). A large number of parties would make it more difficult to form minimum winning coalitions, which in turn are considered to be the most durable type of cabinets, as argued in Chapter 5. One could try to use cabinet status to explain cabinet duration; however, coalition variables such as cabinet status are endogenous to exchange rates and to cabinet duration. Cabinet status is at any rate an intervening variable between parliamentary fragmentation and cabinet duration (Grofman, 1989). Thus, it is better to explain cabinet duration with parliamentary fragmentation rather than cabinet status.

Some scholars use the number of coalition parties as a measure of fragmentation (Frieden, 2002; Keefer, 2002; Keefer and Stasavage, 2002). A simple count of parties in parliament would overstate fragmentation, however, giving similar weights to large as well as small parties. The effective number of parties, N, which is the inverted sum of the squares of the parties' shares in parliament, is a better measure of fragmentation (Laakso and Taagepera, 1979). It returns the simple count of parties only if their shares in parliament are equal, and a lower number otherwise.

Table 6.1 details the period average N level for each sample country. N

is calculated in each quarter, and the quarterly values are then averaged in the table. In bicameral democracies, calculations are based on lower chamber data. Data on parties is based on *Keesing's Record of World Events* and the *Statesman's Yearbook*. There was very little difference in the extent of parliamentary fragmentation between the current euro zone countries and the transition countries in the 1990s. Malta was the least fragmented, always with exactly two parties. In fact, with the exception of Denmark, all non–euro zone nontransition countries featured relatively nonfragmented legislatures. Italy and Belgium top the fragmentation parade with the equivalent of, respectively, 6.6 and 8 equally sized parties. Superficially, therefore, N does not seem to be a good predictor of cabinet duration.

N is the more tangible version of Rae's (1971, 53–58) and Rae and Taylor's (1970, 22–44) fragmentation index, often denoted by F, which returns 0 when there is only one party in parliament, and gets closer to 1 as parties proliferate and shrink. Specifically, $F = 1 - 1/N$. Still, F may be endogenous to various political variables and thus needs to be instrumented. The literature expects F to rise with social cleavages, a proportional representation rather than a majoritarian electoral formula, low parliamentary minimum thresholds, high district magnitude, and the total number of seats in parliament (Amorim Neto and Cox, 1997; Lijphart, 1999, 55–61, 144–157; Ordeshook and Shvetsova, 1994).

FETHNICITY, *FRELIGION*, and *FLANGUAGE* represent social fragmentation indices calculated for each country similar to F, based on the ethnic, religious, and linguistic compositions of society in each country. Ethnic and religious composition data are based on the *CIA World Factbook*, and linguistic composition data, which relate to mother tongue languages, are based on Gordon (2005). All three social fragmentation indices are expected to be positively associated with parliamentary fragmentation. Table 6.1 shows that transition countries are more fragmented than the euro zone member states by all three indices, and especially so when compared with the five non–euro zone, nontransition countries. Latvia, Estonia, and Belgium are, respectively, ethnically, religiously, and linguistically the most fragmented countries in the sample. Malta has the most homogenous society, followed by Denmark, Greece, Ireland, Poland, and Portugal.

MAJORITARIAN is a dummy variable coding 1 when countries feature a majoritarian electoral formula and 0 for a proportional representation formula. A majoritarian formula is expected to be negatively associated with fragmentation in the legislature because competing for single seat districts tends to benefit the large parties. Only France, Lithuania, and the UK have a full majoritarian electoral formula. Hungary is a borderline case because 176 of its legislature's 386 seats are allocated to single member districts, and the other 210 seats are allocated according to the proportional representation formula. Thus, Hungary's value is 0.46 (= 176/386).

THRESHOLD is an index of parliamentary minimum thresholds, taking for each country the higher of either the official threshold or the implied threshold arising from electoral district magnitude. The district magnitude (the number of seats allocated in the legislature to representatives of the district) is converted to an implied parliamentary minimum threshold by using the formula suggested by Lijphart (1999, 153–154): $T = 75\%/(M+1)$, where M (district magnitude) is the average number of seats per electoral district in the (lower chamber of) parliament.[1]

In all sample countries, district magnitude as well the demarcation of districts are enshrined in the law, typically adjusted once in a couple of decades by an apolitical body to account for demographic changes. The exception is Finland, in which redistricting is carried out ahead of each election by political parties. Thus, Finland's implied parliamentary minimum threshold (as well as its THRESHOLD value, in the absence of an official threshold) is 0. Interestingly, the current euro zone member states tend to have relatively low effective parliamentary thresholds.[1]

Small parliaments produce disproportional representation of parties in the legislature, especially harming the small ones. Unsurprisingly, the transition countries, which have relatively small populations, tend to feature smaller legislatures than other sample countries. SEATS100 is a dummy variable coding 1 when countries feature a (lower chamber of) parliament with fewer than 100 seats (a cutoff point suggested by Lijphart [1999]) and 0 otherwise (see Table 6.1). It is expected to be negatively associated with fragmentation. Only three countries in the sample feature such small chambers—Cyprus, Malta, and Slovenia.

Table 6.2 summarizes attempts to instrument F. The two equations differ in their choice of proxy for the electoral formula. Results fit expectations. All three measures of social diversity (ethnicity, religion, and language) are positively associated with political fragmentation, their coefficients reflecting the elasticity of political fragmentation, or its sensitivity to social diversity. These sensitivities are surprisingly low. For example, in 1990s Europe, a rise of 1 percent in religious diversity led to a rise of only 0.05 percent on average in political fragmentation. The alignment of political parties in Europe was, as a general rule, even less sensitive to ethnic or linguistic divisions.

Higher entry thresholds to the legislature and a majoritarian electoral formula are both expectedly negatively associated with political fragmentation. A rise of 1 percent (not a percentage point) in the implied threshold was associated with a decline of 0.063 percent in political fragmentation. A majoritarian formula was more effective, chopping off some 11 percent from fragmentation. Likewise, small legislatures resulted in marginally lower fragmentation.

In spite of their low effects on political fragmentation, most of the esti-

Table 6.2   Ordinary Least Squares Equations of Parliamentary Fragmentation *(F)*

Equation number	(6.1)	(6.2)
CONSTANT	-0.06***	-0.19***
	(0.02)	(0.01)
ln.*FETHNICITY* (+)	0.02***	0.03**
	(0.01)	(0.01)
ln.*FRELIGION* (+)	0.05***	0.05***
	(0.01)	(0.01)
ln.*FLANGUAGE* (+)	0.03***	0.02**
	(0.01)	(0.01)
ln.*THRESHOLD* (−)	-0.06***	
	(0.01)	
MAJORITARIAN (−)		-0.12***
		(0.02)
SEATS100 (−)	-0.02	-0.03
	(0.02)	(0.02)
Number of observations	325	325
Sum of Squared Residuals (SSR)	1.47	1.84
R^2	0.49	0.36
F-statistic	61.4***	36.3***

Notes: Estimates are corrected with White heteroskedasticity-consistent standard errors and covariance. The dependent variable is the logarithmic transformation of the bilateral average of national values of Rae's parliamentary fragmentation index (Rae, 1971). All variables are dyadic averages. The "ln" prefix denotes a logarithmic transformation of the variable. Standard error values are indicated in parentheses. * $.05 < p \leq .10$. ** $.01 < p \leq .05$. *** $p \leq .01$ The signs by the names of the independent variables indicate their expected relationship with the dependent variable.

mated coefficients are quite robust. In contrast, *SEATS100*, the dummy for small parliaments, tends to return weak coefficients. Equation (6.1) has the advantage of including *THRESHOLD*, which is more sensitive than *MAJORITARI-AN* as a proxy for the electoral formula and richer in data. Thus, Equation (6.1) is chosen to instrument *F*.

Parliamentary Committees

Scholars argue that in democracies that allow a constructive and effective role for the opposition parties in legislation and government, as reflected in powerful parliamentary committees, the opposition is less eager to bring the government down and cabinets are more durable. Strøm's (1984) index of the power of parliamentary committees has five criteria: (1) the existence of at least ten permanent committees, (2) the assignment of permanent and specialized issue areas to the committees, (3) issue-area overlap between committees and cabinet portfolios, (4) limits on the number of committees in which a member of parliament can participate, and (5) a stipulation that committee seats be allocated among parties in proportion to their parliamentary seats. For each criterion, a country can be coded between 1 if the criterion is fulfilled, and 0. The scores in the five criteria are then summed and divided by five, to produce an index with a range between 0 for weak committees and 1 for strong committees. According to Strøm (1984), this index should be positively correlated with cabinet duration.

Table 6.3 presents the countries' scores according to the relevant legislation. There was no difference between the current euro zone member states and the transition countries in terms of committee power. In Ireland and the UK, the law does least to support committee work. In contrast, the most legally powerful committees are in Bulgaria, Denmark, Estonia, Italy, and Romania. Superficially, therefore, there seems to be a negative relationship, if any, between committee power and cabinet duration. Indeed, opposition parties can use the committees as power bases to bring down the government by blocking legislation and sabotaging the government's work. Thus, the effect of this variable on cabinet duration is ambiguous. Another problem with this variable is that committee work is rarely regulated by constitutions. More often, it is decided by regular laws or even by the committees themselves, making this variable quite endogenous to political dynamics. In light of these considerations, the power of parliamentary committees is dropped as a possible instrument for cabinet duration.

Cabinet Installation and Dismissal Procedures

This section specifies instruments that determine the legal framework for installing and dismissing cabinets. The first of these is CONSTRUCTIVE—a dummy instrument for a legal requirement to present an alternative cabinet before the current cabinet can be voted out of office by the legislature. This stipulation, henceforth referred to as a requirement for a constructive vote of no confidence, is considered to be an important measure that enhances cabinet duration (Lijphart, 1999, 96–103). Its incidence is expected to be positively correlated with cabinet duration.

A requirement for a constructive vote of no confidence exists in Belgium, Germany, Hungary, Malta, Slovenia, and Spain, as Table 6.3 shows. In addition, Poland adopted this requirement in its 1997 constitution, and CONSTRUCTIVE is adjusted to reflect the relevant proportion of the sample period in this case. For Cyprus, the equivalent of a vote of no confidence is a requirement that the president cannot be impeached without a (nonelected) replacement—a stipulation that, of course, does not exist.

Cabinets can also be more durable, or at least elections should be less frequent, if the law prohibits early elections (as in Norway), or stipulates that the new parliament merely completes its predecessor's term (Strøm et

Table 6.3   Potential Instruments of Cabinet Duration (1992–1998)—Part 2

	COMMITTEE INDEX[a]	CONSTRUCTIVE[a]	EARLY[a]	(HEADSELECT[a])	HEADVETO[a]	(PMDISS[a])	LINKAGE[a]	FREQUENCY[a]
Austria	0.80			1				4
Belgium	0.80	1			1			4
Bulgaria	1.00							4
Cyprus	0.80			1		1		5
Czech Rep.	0.16			1	1			4
Denmark	1.00			1		1	1	4
Estonia	1.00			1	1			4
Finland	0.40			1	1			4
France	0.64				1	1		4.80
Germany	0.80	1		1	1			4
Greece	0.44			1				4
Hungary	0.24	1		1				4
Ireland	0.00				1			5
Italy	1.00			1				5
Latvia	0.60			1				3.15
Lithuania	0.40	1		1	1			4
Malta	0.40			1	1			5
Netherlands	0.80							4
Poland	0.80	0.29		1				4
Portugal	0.80			1	1			4
Romania	1.00			1	1			4
Slovakia	0.36			1	1			4
Slovenia	0.40	1		1				4
Spain	0.20	1		1				4
Sweden	0.80		1					3.57
UK	0.00			1	1		1	5
Average	0.60							4.17
Euro zone average	0.60							4.20
Transition countries	0.60							3.92
Other 5 sample countries	0.61							4.64

Note: Variables in parentheses are not used as instruments for cabinet duration. Data are based on national legal text, as well as on Berglund et al. (1998); Strøm and Swindle (2002, 577); and Kurian (1998).
a. Based on the explicit letter of the law.

al., 1994). For presidential democracies, the equivalent stipulation would be that the term of a new president merely completes its impeached predecessor's term. In none of the countries in the sample are early elections actually prohibited, but in Sweden the electoral calendar is unaltered by early elections. Thus, EARLY is a dummy instrument, coding 1 for Sweden and 0 otherwise. It is expected to be positively correlated with cabinet duration, especially when measured by the effective interval between elections.

Uncertainty regarding the composition of a new cabinet and the identity of the new top executive can discourage political players from bringing down the cabinet. Such uncertainty would increase if a nonpolitical actor has the prerogative to select the first candidate to form a cabinet (Strøm et al., 1994). However, determining who is a political figure and who is not is tricky and subjective, especially in republics. HEADSELECT is a dummy instrument, coding 1 for countries where a nonexecutive head of state (such as monarch or president) has by law the prerogative to select the first candidate to form a cabinet and 0 otherwise (see Table 6.3). This is based on the assumption that the nonexecutive head of state is a nonpolitical actor. For Cyprus, HEADSELECT = 0 because the president is simultaneously the head of state and the top executive. In only eight sample countries does the law not involve the head of state in cabinet formation, as detailed previously, and four of these are current euro zone member states. However, given the difficulty of objectively determining the innocence of heads of state, HEADSELECT is not used as an instrument for cabinet duration.

When parliament is dissolved in a parliamentary democracy, the cabinet is either formally or effectively dismissed, and a transition cabinet ensues. Dissolution should be more prevalent when the top executive can unilaterally call early elections because the top executive is expected to act on opportunistic considerations. However, the existence of *veto players*, whose consent for dissolution is necessary but not sufficient, diminishes the odds for dissolution (Strøm and Swindle, 2002; Tsebelis, 2002).

HEADVETO is a dummy instrument, coding 1 for countries in which the nonexecutive head of state (whether a political actor or not) is by law a veto player, and 0 otherwise. PMDISS is another dummy instrument, coding 1 for countries in which the top executive can unilaterally call early elections, and 0 otherwise. In presidential democracies, calling early presidential elections, which is impossible under normal circumstances, is the equivalent of parliament dissolution in parliamentary democracies. As Table 6.3 shows, the nonexecutive head of state is a veto player in twelve countries, six of which are current euro zone member states, but only four are transition countries. It is expected that HEADVETO is positively associated with cabinet duration. However, the top executive can unilaterally call early elections only in Cyprus (where the president can resign) and France. Thus, PMDISS overlaps PRESIDENT, if imperfectly, and is dropped as a possible instrument of cabinet duration.

When cabinet dismissal automatically triggers dissolution of the legislature, opposition parties or defecting coalition partners will bring a cabinet down only if they expect electoral gains. This should make it more difficult to vote cabinets out of office (Strøm et al., 1994). However, if a cabinet is dismissed for reasons external to electoral considerations, the dismissal-dissolution linkage would cause elections to be more frequent. *LINKAGE* is a dummy instrument, coding 1 for Denmark and the UK, the only countries in which, by law, cabinet dismissal triggers parliament dissolution; and 0 otherwise. It is expected that *LINKAGE* is positively correlated with coalition duration, but increases the frequency of elections (reduces *ELECTION*).

Constitutional Frequency of Elections

Early dissolution of the legislature is more likely the longer its constitutional term because the term of the next legislature (to be gained by the winner of the early elections) is longer (Balke, 1990; Lupia and Strøm, 1995; Strøm and Swindle, 2002). However, short constitutional terms obviously also increase the actual frequency of elections, so the relationship between cabinet duration and the constitutional term of the legislature is a balance of these two effects.

FREQUENCY is the number of years specified by law as the official term of parliament in each parliamentary country, or the president's term in presidential democracies. Latvia and Sweden's parliamentary terms were changed during the sample period, and the relevant proportions of the sample period are adjusted for. The French value is an average between the constitutional frequency of elections to the national assembly and elections to the presidency, weighted by the proportion of the sample period in which there was a cohabitation government. The change in the French president's term from seven to five years since 1995 is also adjusted for. All told, there is very little difference between transition countries and euro zone member states in terms of constitutional frequency of elections (see Table 6.3). It is expected that *FREQUENCY* is either positively or negatively correlated with cabinet duration.

Instrumenting Cabinet Duration

Table 6.4 presents instrument equations for four of the six measures of cabinet duration presented in Table 5.2. *COALITION* and *EXECUTIVE*, the two measures defined by, respectively, coalitions and executive changes, are not instrumented due to the censoring problem explained in Chapter 5. All variables in Table 6.4 are dyadic averages of the national values surveyed earlier. The dependent variable is the logarithmic transformation of the bilateral average of cabinet duration in years.

Table 6.4 confirms that the age of democracy is positively and robustly associated with cabinet duration in 1990s Europe, except when defined in terms of elections. In other words, the frequency of elections is relatively weakly related to experience with democracy, and higher, if related at all, among mature democracies. Regime maturity has a relatively stronger effect on the turnover of cabinet ministers than on other measures of cabinet stability. As democracies grew 1 percent older, their ministers could expect to stay in the cabinet 0.276 percent longer.

Table 6.4   Ordinary Least Squares Equations of Cabinet Duration

Equation number	(6.3)	(6.4)	(6.5)	(6.6)
Variable name:	*ELECTION*	*SHARE*	*ALL*	*RESHUFFLES*
Cabinet change defined by:	An election	A change in coalition parties and/or an election	A change in coalition, the top executive, and/or an election	A gradual replacement of the entire college of ministers
CONSTANT	3.10***	3.58***	3.55***	5.53***
	(0.10)	(0.24)	(0.24)	(0.28)
ln.AGE (+)	−0.01***	0.08***	0.10***	0.27***
	(0.01)	(0.02)	(0.02)	(0.02)
PRESIDENT (+)	0.25***	0.62***	0.78***	0.75***
	(0.04)	(0.08)	(0.08)	(0.09)
fit.ln.F (−)	−0.21**	−1.40***	−0.88***	−0.36*
	(0.09)	(0.20)	(0.20)	(0.21)
CONSTRUCTIVE (+)	0.05***	0.19***	0.26***	0.27***
	(0.02)	(0.03)	(0.03)	(0.04)
EARLY (+) (with elections)	0.16***	−0.10	−0.04	−0.09
	(0.03)	(0.08)	(0.08)	(0.09)
HEADVETO (+)	0.13***	0.27***	0.36***	0.32***
	(0.01)	(0.04)	(0.04)	(0.04)
LINKAGE (−) (with elections)	−0.04	−0.11	−0.08	−0.01
	(0.03)	(0.07)	(0.08)	(0.05)
ln.FREQUENCY (+/−)	0.38***	−0.66***	−0.66***	−2.34***
	(0.09)	(0.20)	(0.21)	(0.23)
Number of observations	325	325	325	325
Sum of Squared Residuals (SSR)	1.96	10.5	10.9	11.5
R^2	0.43	0.44	0.52	0.67
F-statistic	29.9***	31.0***	42.5***	80.5***

Notes: Estimates are corrected with White heteroskedasticity-consistent standard errors and covariance. The "ln" prefix denotes a logarithmic transformation of the variable. Standard error values are indicated in parentheses. * $.05 < p \leq .10$. ** $.01 < p \leq .05$. *** $p \leq .01$. The signs by the names of the independent variables indicate their expected relationships with the dependent variable. Variables underscored with a dotted line are calculated as bilateral averages of national values.

Presidential democracies have distinctly more durable cabinets than parliamentary democracies. PRESIDENT's large and robust coefficients imply that cabinet duration was roughly doubled (exp[0.783] = 2.2). FIT.ln.*F* is the fitted value of the logarithmic transformation of parliamentary fragmentation, as instrumented by Equation (6.1). Again, results are both robust and compatible with expectations. Political fragmentation is found to have had the highest effect on cabinet duration when the latter is defined in terms of both coalition change and elections. This measure, approximating changes in the number of seats in the legislature commanded by the governing coalition, decreases by 1.4 percent for every 1 percent increase in fragmentation. However, fragmentation's effect on cabinet reshuffles and especially on the frequency of elections is much smaller.

A requirement for a constructive vote of no confidence has a clear positive effect on cabinet duration, as expected, especially on cabinet reshuffles. Ministers' office terms are extended by 30 percent as a result of this measure (exp[0.27] = 1.3), but elections are only 5 percent less frequent. Sweden's stipulation that a new parliament following early elections merely completes its predecessor's term indeed is found to have slightly postponed elections. Similarly, giving the head of state the right to veto cabinet dismissal is estimated to have made cabinets more durable. Elections are 14 percent less frequent when this condition applies, and cabinets are more durable by 44 percent when elections and changes in coalitions and top executives are all considered as cabinet changes.

Linking cabinet dismissal with dissolution of the legislature is found to have reduced cabinet duration according to all four definitions, but the effect is statistically insignificant. Higher constitutional electoral intervals are found to have significantly shortened the lives of the cabinets. For example, parliaments with a five-year tenure, 25 percent longer than those with a four-year tenure, are associated with ministerial posts that are 58 percent shorter. In contrast, the actual frequency of elections is 10 percent lower. In other words, longer constitutional tenures of the legislature do make elections a little less frequent, but at the price of a higher turnover in cabinet.

The discussion and empirical evidence presented in this chapter supports arguments that durable cabinets are generally associated with mature and presidential democracies, social homogeneity, high entry thresholds to the legislature, small legislatures, constructive votes of no confidence, penalties for early elections, a multitude of veto players in cabinet dismissal games, and short constitutional parliamentary tenures. All of these institutional features are suggested as instruments for cabinet duration. In addition, all four measures of cabinet duration are well explained by these instruments and all are useful as proxies of cabinet duration.

Notes

1. Lijphart uses the median number of seats per electoral district for M. However, that requires data on the specific number of seats for each district in each country, which is difficult to obtain for many sample countries. The average number of seats in contrast is a simple ratio of total seats in parliament to the number of electoral districts.

7

The Burden of Adjustment

The previous chapters discussed the economic and political potential sources of costs to membership in the euro zone. This chapter forecasts the magnitude of these costs for each dyad in the sample. To that end, it first estimates the relationship between the factors studied in Chapters 3 through 5 and the alternative measures of adjustment that are discussed in Chapter 3. This analysis is performed with instrumented variables (IV) estimation within a generalized method of moments (GMM) framework.

The Generalized Method of Moments: A Brief Description

Instrumented variables estimation within a generalized method of moments framework is a two-step procedure for estimating an equation (henceforth the structural equation) that has simultaneous explanatory variables. Simultaneous variables are characterized by being correlated with the disturbance in the equation, biasing ordinary least squares estimates, and making them inconsistent.

Under the GMM's two-step procedure, variables that are uncorrelated with the disturbance (instruments) are used to find the component of a simultaneous variable that is attributable to the instruments. This is done by running an ordinary least squares regression in which the dependent variable is a simultaneous variable and the instruments are independent variables. This regression is called a first-step regression. There is one first-step regression for each simultaneous explanatory variable in the structural equation. In the second step of the procedure, a GMM regression is run on the structural equation, with first-step fitted values replacing the simultaneous variables, and adjusting the estimates for heteroskedasticity (see Box 7.1); this is the second-step regression (see Box 7.2 for a comparison of GMM and the two-step least squares [2SLS] procedure).

In this book, the structural equation consists of one of EMU's adjustment burden indicators as a dependent variable. Chapter 3 discusses the four alternative indicators that drive the four variations of this equation.

Box 7.1   What Is Heteroskedasticity?

Heteroskedasticity is a feature of a dataset. A sequence or a vector of random variables is heteroskedastic if the random variables in the sequence or vector may have different variances. This means that in estimating an equation, the error term might not feature a constant variance. Rather, the error term is correlated with some of the independent variables. As a result, ordinary least squares estimation could not correctly estimate the standard errors of coefficients and their significance. Heteroskedasticity often occurs when there is a large difference in the values of observations. This indeed is the case in the dataset used in this book, which features very diverse countries. For example, some countries experienced hyperinflation during the 1990s while others experienced price stability.

Box 7.2   How Are GMM and 2SLS Different?

The generalized method of moments is the conventional method for estimating causal relationships in cross-sectional data when heteroskedasticity is present. The GMM procedure is much like the 2SLS procedure, but it corrects for heteroskedasticity in a different way. The 2SLS procedure corrects for heteroskedasticity by using heteroskedasticity-consistent standard errors for the first-step regressions. The conventional IV estimator is thus consistent (i.e., it has a high probability of being close to the true value of the parameter when the sample is very large), yet inefficient (i.e., it features high bias). In the GMM procedure estimates are chosen to minimize the weighted distance between theoretical and actual values.

There are four simultaneous explanatory variables and two exogenous variables based on optimum currency area theory and the domestic political theories. The simultaneous explanatory variables are business cycle correlation, openness, bilateral inflation differences, and cabinet duration. The exogenous variables are partisanship and political business cycle correlation. Each of the simultaneous variables is initially instrumented in the first step by the same group of instruments, representing idiosyncratic and institutional country features, as well as the exogenous explanatory variables, which do not need to be instrumented.

The choice of instruments must satisfy a few potentially conflicting requirements (Bartels, 1991). First, instruments should be exogenous and uncorrelated with the disturbances. Second, instruments should be correlated with the simultaneous variable for which they proxy. Third, to be meaningful, forecasts of the dependent variable in the structural equation should have low standard errors. There are trade-offs among these requirements with no obvious way to balance them—only a few general rules.

The first requirement is satisfied by tests for overidentification, also known as *J*-tests (see Box 7.3). The second requirement is satisfied by examining the results of the first-stage equation. Generally, instruments are considered to be correlated with the simultaneous variable for which they proxy if their standard errors are low and if the *F*-tests for the first-step equations are higher than 10. The potential for satisfying the third requirement is indicated by a number of measures—the Theil inequality coefficient, and the bias, variance, and covariance proportions (see Box 7.4).

After reliable estimates of the structural equation are obtained, EMU's adjustment burden indicators can be forecast for any pair of countries by substituting values of the simultaneous variables in the estimated structural equation. The sensitivity of forecasts to changes in instruments can be derived from the products of the instruments' first-step equation coefficients and the second-step regression's coefficients.

An Integrated Analysis of Economic and Political Costs

The first variable to be instrumented is business cycle correlation, which is hypothesized in Chapter 4 to reduce the extent of adjustment as it improves. The second is openness, which is hypothesized to reduce exchange rate

---

Box 7.3   What Are *J*-Tests?

Once the structural equation is estimated, heteroskedasticity-robust tests for overidentification, also known as *J*-tests, are run to find whether the instruments are indeed uncorrelated with the disturbance in the equation. A *J*-test has a chi-square distribution with degrees of freedom equal to the difference between the number of instruments and the number of simultaneous variables in the second-step equation. For example, if there are sixteen instruments and seven simultaneous variables, then there are nine degrees of freedom. The null hypothesis is that the group of instruments used is not correlated with the disturbance in the second-step equation. High *J*-test values allow a safe rejection of this hypothesis and indicate that at least some of the instruments in the group are correlated with the disturbance (Wooldridge, 2002, 123–124).

Box 7.4   Forecast Quality Indicators

A number of measures indicate the quality of forecasts. Ranging between 0 and 1, the Theil inequality coefficient is the ratio between the root of the mean squared forecast error and the sum of the roots of mean squares of fitted values and of actual dependent variable values. When the equation's fit is perfect, the Theil inequality coefficient is 0. The bias, variance, and covariance proportions are three indicators that decompose the mean squared forecast error. All three are ratios with the mean squared forecast error in their denominators; all three range between 0 and 1, and all together add up to 1. The numerator in the bias proportion is the squared difference between the mean of the forecast and the mean of the actual series. The numerator in the variance proportion is the squared difference between the variation of the forecasts and the variation of the actual series. The covariance proportion measures the remaining nonsystemic forecasting errors. As the equation's fit improves, the covariance proportion gets closer to 1, and the bias and variance proportions get closer to 0 (Pindyck and Rubinfeld, 1991).

---

adjustment but to increase adjustment through other channels. The third variable is bilateral disparity of the rate of inflation, which is hypothesized to increase the extent of adjustment. A fourth simultaneous determinant of adjustment is cabinet duration, which is hypothesized in Chapter 5 to be negatively associated with indicators of adjustment.

In each first-step equation, one of these determinants is the dependent variable. The independent variables are the exogenous determinants of the adjustment and the instruments. The two exogenous determinants of adjustment offered in Chapter 5 are partisanship policy bias and political business cycle correlation. Both can be either positively or negatively associated with the extent of adjustment and are regarded as control variables. In other words, in order to accurately measure the effect of the determinants of adjustment, the effects of partisanship bias and the political business cycle must be cleared, although they do not represent an idiosyncratic country feature.

In the first-step equations, the GMM procedure runs an identical set of instruments, as well as the two exogenous control variables, on each simultaneous determinant of adjustment. In accordance with the discussion in Chapter 4, this set of instruments should include area, which is expected to reduce openness (see Equation [4.4]); and bilateral disparity of the extent of central bank political independence from the government, which is expected to make national rates of inflation more disparate as well (see Table 4.7).

Furthermore, the set of instruments should include distance and sea access, which are expected to impede trade, as well as language similarity, trade agreements, and adjacency, which are expected to enhance trade (see Equation [4.3]).

Ideally, the set of instruments should also include the products of these trade-related instruments with the rate of transposition of internal market directives. This would allow the first-step equation that explains business cycle correlation to reflect the different effects that trade may have on business cycle correlation (see Equation [4.2]). Because fitted values of trade are positively associated with business cycle correlation, the direction of association of each instrument with business cycle correlation would be expected to be similar to its direction of association with trade. Similarly, the direction of association with business cycle correlation of the product of each instrument and the rate of transposition would be expected to be the opposite of its direction of association with trade.

However, as argued in Chapter 4, the rate of transposition of directives is endogenous to other instruments and variables and would cause business cycle correlation and the other determinants of adjustment to be overidentified. For this reason, distance, sea access, language similarity, trade agreements, and adjacency are used as instruments, but not their products with the rate of transposition. As a result, these instruments can be either positively or negatively associated with business cycle correlation, depending on the type of trade with which they are mostly associated.

Chapter 6 supports arguments that cabinet duration can be explained by a set of institutional features. Tables 6.2 and 6.4 show that durable cabinets are generally associated with mature and presidential democracies, social homogeneity, high entry thresholds to the legislature, small legislatures, constructive votes of no confidence, penalties for early elections, a multitude of veto players in cabinet dismissal games, and short constitutional parliamentary tenures.

Thus, all of these institutional instruments seem suitable for explaining cabinet duration in 1990s Europe. Instruments that code for conditions that apply in only three or fewer countries are dropped at this point. These instruments are those that code for presidential democracies, small legislatures, penalties for early elections, and a linkage between cabinet dismissal and dissolution of the legislature. The reason is that the lower the number of countries for which a certain instrument codes, the greater the risk that it captures, in practice, effects other than those of the intended feature, or that it is based on coincidence. On a practical level, such instruments should also be dropped in order not to draw conclusions for all EU member states based on the experience of a small number of countries. This is also why other institutions, such as federalism or corporatism, which the literature relates to exchange rate and fiscal policies, are not represented in the set of instruments.

Table 7.1   First-Step Ordinary Least Squares Equations of Determinants of Adjustment

Equation number: Dependent variable: Cabinet change defined by:	(7.1) ln.CYC	(7.2) ln.OPEN	(7.3) ln.INFLATION	(7.4) ln.ELECTION An election	(7.5) ln.SHARE A change in coalition parties and/or an election	(7.6) ln.ALL A change in parties, the top executive, and/or an election	(7.7) ln.RESHUFFLES Gradual replacement of the entire college of ministers
CONSTANT	-1.69***	5.96***	-0.07	3.52***	2.47***	2.23***	2.56***
	(0.41)	(0.19)	(0.60)	(0.08)	(0.16)	(0.18)	(0.20)
Instruments of economic sources of adjustment:							
ln.DISTANCE (+/–)	-0.09*	-0.05**	0.03	0.03***	0.10***	0.11***	0.06**
	(0.05)	(0.02)	(0.06)	(0.01)	(0.02)	(0.02)	(0.02)
LANGUAGE (+/–)	0.14	0.20*	0.46	0.09	0.15	0.17	0.10
	(0.20)	(0.12)	(0.42)	(0.05)	(0.12)	(0.14)	(0.13)
FREETRADE (+/–)	-0.80***	-0.19***	-2.06***	-0.01	0.12***	0.12***	0.19***
	(0.07)	(0.03)	(0.12)	(0.01)	(0.03)	(0.03)	(0.03)
ADJACENCY (+/–)	-0.07	-0.10**	-0.12	0.01	0.03	0.03	0.02
	(0.11)	(0.04)	(0.11)	(0.02)	(0.04)	(0.04)	(0.05)
LANDLOCKED (+/–)	-0.03	-0.08*	-0.78***	-0.03	0.31***	0.33***	0.18***
	(0.09)	(0.05)	(0.18)	(0.02)	(0.04)	(0.05)	(0.05)
ln.AREA (–)	0.03	-0.23***	0.03	-0.03***	-0.05***	-0.02	-0.04***
	(0.03)	(0.02)	(0.06)	(0.01)	(0.01)	(0.01)	(0.01)
ln.BANK (+)	0.04	-0.12	0.71***	-0.04	-0.21***	-0.27***	0.01
	(0.13)	(0.07)	(0.24)	(0.03)	(0.05)	(0.06)	(0.06)
Instruments of political sources of adjustment:							
ln.AGE (+)	-0.15***	0.01	0.57***	0.02***	0.06***	0.08***	0.21***
	(0.03)	(0.01)	(0.06)	(0.01)	(0.01)	(0.02)	(0.02)
ln.FRELIGION (–)	-0.17**	0.06*	0.12	0.01	-0.02	-0.01	0.07***
	(0.08)	(0.03)	(0.08)	(0.01)	(0.02)	(0.02)	(0.02)

(continues)

Table 7.1 Continued

Equation number: Dependent variable: Cabinet change defined by:	(7.1) ln.CYC	(7.2) ln.OPEN	(7.3) ln.INFLATION	(7.4) ln.ELECTION An election	(7.5) ln.SHARE A change in coalition parties and/or an election	(7.6) ln.ALL A change in parties, the top executive, and/or an election	(7.7) ln.RESHUFFLES Gradual replacement of the entire college of ministers
ln.THRESHOLD (+)	0.05	0.01	0.08	0.05***	0.11***	0.04**	-0.10***
	(0.04)	(0.02)	(0.05)	(0.01)	(0.02)	(0.02)	(0.02)
CONSTRUCTIVE (+)	-0.35***	0.07*	-0.24*	0.02	0.15***	0.22***	0.29***
	(0.08)	(0.04)	(0.12)	(0.02)	(0.03)	(0.03)	(0.03)
HEADVETO (+)	-0.12*	0.10**	-0.11	0.09***	0.18***	0.23***	0.18***
	(0.07)	(0.04)	(0.13)	(0.02)	(0.03)	(0.04)	(0.05)
Exogenous political sources of adjustment:							
PARTY	-0.10*	-0.09***	0.25**	-0.01	-0.01	-0.05*	0.11***
	(0.06)	(0.03)	(0.10)	(0.01)	(0.02)	(0.03)	(0.03)
POLICYC	-0.39**	-0.03	-0.02	-0.04	0.02	0.05	0.04
	(0.19)	(0.10)	(0.33)	(0.04)	(0.08)	(0.09)	(0.09)
Sum of Squared Residuals	45.5	12.0	132	2.43	8.47	9.95	12.5
R²	0.57	0.61	0.60	0.29	0.55	0.56	0.64
F-test	29.1***	35.3***	33.5***	9.18***	26.8***	28.3***	39.7***

Notes: All equations are estimated on 325 dyadic observations. Column entries are parameter estimates, and standard error values are indicated in parentheses. Estimates are corrected with White heteroskedasticity-consistent standard errors and covariances. Instruments and variables underscored with a dotted line are calculated as bilateral averages of national values. The 'ln' prefix denotes a logarithmic transformation of the variable. * $.05 < p \leq .10$. ** $.01 < p \leq .05$ *** $p \leq .01$. The signs by the names of the instruments indicate their expected relationship with one of the dependent variables; the boxed cells highlight the column of the relevant dependent variable in each row.

In addition, two of the three proxies representing social diversity are dropped from the set of instruments. This is done so as not to overidentify cabinet duration in the GMM procedure. An excess of instruments might increase their correlation with the residuals of the second-step equation, especially if there is growing correlation among the instruments. As an example, the index of linguistic fragmentation might be related to the index of bilateral language similarity, which is associated with trade. There may also be some degree of overlapping among the three social cleavages. The preferred proxy to be kept in the set of instruments is the one representing religious divisions. It has a certain advantage over the other two proxies in that it is estimated in Table 6.2 to have a stronger effect on parliamentary fragmentation and hence on cabinet duration.

Table 7.1 details first-step ordinary least squares equations for the determinants of adjustment. All equations are estimated on 325 dyadic observations. The dyadic values of variables and instruments underscored with a dotted line are averages of their national values. The values of most other variables and instruments are identical to those used in Chapter 4. The only exceptions are *INFLATION* and *BANK*. *INFLATION* is the ratio of the two countries' transformed annual rates of consumer price inflation *(D)*, such that the lower rate is in the denominator (see Chapter 4). It returns a value of 1 for dyads with perfectly similar rates of inflation, and increases with bilateral disparity in inflation. *BANK* is calculated similarly, as the ratio of the two countries' indices of central bank independence *(CBI)*, such that the lower index is in the denominator (see Chapter 4). The four measures of cabinet duration are studied in Table 7.1 as alternatives to each other.

As already stated, the GMM procedure runs the entire set of instruments on each dependent variable. Thus, in each equation some of the instruments are not expected to have any particular relationship with the specific determinant. Cells of entries that do refer to relationships discussed in Chapters 3 and 5 are boxed in Table 7.1.

The distance between trade partners *(DISTANCE)* and a lack of access to the sea *(LANDLOCKED)* are shown in Chapter 4 to reduce trade. The negative coefficients of the proxies of these factors in Equation (7.1) may be indications that this reduction in trade was associated in 1990s Europe with enhanced business cycle correlation, which in turn suggests that these factors are associated mostly with specialization-driven trade. In contrast, language similarity, trade agreements, and adjacency support trade. The negative coefficients of the latter two in Equation (7.1) can be interpreted as indications that they are mostly associated with intra-industry trade, driven by economies of scale. However, the positive coefficient of the proxy for language similarity may mean that it too supports mostly classic specialization-based trade.

Table 7.1 shows that most of the instruments that are theoretically expected to be associated with business cycle correlation return weak coefficients in Equation (7.1). The only factor with a clear and strong effect on business cycle correlation is trade agreements (*FREETRADE*). The exponential transformation of its proxy's coefficient reveals that a fully operational free trade area in 1990s Europe was associated with 55 percent greater business cycle correlation compared with the absence of a free trade area.

The weakness of most of the boxed coefficients in Equation (7.1) could be interpreted as evidence that the distinction between the two types of trade is not clear-cut. Rather, most of the factors that affect trade influence both of its types, with contradicting and often mutually offsetting effects on the business cycle. This duality may in turn be attributed in part to the existence of two groups of countries in the sample—the EU member states, which tended to intra-industry trade among themselves, and the other sample countries, which tended to specialization-driven trade (see Chapter 4).

However, the duality may also be attributed to the specific characteristics of the determinants of trade. This is especially clear when comparing the coefficients of the instruments in Equation (7.1) with the sum of products of their coefficients in Equations (4.2) and (4.3). For example, the coefficient of adjacency's proxy in Equation (7.1) is −0.07, whereas if assuming a perfect rate of transposition of internal market directives, the coefficient should have been −0.05.[1] This means that for some reason, adjacency has an inherent tendency to foster trade of the type that encourages business cycle correlation even beyond the effect of membership in the internal market.

The same can be said about free trade agreements, which return a coefficient of -0.80 in Equation (7.1) compared with an implied coefficient of −0.33 under the perfect transposition scenario [(0.13 − 0.39) x 1.28]. In contrast, the proxy for language similarity has a coefficient of 0.14 compared with an implied coefficient of 0.10, assuming a 0 rate of transposition of directives (0.13 x 0.73). This means that language similarity tends to encourage trade of the type that causes business cycles to diverge, even when the effect of staying out of the internal market is controlled for.

A final observation with respect to Equation (7.1) in Table 7.1 regards the relationship between economic business cycle correlation and political business cycle correlation. As argued in Chapter 5, bilateral correlation of political business cycles is, to a great extent, a matter of coincidence and is not endogenous to other variables and instruments in this study. Thus, any meaningful relationship between economic and political business cycle correlations depends on the ability of political cycles to generate real economic effects, as suggested in the traditional literature on the political business cycle. However, as argued in Chapter 5, there is very little evidence for the existence of such real effects. The negative coefficient between the two cycles in Equation (7.1) is counterintuitive, even according to the traditional approach, and therefore can be considered as spurious.

Thus, the correlation of economic business cycles and the correlation of political business cycles remain independent from one another. Indeed, an attempt to regard political business cycle correlation as a simultaneous variable and run a first-step equation that explains it with the set of instruments returned an F-test of 0.5, well below the minimum threshold of 10 suggested above for evaluating the robustness of first-step equations. Thus, the theoretical conclusion that the political business cycle correlation is exogenous to other variables and instruments in this study is empirically vindicated.

Equation (7.2) studies openness. As expected, geographically large countries tend to be economically less open. A 1 percent more spacious country is estimated to have been 0.23 percent less open in 1990s Europe. This effect is statistically highly robust and very similar to the coefficient (0.21) estimated in Equation (4.4). In addition, landlocked countries tend to be less open. Although this possibility is not discussed in Chapter 4, it seems consistent with the same logic that explains why lack of access to the sea hampers bilateral trade. Another interesting observation is that left-wing governments had a robust, though small, tendency to rule over open economies. Due to the short sample period, it is difficult to say whether this is just a matter of coincidence or indeed whether the new European left of the 1990s was eager to attract foreign business. Of course, reverse causality is also possible: Perhaps voters in open economies sought left-wing policies to cushion the social effects of globalization.

Equation (7.3) focuses on bilateral disparity in national rates of inflation. As expected, the closer the two central banks are in terms of the degree of political independence from the government, the more similar the rates of inflation in the two economies. Another interesting observation is that young democracies tend to feature similar levels of inflation among themselves compared with mature democracies. This mostly reflects the common tendency for high rates of inflation in young democracies, which can be explained as a result of their low cabinet duration (see Chapter 6). Finally, right-wing governments in 1990s Europe also were associated with similar levels of inflation. This could be a matter of coincidence, or it could reflect the common emphasis on price stability among the right, whereas not all left-wing politicians accept this discipline.

The last four equations in Table 7.1 explain alternative measures of cabinet duration. As a general rule, all estimated coefficients of the five theoretically relevant instruments are in line with expectations, as discussed in Chapter 6, and all are statistically highly robust. The exceptions are religious cleavages (*RELIGION*), which appear to have a weak or even an implausible positive effect on cabinet duration; parliamentary minimum thresholds (*THRESHOLD*), which are estimated to have a negative effect on ministerial tenures; and the requirement for a constructive vote of no confidence (*CONSTRUCTIVE*), which does not have a strong effect in postponing elections.

Regime maturity has a large impact on the personal tenure of cabinet members but only a small impact on the frequency of elections. Countries with high entry thresholds to the legislatures and, therefore, potentially less fragmented legislatures, are more characterized by durable coalitions than by less frequent elections or more durable top executives. Finally, left-wing cabinets happen to be more durable than right-wing cabinets in 1990s Europe, especially when cabinet duration is represented by *ALL*.

According to Table 7.1, using the frequency of elections (ln.*ELECTION*) as a measure of cabinet duration has the disadvantage of having weak coefficients. Equation (7.4) is also the only equation in Table 7.1 to feature an *F*-test that is lower than 10. In contrast, using cabinet reshuffles (ln.*RESHUF-FLES*) as a measure of cabinet duration returns robust coefficients but two of them conflict with theoretical expectations. There is also a concern that this measure reflects not only the duration of cabinets as policymaking bodies but also changes in cabinet due to personal affairs. Thus, *SHARE* and *ALL* seem more promising as determinants of adjustment. The other two measures of cabinet duration are dropped at this point.

Evidence of the Political Economy of Adjustment

Table 7.2 details two second-step GMM equations for each of the four alternative dependent variables that represent the extent of adjustment between European countries, which were developed in Chapter 3. Each of these adjustment indicators is estimated alternatively with *SHARE* and *ALL*. As explained in Chapter 3, real exchange rate data are unavailable for the three Baltic countries and Slovenia. As a result, values of two of the adjustment indicators (*RERV* and *RADJUSTMENT*) are available in only 231 dyads (the restricted sample). This makes comparisons across columns in Table 7.2 potentially sensitive to sample bias. To avoid such bias, references to results in restricted-sample versions of equations explaining *ERV* and *ADJUSTMENT* are given wherever the discussion so merits. However, these versions are not tabulated here so as not to overburden the reader with tables.

The results presented in Table 7.2 tend to support Hypotheses 1, 2, 3, and 6. Hypothesis 1 argues in Chapter 4 that as business cycles become less correlated between European partners, adjustment between them rises. The proxy for business cycle correlation (ln.*CYC*) is positively associated with all four indicators of adjustment and under both measures of cabinet duration. The only exception is its coefficient in Equation (7.11). Thus, Hypothesis 1 is supported.

The effect of business cycle correlation on adjustment is in general also highly robust, with the exception of Equations (7.10) and (7.11). Business cycle correlation had the greatest effect in 1990s Europe on variation in

Table 7.2 Second-Step GMM Equations of Adjustment Indicators

Equation number: Dependent variable	(7.8) ln.ERV	(7.9)	(7.10) ln.RERV	(7.11)	(7.12) ln.ADJUSTMENT	(7.13)	(7.14) ln.RADJUSTMENT	(7.15)
Factors considered in dependent variable	Nominal exchange rate variation only.		Real exchange rate variation (ERV + price adjustments).		Nominal exchange rate variation and bilateral variation in fiscal and monetary policies.		Real exchange rate variation and bilateral variation in fiscal and monetary policies (ADJUSTMENT + price adjustments).	
CONSTANT	12.1***	10.3***	2.20	0.43	3.25*	2.47	3.56	1.83
	(4.09)	(3.72)	(2.87)	(2.98)	(1.74)	(1.72)	(3.84)	(3.66)
ln.CYC (+)	1.24***	1.02***	0.18	−0.03	0.90***	0.80***	0.97***	0.94**
	(0.23)	(0.24)	(0.22)	(0.26)	(0.17)	(0.19)	(0.36)	(0.39)
ln.OPEN (+) (−) with ERV	−1.09***	−0.93***	0.05	−0.02	−0.25	−0.21	0.23	0.01
	(0.34)	(0.33)	(0.38)	(0.40)	(0.19)	(0.19)	(0.57)	(0.58)
ln.INFLATION (+)	0.03	0.09	0.29**	0.44***	0.13**	0.15**	−0.14	−0.01
	(0.09)	(0.08)	(0.14)	(0.14)	(0.07)	(0.07)	(0.23)	(0.21)
ln.SHARE (−)	−1.17***		−2.29***		−0.89***		−2.36**	
	(0.38)		(0.62)		(0.30)		(1.03)	
ln.ALL (−)		−1.31***		−1.99***		−0.87***		−1.60
		(0.36)		(0.65)		(0.32)		(0.99)
PARTY (+/−)	−1.02***	−1.00***	−0.39*	−0.38*	−0.54***	−0.54***	−1.14***	−1.07***
	(0.24)	(0.22)	(0.20)	(0.21)	(0.17)	(0.17)	(0.30)	(0.29)
ln.POLICYC (+/−)	−4.27	−2.93	4.36*	4.61*	2.61	2.85	7.65**	7.05*
	(4.70)	(4.35)	(2.61)	(2.73)	(1.65)	(1.75)	(3.54)	(3.65)

(continues)

Table 7.2 Continued

Equation number:	(7.8)	(7.9)	(7.10)	(7.11)	(7.12)	(7.13)	(7.14)	(7.15)
Dependent variable	ln.*ERV*		ln.*RERV*		ln.*ADJUSTMENT*		ln.*RADJUSTMENT*	
Factors considered in dependent variable	Nominal exchange rate variation only.		Real exchange rate variation (*ERV* + price adjustments).		Nominal exchange rate variation and bilateral variation in fiscal and monetary policies.		Real exchange rate variation and bilateral variation in fiscal and monetary policies (*ADJUSTMENT* + price adjustments).	
Number of observations	325	325	231	231	325	325	231	231
Sum of Squared Residuals (SSR)	347	304	132	140	162	168	345	313
J-test	14.6	15.2	14.0	14.9	5.47	5.92	5.88	9.10
(*p* value)	(0.07)	(0.06)	(0.08)	(0.06)	(0.71)	(0.66)	(0.66)	(0.33)
Indicators of the reliability of forecasts:								
Theil Inequality Coefficient	0.16	0.15	0.11	0.11	0.18	0.18	0.24	0.23
Bias Proportion	0.00	0.00	0.00	0.00	0.00	0.00	0.00	0.00
Variance Proportion	0.00	0.01	0.02	0.03	0.00	0.00	0.05	0.03
Covariance Proportion	1.00	0.99	0.98	0.97	1.00	1.00	0.95	0.97

Notes: See notes in Table 7.1. The lower numbers of observations in Equations (7.10), (7.11), (7.14), and (7.15) are due to the lack of real exchange rate data for four sample countries (see Chapter 3). Indicators of the reliability of forecasts are calculated for the forecasting of the sample's observations and rounded to two decimals. * $.05 < p \leq .10$. ** $.01 < p \leq .05$. *** $p \leq .01$.

nominal exchange rates (*ERV*), where a 1 percent improvement in correlation (decline in *CYC*) brought variation down by 1.02–1.24 percent. The sensitivity of the other indicators of adjustment to business cycle correlation is only slightly lower, which means that the fiscal and monetary channels did respond to the business cycle. However, the variation of real exchange rates is not strongly related to business cycle correlation. This could be explained by a countercyclical adjustment of domestic prices that perhaps tends to offset adjustments in nominal exchange rates. Of course, Equations (7.8) through (7.11) are not based on the same sample, and the absence of dyads involving the three Baltic countries and Slovenia in the latter two equations may bias the results. However, running Equations (7.8) and (7.9) on the restricted sample still returns larger and stronger coefficients for *CYC* than for Equations (7.10) and (7.11).

Hypothesis 2 argues in Chapter 4 that the greater the openness, the smaller the nominal exchange rate variation but the greater the overall extent of adjustment between European economies. The first part of this hypothesis relating to nominal exchange rate variation is definitely supported in Equations (7.8) and (7.9). A 1 percent increase in openness resulted in roughly a 1 percent decline in nominal exchange rate variation in 1990s Europe. However, only some of the other indicators of adjustment are positively associated with openness. Thus, the last part of Hypothesis 2 is not well supported in Table 7.2.

Nevertheless, the small (in absolute terms) and weak coefficients of the openness proxy (ln.*OPEN*) in Equations (7.12) and (7.13) compared with those in Equations (7.8) and (7.9) do suggest that in open economies greater adjustment was taking place through the fiscal and monetary channels than through nominal exchange rates. In other words, these other mechanisms of adjustment compensated for the stability of exchange rates. The role of price adjustments in open European economies is less certain. Versions of Equations (7.8) and (7.9) based on the restricted sample return coefficients for the openness proxy that are positive, small, and weak, as are those obtained in Equations (7.10) and (7.11). These results do not point to any advantage for domestic prices over nominal exchange rates in affecting adjustment.

Hypothesis 3 argues in Chapter 4 that greater bilateral disparity in rates of price inflation increases adjustment between European countries. This hypothesis is strongly supported in Equations (7.10) through (7.13). The results show that nominal exchange rates were only weakly related to differences in inflation between European countries in the 1990s, probably as a result of the exchange rate policies discussed in Chapter 3. These differences are reflected, of course, in price adjustments, as shown in Equations (7.10) and (7.11).

The dependent variable in Equations (7.12) and (7.13) considers adjustment through nominal exchange rates as well as through fiscal and monetary stances, but disregards adjustment in domestic prices. The positive and robust coefficients of *INFLATION* in these equations compared with Equations (7.8) and (7.9) in the table are consistent with the argument developed in Chapter 2 that a loss of competitiveness as a consequence of high inflation can be compensated for with fiscal and monetary cushioning. The weak and negative coefficients in Equations (7.14) and (7.15) compared with those in Equations (7.10) and (7.11) are further evidence that adjustment through the fiscal and monetary channels offsets inflation-driven price adjustments.

Hypothesis 6 argues in Chapter 5 that higher cabinet duration reduces the extent of adjustment in Europe. This hypothesis is supported in Table 7.2 by the robust and negative coefficients of both measures used for cabinet duration (*SHARE* and *ALL*), with the sole exception of the weak coefficient in Equation (7.15). The estimated decline in the extent of adjustment required between European countries in the 1990s in response to a 1 percent increase in cabinet duration ranges between 2.36 percent in Equation (7.14) and 0.87 percent in Equation (7.13).

SHARE, which considers elections and coalition changes as defining cabinet changes, appears across most of the eight equations to have a somewhat stronger effect on adjustment than *ALL*, which considers changes in the top executive as well. Comparing the coefficients of cabinet duration in Equations (7.8) and (7.9) with those in Equations (7.12) and (7.13) nominal exchange rate variation appears to have been a little more sensitive to cabinet duration than fiscal and monetary adjustments. Running Equations (7.8) and (7.9) on the restricted sample returns higher coefficients (in absolute terms) than running Equations (7.10) and (7.11). This implies that domestic prices are also less responsive to cabinet duration than nominal exchange rate variation.

Frieden's (2002) and Leblang's (2003) argument that left-wing governments try harder to stabilize exchange rates is well supported in Table 7.2. Interestingly, it seems that the European left of the 1990s was fiscally and monetarily restrained as well. *PARTY* has a robust and negative coefficient in each of that table's equations. The estimated decline in the extent of adjustment required between two European countries governed by left-wing parties throughout the sample period compared with two center-government countries ranges between 68 percent in Equation (7.14) and 32 percent in Equation (7.11). The corresponding range is 90 and 53 percent when left-wing governments are compared with right-wing ones, respectively. Versions of Equations (7.8) and (7.9) run on the restricted sample return robust, although lower, coefficients.

The proxy for political business cycle correlation (ln.*POLICYC*) seems in Table 7.2 to be mostly positively associated with indicators of adjustment.

Many of its coefficients are of low statistical significance, but in the last two equations a robust positive relationship is established between *POLICYC* and *ADJUSTMENT*. In addition, the restricted-sample versions of Equations (7.8) and (7.9) return coefficients similar to those of Equations (7.14) and (7.15) in terms of magnitude and robustness. Restricted-sample versions of Equations (7.12) and (7.13) also return stronger coefficients than the regular-sample versions. Even by the lowest positive estimate of this effect (in Equation (7.12)), a hypothetical case of perfect political business cycle correlation is estimated to have been associated in 1990s Europe with an 80 percent decrease in adjustment compared with the average dyad in the sample.

This result has three implications. First, the three Baltic countries and Slovenia defied in the 1990s an otherwise strong continental trend for greater adjustment between countries with unsynchronized electoral cycles. Second, this trend was especially apparent in nominal exchange rates and in fiscal and monetary stances, but was seen to a lesser extent, if any, in domestic price adjustment. Third, this effect could materialize with respect to nominal exchange rates only to the extent that all sample countries underwent a traditional political business cycle, or all underwent a rational cycle, but not a continental mixture of the two.

Which of the equations presented in Table 7.2 should be selected for the purpose of forecasting the adjustment burden for membership in the euro zone? Equations (7.10) and (7.11) score a little better than the others on the Theil coefficient, and Equations (7.8), (7.12), and (7.13) do a little better on the bias, variance, and covariance proportions. These differences are small, however, and all of the equations can be considered to produce reasonably precise forecasts. However, Equation (7.12) has a clear advantage over the others in terms of its *J*-test. The p value of this test means that there is a 71 percent chance that it would be wrong to reject the null hypothesis that the instruments are not correlated with the disturbance in Equation (7.12). This means that it is relatively safe to assume that the instruments used are indeed exogenous to the independent variables in the table, and to the specific indicator of adjustment that is being estimated, namely, *ADJUSTMENT*. Thus, Equation (7.12) is selected for the purpose of forecasting the adjustment burden.

Endogenous Effects

According to the discussion in Chapter 4, the endogenous theory of optimum currency areas argues that currency unions enhance trade, which may then affect business cycle correlation either positively or negatively. Exchange rates may affect the business cycle through other channels as well. For example, devaluation reduces the purchasing power of consumers and weakens local aggregate demand for goods. Thus, the more exchange rates vary, the weaker the business cycle correlation.

Of the GMM equations in Table 7.3, Equation (7.16) estimates the effect of exchange rate variation on business cycle correlation. It specifies the five trade-related instruments as exogenous independent variables, alongside nominal exchange rate variation *ERV*, and *TRANSPOSE*, the rate of transposition of internal market directives, both of which are simultaneous independent variables.

Exchange rate variation is included as an explanatory variable in the equations of Table 7.3 with its original values, not its logarithmic transformation, in order to later consider the effects of post-EMU total lack of exchange rate variation. The rest of the instruments that are used in the previous sections, as well as *PARTY* and *POLICYC*, are specified again as instruments in two first step-equations of Equation (7.16) because they explain openness, inflation disparities, and cabinet duration, which in turn explain exchange rate variation. For brevity's sake, these first-step equations are not presented here; both return F-test values above the 10 threshold.

This specification admittedly is not ideal. In accordance with Equations (4.2) and (4.3), it would have been theoretically more appropriate to run all variables in Equation (7.16) alongside their products with *TRANSPOSE*, thus distinguishing the effect of each of them on members and nonmembers of the internal market. However, this is technically impossible in the GMM procedure because the number of independent variables would exceed the number of instruments, and the equation would be underidentified.

Exchange rate variation and all of the other trade-related exogenous variables in Equation (7.16) can be either positively or negatively associated with business cycle correlation, depending on the type of trade with which they are related. In contrast, the rate of transposition is expected to be negatively associated with business cycle correlation because a high level of integration in the internal market is expected to improve business cycle correlation.

Exchange rate variation (*ERV*) returns a positive and robust coefficient, which means that lower exchange rate variation did lead to more correlated business cycles in 1990s Europe. *ERV*'s mean value is 0.07 (see Table 8.2). Bringing this value to 0 is calculated to potentially improve business cycle correlation by 28 percent. The other variables in Equation (7.16) are not very significant, but the rate of internal market directives transposition (*TRANSPOSE*) is negatively related to business cycle correlation, as expected. The proxies for trade agreements and language similarity return the same signs as in Equation (7.1). However, the proxies for distance, adjacency, and lack of sea access return positive coefficients in Equation (7.16), which controls for exchange rates and the internal market, compared with the neg-

Table 7.3 Second-Step GMM Equations of Endogenous Effects

Equation number:	(7.16)	(7.17)	(7.18)
Dependent variable:	ln.*CYC*	ln.*INFLATION*	ln.*SHARE*
CONSTANT	−7.99	0.07	3.33***
	(5.21)	(0.20)	(0.36)
ERV [(+) with INFLATION]			
[(−) with SHARE]	4.63***	22.4***	−3.22***
	(1.21)	(2.58)	(0.49)
ln.DISTANCE (+/−)	0.65		
	(0.69)		
LANGUAGE (+/−)	0.31		
	(2.63)		
FREETRADE (+/−)	−0.21		
	(0.73)		
ADJACENCY (+/−)	0.66		
	(1.47)		
LANDLOCKED (+/−)	1.18		
	(0.73)		
TRANSPOSE (−)	−0.30		
	(0.67)		
ln.BANK (+)		−0.40	−0.12**
		(1.23)	(0.05)
ln.AGE (+)			−0.12**
			(0.05)
ln.FRELIGION (−)			−0.20*
			(0.12)
ln.THRESHOLD (+)			0.20
			(0.14)
CONSTRUCTIVE (+)			−0.02
			(0.32)
HEADVETO (+)			0.34***
			(0.12)
Number of observations	325	325	325
Sum of Squared Residuals	89.7	908	30.3
J-test	2.07	51.4	12.9
(p value)	(0.96)	(0.00)	(0.11)
Indicators of the reliability of forecasts:			
Theil Inequality Coefficient	0.09	0.41	0.04
Bias Proportion	0.00	0.01	0.00
Variance Proportion	0.00	0.25	0.06
Covariance Proportion	1.00	0.74	0.94

Notes: See notes in Tables 7.1 and 7.2. All instruments used in Equations (7.1) through (7.7) are used in Equations (7.16) through (7.18), too, whether as instruments or as explanatory variables. * $.05 < p \leq .10$. ** $.01 < p \leq .05$. *** $p \leq .01$.

ative coefficients. All the same, the *J*-test for Equation (7.16) is remarkably weak and the indicators of the reliability of forecasts are good.

Hypothesis 4 argues in Chapter 4 that greater nominal exchange rate variation increases bilateral disparity in rates of price inflation between European countries. Equation (7.17) in Table 7.3 supports this hypothesis.

The same set of instruments as for the equations in Table 7.1 is used, this time specifying the proxy for disparities in central bank independence as an exogenous independent variable alongside nominal exchange rate variation, which is a simultaneous variable. Equation (7.17)'s one first-step equation, which explains exchange rate variation, is identical to one of the first-step equations estimated for Equation (7.16), which was shown above to be robust. In contrast to expectations, however, disparities in central bank independence are negatively associated with disparities in inflation (ln.*INFLATION*) in this equation. In addition, the *J*-test is highly robust, and indicators of the reliability of forecasts are weak. Thus, Equation (7.17) seems unreliable for the purpose of forecasting the disinflationary effect of fixed exchange rates.

Nevertheless, EMU's disinflationary effect is assessed by using the equations presented in the previous sections (see Box 7.5). Assuming that complying with the Maastricht Treaty's stipulations on central bank independence would lead member states to identical levels of legal central bank independence, *BANK*'s value would drop from 1.27 in the average dyad to 1 (see Table 8.2 on page 144). This would chop off 7.1 percent from the adjustment burden, which may seem minor. However, in the German-Romanian dyad, which has the greatest disparity in central bank independence (*BANK* = 2.45), the same assumption generates a 19 percent effect.

Hypothesis 5 argues in Chapter 5 that higher exchange rate variation reduces cabinet duration in Europe. Equation (7.18) in Table 7.3 supports this hypothesis and estimates that reducing nominal exchange rate variation from 0.07 (see ERV in Table 8.2) in the average dyad to 0 would improve cabinet duration by 25 percent.[2] Again, the same set of instruments as for the equations in Table 7.1 is used, this time specifying the five instruments related to cabinet duration as exogenous independent variables, with the same robust single first-step equation. *SHARE* is chosen as a measure for cabinet duration because it is used in Equation (7.12), which was selected for the purpose of forecasting the adjustment burden. Most coefficients in Equation (7.18) return the expected signs, and nominal exchange rate variation (*ERV*) is indeed shown to reduce cabinet duration. However, the *J*-test in Equation (7.18) is again too robust to allow a safe assumption of exogeneity of instruments.

The Burden of Adjusting to EMU

Table 7.4 presents forecasts of the broad adjustment indicator (*ADJUSTMENT*) for 2004. The forecasts show the extent of adjustment that is expected in each dyad based on data for the period 1998–2004, given the idiosyncratic

Table 7.4   Forecasts of Broad Adjustment Indicator Levels (*ADJUSTMENT*) for 2004

France		Germany		Italy		UK	
Hungary	1.0	Latvia	0.9	UK	0.5	**Italy**	0.5
Netherlands	1.1	Slovakia	1.1	Bulgaria	1.3	Bulgaria	0.7
Czech Rep.	1.1	Hungary	1.5	Slovenia	1.6	Poland	0.8
UK	1.5	Czech Rep.	1.7	Poland	1.7	Slovenia	1.0
Slovakia	1.5	Sweden	1.9	Hungary	2.2	**Spain**	1.2
Ireland	2.0	Estonia	2.2	Czech Rep.	2.7	**France**	1.5
Latvia	2.0	Cyprus	2.2	Slovakia	2.7	Hungary	1.6
Sweden	2.1	Poland	2.8	**France**	3.2	Czech Rep.	1.6
Slovenia	2.1	**Netherlands**	3.2	**Belgium**	3.3	Slovakia	1.8
Poland	2.1	**Finland**	3.6	**Spain**	3.6	Latvia	2.0
Italy	3.2	Bulgaria	3.8	**Netherlands**	3.6	**Belgium**	2.1
Belgium	3.3	Slovenia	3.8	Latvia	3.8	**Netherlands**	2.1
Austria	3.5	UK	4.3	**Austria**	4.3	Sweden	2.3
Spain	3.5	**Belgium**	4.3	Sweden	4.4	**Austria**	2.5
Cyprus	3.8	Malta	4.7	Lithuania	5.0	Romania	2.8
Finland	4.6	**France**	4.8	Romania	5.1	Lithuania	3.1
Lithuania	4.7	**Austria**	5.0	Cyprus	5.7	Estonia	3.3
Bulgaria	4.8	Romania	5.3	**Finland**	6.4	Cyprus	3.4
Germany	4.8	**Ireland**	6.7	Denmark	6.9	Denmark	3.9
Portugal	4.9	**Italy**	7.6	Estonia	7.0	**Germany**	4.3
Estonia	5.0	**Portugal**	7.6	**Portugal**	7.1	**Finland**	4.3
Romania	5.3	**Spain**	7.7	**Germany**	7.6	**Portugal**	4.5
Denmark	6.3	Denmark	10.2	**Ireland**	7.9	**Ireland**	5.0
Malta	8.1	Lithuania	12.7	Malta	9.8	Malta	6.8
Greece	11.9	**Greece**	14.5	**Greece**	11.8	**Greece**	6.8
Average	3.8		5.0		4.8		2.8
Euro zone average	4.3		6.5		5.9		3.2
Transition countries	3.0		3.6		3.3		1.9
Other 5 sample countries	4.4		4.7		5.5		4.1

Notes: ADJUSTMENT is the sum of the standardized values of bilateral variations in exchange rates and fiscal and monetary policies during the sample period, expressed in percent change of exchange rates. Averages are simple and not weighted. Forecasts are based on Equation (7.12) and data for the period 1998–2004, and consider endogenous effects of membership in the euro zone.

and institutional features of the countries, and clearing out the simultaneous relationships among variables. The forecasts assume that all sample countries are members of the euro zone, as explained next (see Box 7.5 for technical explanations). Thus, these forecasts are estimations of EMU's adjustment burden.

The 2004 forecasts of the broad adjustment indicator in Table 7.4 adjust for changes in values of instruments that have occurred between the sample period and 2004. Aside from the natural aging process of democracies, these include only two developments: Poland's adoption in 1997 of a requirement for a constructive vote of no confidence, and the rise in the Latvian parliament's effective minimum entry threshold from 4 to 5 percent

---

Box 7.5   How Are the 2004 Forecasts of *ADJUSTMENT* Calculated?

The forecasts in Table 7.4 are calculated by substituting actual values of the independent variables for the period 1998–2004 in Equation (7.12). However, values for *SHARE* and *PARTY* are unchanged from the period 1992–1998 due to the censuring problem in the former and lack of data for the 2000s in available databases of the latter. The standard errors of these forecast values, which give an indication of the confidence interval of forecasting, are not reported here for brevity's sake but are more than two times smaller than each of the forecasts in the table. The exceptions are the forecasts that relate to Romania in the first three columns, and to Italy in the cases of Estonia and Malta. The average factor is 3 or higher in all four columns. These results are robust.

The forecasts in Table 7.4 adjust the fitted values of *ADJUSTMENT* for changes that have occurred in various instruments as of 2004, as explained in the text. This is done by multiplying the change in the instrument's value separately by its coefficient in each of the four first-step equations, one for each of the simultaneous variables in Equation (7.12). Each of these four products is then multiplied by the coefficient of the relevant variable in Equation (7.12). The four products are then summed and exponentially transformed.

The forecasts are also adjusted for EMU's endogenous effect estimated above. The effect on *ADJUSTMENT* of reducing *ERV* to 0 is calculated as an exponential transformation of the product of *ERV*, *ERV*'s coefficient in Equation (7.16), and ln.*CYC*'s coefficient in Equation (7.12). For example, in the average dyad, *ADJUSTMENT* is multiplied by the factor exp(–0.023 X 0.90 X 4.63), where 0.023 is *ERV*'s average for the period of 1998–2004. The endogenous disinflationary effect of EMU is factored in by substituting a value of 1 for *BANK* in all dyads. Finally, a value of 1 is substituted for *FREETRADE* because all euro zone member states are expected to belong to the internal market. Technically, the effects of these substitutions are calculated similarly to the effects of changes in instruments described in the second paragraph above.

---

in 1995. These are only partially reflected in the 1992–1998 period averages used in the estimations, but are fully reflected in the 2004 values.

Forecasts are adjusted for the euro zone membership assumption by factoring in the endogenous effect that fixed exchange rates are estimated to have on business cycle correlation. In addition, forecasts assume that all dyads share a fully operational free trade area, as they would inside the euro zone, and that central banks in all countries are equally independent from their governments. In reality the extent of central bank independence grant-ed by law, at least as it is interpreted by Cukierman's (1992) index, is not identical across EU member states. Some differences are allowed in the pro-cedures for appointing and dismissing governors, in their terms of office, and in the extent of involvement of the central bank in the formulation of fiscal policies. However, these differences are small and the unitary central bank independence assumption is convenient.

The main and immediate observation about the figures in Table 7.4 is their low levels compared with those in Table 3.4. In other words, consider-ing EMU's endogenous effects and developments during the 2000s in open-ness, inflation, and economic as well as political business cycle correlation, the burden of adjustment to EMU by the EU member states is much lower than the observed levels of adjustment during the 1990s would suggest.

One reason for this is that business cycle correlation improved in most dyads, between the 1992–1998 period and the 1998–2004 period, especially those involving the transition economies. Bulgaria and Poland more than halved their CYC values with the four major EU member states. In contrast, business cycles in Denmark, Greece, and especially in Malta grew less cor-related with the major economies. Perhaps the most important development was the deterioration of Germany's cycle correlation with all of the pre-2004 EU member states except Austria and Belgium.

Almost all countries have grown more open between the 1990s and the early 2000s. This is especially true for Hungary, which doubled its openness ratio to 135 percent (compare with Table 4.5), and for Germany and Poland, which increased their ratios by a third. In Greece, Ireland, Italy, and Spain, the openness ratios increased by more than a fifth. In contrast, in Latvia the openness ratio declined from 114 to 96 percent. Small declines were also recorded in Lithuania, Malta, and Slovenia.

Consumer price inflation was reduced in the 2000s in almost all of the sample countries. Stabilization in Bulgaria brought inflation down from an annual average of 130 percent in the period 1992–1998 (see Table 4.6) to an average of 7.5 percent in the period 1998–2004. In the Baltic countries, Poland, and Slovenia, inflation was reduced from an annual rate of more than 25 percent to single digit rates. However, inflation remained high in Romania (35 percent), and rose marginally in Ireland from 2.1 to 3.5 per-cent.

Trends in political business cycle correlation in the 2000s compared with the 1990s were generally moot, as expected from such a haphazard variable, but still pointed at some improvement, especially in dyads involv-ing France. This could be explained by the official harmonization of presi-dential and parliamentary tenures there. In contrast, elections in Belgium, Greece, Romania, and Slovenia happened to fall a little out of sync with those in the major EU member states.

A rather surprising observation about the figures in Table 7.4 is the greater potential for adjustment between the four major EU member states and the current euro zone member states compared to that between the four majors and the transition countries. This is reflected both in the groups' averages at the bottom of Table 7.4 and in the distribution of the countries in the columns of the table. Again, this result is based on the scenario that all countries participate in the third stage of EMU. The five nontransition non-euro countries feature, on average, levels of adjustment burden similar to those of the current euro zone member states.

Differences in the countries' scores in Table 7.4 also reflect the maturing effect of democracies, which is stronger in the transition economies, and the magnitude of EMU's calculated endogenous effect on business cycle correlation. The latter effect is strong in countries that experienced relatively high exchange rate variation during the period 1998–2004. In contrast, the calculated endogenous effect on business cycle correlation is virtually nonexistent among the current member states of the euro zone, which fixed their exchange rates since 1999, and between these countries and Estonia and Bulgaria, which adopted currency boards anchored on the euro at the same time.[3]

This is not to say that these countries did not experience such an endogenous effect upon fixing their exchange rates—only that this effect should already be reflected in their levels of business cycle correlation for the period 1998–2004. The calculated endogenous effect on business cycle correlation especially improves the scores of Lithuania (which anchored its currency on the euro only in 2002), Poland, and Romania with France, Germany, and Italy in Table 7.4. This effect also significantly affects the scores of Bulgaria, the Czech Republic, Greece, Poland, Romania, and Slovakia with the UK.

A final observation with regard to Table 7.4 is that among the four major EU member states, the UK emerges as the cheapest potential anchor country for the euro zone because the burden of adjusting to a currency link with that country is, on average, lower than the burden of adjusting to a link with any other major country. This is true for the entire sample as well as for the current euro zone member states and the transition countries. Unexpectedly, France comes in second, followed by Germany and Italy, which are disadvantaged mostly by, respectively, deteriorating business cycle correlation and low cabinet duration levels.

Making Sense of the Adjustment Burden

Aside from ranking the different countries according to the costs of adjusting their political economies to EMU, what do the forecasts reported in

Table 7.4 mean in practice? As explained in Chapter 2, adjustment can occur through a number of channels. These chiefly include adjustment in nominal exchange rates and in monetary and fiscal positions. Adjustment can also occur through prices and labor flows, but these are assumed to be of low magnitude in Europe. Evidence presented in this chapter and in Chapter 3 seems to support this assumption, at least with respect to prices.

Under a currency union one monetary policy and one interest rate apply in all member states. Some variation still occurs in national rates of price inflation, so differences in the real interest rates (see Chapter 2) occur. More precisely, variation in real interest rates among the member states is the variation in rates of inflation. Some of this cross-country variation in rates of inflation reflects structural factors, such as the Balassa-Samuelson effect (see Box 7.6), but some of it is cyclical and responds to shocks that affect different countries unevenly. In fact, the resulting variation in real interest rates might be pro-cyclical. For example, in a given member state, as inflation slows during recession against a fixed nominal interest rate, the real interest rate rises. Thus, far from providing a channel of adjustment between member states, monetary policy in this case adds to the burden of adjustment.

The standard deviation of quarterly bilateral differences in the rates of consumer price inflation for dyads of euro zone member states during 1999–2004 was an average of 1.7 percent across dyads. It is assumed that this variance in inflation would prevail among any future member states of the euro zone. According to the European Central Bank (1999), the Balassa-Samuelson effect accounts for some 70 percent of inflation differentials in the euro zone. Thus, the cyclical part of variation in real interest rates among the member states is assumed to be 0.3 of 1.7 percent, or 0.5 percent.

Box 7.6   What Is the Balassa-Samuelson Effect?

The Balassa-Samuelson effect is the effect that changes in factor productivity in different member states of a currency union have on rates of price inflation within them. Higher productivity growth in the tradable goods sector in low-income countries compared with the nontradable goods sector generates pressures for nominal appreciation of the currency. Because this is not possible, in a currency union the real exchange rate is adjusted by a rise in the local price level. Even in long-standing currency unions, regional differences in inflation persist. For example, in the United States such differences amounted in the 1990s to as much as 2 percent (Directorate General for Research, 1999).

This part of the variation in real interest rates is now uniformly added to the forecasts of EMU's adjustment burden presented in Table 7.4.[4]

If all member states are not to exceed public deficits of 3 percent, as required by the Maastricht Treaty and the SGP, and assuming that surpluses are rare and at best governments achieve a balance in their books, then bilateral differences in deficits should range between −3 and +3 percent. If these bilateral differences distribute normally around the midpoint of this range and exceed it only 4.6 percent of the time,[5] the standard deviation of bilateral differences in deficits (*FISCAL*) would be 1.5 percent in each dyad.

The imp.*ERV* columns in Table 7.5 derive the implied adjustment in exchange rates against Germany and the UK from the forecasts of EMU's adjustment burden reported in Table 7.4, given the assumptions regarding monetary and fiscal policies. In other words, imp.*ERV* is the implied standard deviation of quarterly percent change in the bilateral nominal exchange rate that satisfies the reported forecasts of *ADJUSTMENT* and the assumptions made above. Similar data for France and Italy are not reported, in the interest of not overburdening the reader with tables. Germany and the UK are selected for the discussion that follows because the former is conventionally regarded as the political and economic anchor of European monetary cooperation, and Table 7.4 shows the latter to be the potentially cheapest anchor.

The entries for some of the countries are negative, even though, of course, a standard deviation cannot be negative. Negative values indicate that the forecasted burden of adjustment is lower than the assumed level of fiscal flexibility, even when accounting for the effect of monetary policy. Countries with negative values would need to resort to no exchange rate adjustment. In contrast, countries with positive implied exchange rate variation are expected to be under pressure to adjust their exchange rates as member states of the euro zone. This channel of adjustment, however, is available only if a country leaves the euro zone, so these countries are expected to be under pressure to withdraw from it.

For some of these countries, these pressures are low enough to be sustained perhaps through slow adjustment in prices and mild labor flows. Officially, the Maastricht Treaty stipulates that EU member states must maintain their exchange rates within a ±2.25 percent fluctuation margin for two years prior to joining the euro zone. Since the launch of the euro in 1999, these margins center on the euro, but in earlier years, the margins applied for each and every dyad of member states. If this exchange rate criterion is anything to go by, which countries have the potential to fulfill it according to Table 7.5?

According to this exchange rate criterion, the ±2.25 percent margins represent the maximum and minimum values for changes in exchange rates. If quarterly percent changes in exchange rates distribute normally around 0, and the margins are violated only 4.6 percent of the time, the standard devi-

Table 7.5   Implied Adjustment in Exchange Rates and Fiscal Position

Germany	imp.*ERV*	imp.*FISCAL*	UK	imp.*ERV*	imp.*FISCAL*
Latvia	-2.1	0.5	**Italy**	-2.4	0.3
Slovakia	-1.8	0.6	Bulgaria	-2.2	0.5
Hungary	-1.4	0.8	Poland	-2.1	0.5
Czech Rep.	-1.3	0.9	Slovenia	-1.9	0.6
Sweden	-1.0	1.0	**Spain**	-1.8	0.7
Estonia	-0.7	1.2	**France**	-1.5	0.8
Cyprus	-0.7	1.2	Hungary	-1.3	0.9
Poland	-0.1	1.5	Czech Rep.	-1.3	0.9
Netherlands	0.2	1.6	Slovakia	-1.1	1.0
Finland	0.7	1.8	Latvia	-0.9	1.1
Bulgaria	0.9	1.9	**Belgium**	-0.8	1.1
Slovenia	0.9	1.9	**Netherlands**	-0.8	1.1
UK	1.3	2.1	Sweden	-0.6	1.2
Belgium	1.4	2.1	**Austria**	-0.4	1.3
Malta	1.8	2.4	Romania	-0.1	1.4
France	1.8	2.4	Lithuania	0.2	1.6
Austria	2.1	2.5	Estonia	0.3	1.7
Romania	2.4	2.7	Cyprus	0.5	1.7
Ireland	3.8	3.3	Denmark	0.9	2.0
Italy	4.6	3.7	**Germany**	1.3	2.1
Portugal	4.7	3.8	**Finland**	1.4	2.2
Spain	4.8	3.8	**Portugal**	1.6	2.3
Denmark	7.2	5.0	**Ireland**	2.1	2.5
Lithuania	9.8	6.2	Malta	3.8	3.3
Greece	11.5	7.0	**Greece**	3.9	3.4
Average	2.0	2.5		-0.1	1.4
Euro zone average	3.6	3.2		0.2	1.6
Transition countries	0.6	1.8		-1.0	1.0
Other 5 sample countries	1.7	2.3		1.2	2.1

Notes: imp.*ERV* is the implied standard deviation of quarterly percent change in the bilateral nominal exchange rate, given forecasts of *ADJUSTMENT* and assumptions detailed in the text. imp.*FISCAL* is the implied standard deviation of annual bilateral differences in public balances, expressed in percent of GDP. Averages are simple and not weighted. The current euro zone member states are printed in bold type.

ation of percent changes in exchange rates equals half of the margins, which amounts to 1.125 percent. Countries with an implied exchange rate variation (imp.*ERV*) between them that is higher than this threshold are under pressure for exchange rate adjustment that exceeds the extent allowed before joining the euro zone. Had these countries continued to observe the ERM arrangement instead of launching the euro, their implied exchange rate variation, stripped of EMU's endogenous effects, would have been even higher and they would have been pressured into some realignment of their exchange rates.

More than half of the sample countries fall beyond this threshold when Germany is considered as an anchor country. Crucially, these countries include all of the current euro zone member states except for Finland and the Netherlands, and all of the major EU member states. To maintain their actual or potential membership in the euro zone, these countries would either be systematically breaking the stipulations of the SGP on fiscal discipline or would have to try harder to liberalize their economies to enable greater price and wage flexibility and better factor mobility. In contrast, only six countries of the entire sample fall beyond the 1.125 percent threshold with the UK, including only one major country (Germany). These results again underscore the advantage of the UK's economy and politics as an anchor for the euro zone.

Another way to interpret forecasts of the adjustment burden is to assume total lack of exchange rate variation (which, after all, is the case in a currency union), and to isolate the fiscal component of the forecasted adjustment indicator, which is the implied variation in the fiscal positions of the member states. imp.*FISCAL* is the implied standard deviation of annual bilateral differences in public balances, expressed in percent of GDP, that is required to adjust to membership in the euro zone.

Applying a 1.5 percent threshold for the variation in the fiscal positions (*FISCAL*), as suggested previously, would reduce the number of countries with a potential for sustainable membership in the euro zone. In contrast, applying a 2 percent threshold would single out the same countries suggested by imp.*ERV*. Such a threshold would represent a range that is 4 percentage points wide in the distribution of bilateral differences in fiscal positions under the same assumption with respect to this distribution. In other words, to maintain a viable membership in the euro zone, especially including France, and to also respect the SGP's stipulations, member states must occasionally do better than just balance their books. Some surpluses must be acquired if the variation in fiscal positions is to allow sufficient adjustment between them.

Some Suggestions for Reform

As argued previously, only twelve of the twenty-six European countries studied so far can sustain a currency link with Germany by relying on the fiscal adjustment channel without systematically breaking the rules of the SGP. The other countries, eight of which are current euro zone member states, might find the European currency union to be very costly in terms of unemployment or, on the contrary, inflation.

Of course, as explained in Chapter 1, such costs may not deter a specific country from membership in the euro zone if its government and public deems the existence of substantial nontangible benefits from its membership. For example, participating in EMU may play an important part in managing ethnic strife in Belgium or in safeguarding Greece's strategic interests. Such considerations are beyond the scope of this book. Whatever the benefits of the single currency, it is always worthwhile to make it cheaper. This section attempts to suggest reforms that would make the euro zone cheaper to sustain by as many member states as possible.

The first suggestion for reform addresses fiscal policies. The identification of core countries in this book is based on the assumption that member states as a rule do not run significant surpluses. Should European governments be good on their promises to reform their budgets and balance their accounts, they could cushion their political economies from asymmetric shocks without recourse to large deficits. For example, a recession can be eased by reducing a surplus rather than by increasing a deficit. If fiscal positions of member states ranged between surpluses and deficits of 3 percent of GDP, then bilateral differences in these positions would range between +6 and –6 percent of GDP. If these differences distributed normally around 0, symmetrically exceeding these values only 4.6 percent of the time, then their standard deviation would be 3 percent of GDP. Applying this threshold to the implied values of *FISCAL* would leave only seven countries beyond the sustainability threshold with Germany, and only Greece and Malta beyond that threshold with the UK.

Alternatively, the EU can abolish the restrictions on the fiscal performance of its member states, as some economists suggest. However, this might lead to other problems, which are not analyzed in this book. One such problem is the free rider dilemma, for which the SGP was signed in the first place. If only one interest rate prevails in the euro zone, reckless governments are tempted to borrow cheaply at the expense of other governments. Another potential problem is that external policy anchors such as the SGP are often helpful for local politicians to use as scapegoats on which unpopular reforms can be blamed. Finally, large deficits that inflate public debt levels eventually reduce the effectiveness of fiscal measures, as explained in Chapter 2. Doing away with the SGP would not change this.

EU member states could make the euro zone cheaper to sustain by fulfilling their promise, delivered at the European Council in Lisbon in 2000, to make the internal market more competitive. This second suggestion for reform involves making wages and prices more flexible as well as encouraging labor and capital flows. Unfortunately, recent political trends within the member states are pointing in other directions. The failure of the EU's Council of Ministers to adopt the services directives proposed by the Commission in March 2005 and the rejection of the Constitutional Treaty in referendums in France and the Netherlands may signal a rejection by important societal groups of further integration among the member states. This unwillingness to complete the internal market is unfortunate, given the importance of the internal market in improving business cycle correlation among the member states, as shown in Chapter 4. This is especially crucial for many of the new member states.

Opening the economy to international trade and factor flows, which is the third suggestion for reform, is in general a good strategy for any country seeking membership in a currency union. In spite of great recent strides, insufficient openness remains a Mediterranean malaise, shared by Greece, Italy, Portugal, and Spain. Large countries have a natural tendency for lower openness but such objective realities should not become an excuse for complacency and protectionist tendencies.

The fourth suggestion for reform is to increase cabinet duration. This is important for Austria, Belgium, and Ireland, where cabinet duration in the 1990s was close to the sample average when defined by elections and coalition changes (*SHARE*), leaving much scope for improvement. This is all the more so for many of the transition countries, and also for France and Italy (see Table 5.2).

Tables 6.2 and 6.4 provide a menu of institutional reforms for greater cabinet duration. These include applying a majoritarian electoral formula and raising parliamentary entry thresholds. This is especially relevant for Belgium, which has the most fragmented legislature in the continent, doubling the entire partisan spectrum for each major ethnic group. Similar advice should be heeded in Poland, Romania, and Slovenia (see Table 6.1). Other useful institutional reforms include shifting from a parliamentary to a presidential democracy, giving some nonpolitical authority the right to veto early dissolution of the legislature, and enacting a requirement for a constructive vote of no confidence. The latter two measures, if applied in any two member states of the euro zone, are estimated to reduce the potential for adjustment between them by 18 percent per measure.[6]

Finally, correlation between the member states' electoral cycles is very important for reducing EMU's adjustment burden. Perhaps member states of the euro zone should commit to a synchronized electoral schedule, holding elections at the same time across the continent. Occasional early elections, if not banned, as they are in Norway, could at least be prevented from upsetting the continental schedule by restricting the terms of early-elected legislatures, as is the case in Sweden. In other words, a further dose of political integration among EU member states could help sustain their currency union.

Notes

1. *ADJACENCY's* coefficient in Equation 4.3 is 0.18, while *TRADE* and *TRADE/TRANSPOSE's* coefficents in Equation 4.2 are 0.13 and –0.39, respectively, thus $(0.13 - 0.39) \times 0.18 = -0.05$.

2. This value is derived by multiplying a value of –0.07 (which is the differ-

ence between 0 and 0.07) by *ERV*'s coefficient in Equation 7.18 (–3.22), and calculating the exponential transformation of this product.

3. Further data on the calculated endogenous effect of EMU on business cycle correlation is available from the author upon request.

4. The variation in real interest rates is added to forecasts of *ADJUSTMENT* after standardizing it, of course (see Chapter 3 for the calculation method of *ADJUSTMENT*).

5. In a normal distribution, only 4.55 percent of observations fall beyond two standard deviations on either side of the mean.

6. This figure is the exponential transformation of the product of the relevant coefficients in Equations 7.1 through 7.3, and 7.5 in Table 7.1, and Equation 7.12 in Table 7.2. If the relevant reforms took place in only one country their effect on the potential for adjustment with any other country would diminish to 10 percent.

8

Meet the Neighbors

This chapter applies the methodology of the book to a wider set of countries surrounding the EU in an attempt to find how costly adopting the euro would be to these countries compared with adopting the US dollar. The motivation for this chapter is the growing emphasis in the EU on integrating these neighboring countries into its internal market. Because many of these countries are not democratic, the analysis in this chapter measures the effect of autocracy and regime duration on the adjustment burden. Forecasts of this burden are made for selected subperiods since 1975, showing whether the country gravitates in the long term to the euro or to the dollar.

Wider Europe

In 1995, the EU launched the Barcelona process, a policy that aims at enhancing economic development, democracy, and liberal values in the southern and eastern Mediterranean countries (including Jordan and the Palestinian Authority). Euro-Mediterranean cooperation in the Barcelona process encompasses three "baskets": economic, political, and cultural. These baskets are reflected in the Euro-Mediterranean association agreements, which the EU has so far concluded in the framework of the Barcelona process with each of these Mediterranean countries except for Libya. Each Euro-Mediterranean association agreement consists of provisions allowing for a free trade area in industrial goods and some liberalization of trade in agricultural goods, services, capital flows, and government procurement. Other measures in these agreements relate to competition policy and protection of intellectual property rights. Each Euro-Mediterranean association agreement also consists of a bilateral political dialog and cooperation in cultural and social matters.

Within the economic basket, the aim of the Barcelona process is to establish by 2010 a free trade area among the EU and all Mediterranean countries, based on the Euro-Mediterranean association agreements as well as on free trade area agreements to be signed among the non-EU

Mediterranean countries. To this effect, the EU has been pressing for liberalization of Mediterranean economies and for structural adjustments. A financial assistance program has been set up, through which the EU helps in the development of infrastructure and the business communities in these countries. The EU has also been urging the Mediterranean countries to join all of the multilateral agreements and commitments under the World Trade Organization (WTO) (Commission of the European Communities (2000, 6, 8).

To achieve further Euro-Mediterranean economic integration, the Commission of the European Communities (henceforth, the Commission) often convenes interministerial conferences in addition to regular meetings of steering committees and working groups of experts. Business, environmental, research, and cultural networks have been established as well. The initial committee work in the context of the Barcelona process focused on allowing duty-free trade in industrial goods among the Mediterranean partners, and now the focus is increasingly shifting to a plethora of other technical issues that represent nontariff barriers, including industrial cooperation, rules of origin, customs procedures, common standards, regulatory frameworks for investment, harmonization of rules of origin, and liberalization of services (Commission of the European Communities, 2002a, 2002b, 2002c).

The tendency to view the Barcelona process not merely as a scheme for regional trade integration but as a process of profound economic and political change among the participants follows the same neofunctionalist logic that is argued to form the foundation of the EU. Cooperation in supposedly simple, and technical issues spill over to much more fundamental issues, increasingly impinging on state sovereignty. Thus, in its recommendations to countries participating in the Barcelona process, the Commission called in 2002 for the gradual development of a Euro-Mediterranean internal market (Commission of the European Communities, 2002a, 14).

The enlargement of the EU in May 2004 redefined its borders, bringing them closer to Russia and the Middle East. In 2003, in view of this enlargement, the Commission launched the European neighborhood policy, directed toward those countries neighboring the EU to its east and south that are not regarded as potential EU member states in the foreseeable future. Specifically, this neighborhood group originally consisted of the Barcelona process countries, as well as Belarus, Moldova, and Ukraine. In 2004, Armenia, Azerbaijan, and Georgia were added to the list (Sadeh, 2004).

The European neighborhood policy is not directed at candidate countries (Bulgaria, Croatia, Romania, and Turkey) and other Balkan countries, which are considered potential EU member states. The EU also prefers to leave Russia out of the neighborhood policy, developing with it instead the Common European Economic Space, based on their partnership and cooperation agreement. Partnership and cooperation agreements, which were signed during the 1990s with many ex-Soviet countries, apply the tariff schedule agreed to in the WTO to their trade with the EU, but do not establish free trade areas as the Euro-Mediterranean association agreements do with the Mediterranean countries.

According to the Commission, the European neighborhood policy aims at enhancing political stability around the EU, creating a "ring of friends," by promoting democracy, pluralism, and respect for human rights and the rule of law (Commission of the European Communities, 2003). The lack of these so far is deemed by the Commission to pose an increasing threat to the political stability of the EU. To stabilize the EU's neighborhood, the Commission is proposing to allow the neighborhood countries unhindered access to the EU's internal market, including labor mobility in the distant future (Commission of the European Communities, 2004). According to Romano Prodi, the previous head of the Commission, the EU proposes "sharing everything but institutions" (Prodi, 2002). The European Economic Area, which the EU shares with Iceland, Lichtenstein, and Norway, was considered, at least at some point, as a model for EU–neighborhood relations (Commission of the European Communities, 2003; Prodi, 2002).

Time will tell whether indeed the sky is the limit, at least in the economic aspect of these relations. However, as this political-economic integration process spills over to ever-deeper issue areas, and as the neighborhood countries integrate with the internal market, the question of unilateral adoption of the EU's single currency by the neighbors will surely be raised (Sadeh, 2004). The purpose of this chapter is to explore whether the euro is potentially a cheaper external anchor to the countries of the wider Europe region compared with the US dollar.

Unfortunately, existing optimum currency area studies of the EU and the neighborhood countries are few. With some exceptions (Bénassy-Quéré and Lahrèche-Révil, 1999, 2000) they focus on specific criteria of specific countries, such as trade relations, immigration, and institutional issues (Barber, 1998; Brenton et al., 1997; Flam, 2004; Sayek and Selover, 2002; Tovias, 2003; White, 1999). Thus, this chapter is meant to be a significant contribution to the debate.

Basing its sample on the same period used in previous chapters (1992–1998), this chapter broadens the sample's country coverage. In addition to the twenty-six European countries studied so far (henceforth, the small sample), the new large sample includes Belarus, Moldova, Russia, Ukraine, three member states of EFTA, the ten Mediterranean non-EU countries, and the United States—a total of forty-four countries. These potentially make for 946 dyadic observations, but in practice some observations are lost due to insufficient data in the neighborhood countries.

Russia is included because it is an important neighbor of the EU, even if the neighborhood policy does not officially apply to it. The adoption of the euro as an anchor currency in Russia is an intriguing if very distant possibility, especially because the EU softly promotes the use of the euro as an international reserve currency. Using the euro as an anchor currency is less fictional for the EFTA countries—Iceland, Norway, and Switzerland— which are already very well integrated with the EU.

The Mediterranean non-EU countries in the sample do not include the Palestinian Authority due to the lack of an independent currency and reliable and consistent data in important variables during the sample period. However, the sample does include Jordan, which does not have a Mediterranean coast but is politically grouped by the EU with these countries. Libya is also included, in spite of being excluded from the Barcelona process until recently, because its new policy is expected to lead it on the same path of Euro-Mediterranean integration. Turkey is included in the sample, in spite of being officially regarded as a candidate rather than a neighbor country, because in practice it is expected to stay outside the EU for many years to come and because it has not been analyzed in previous chapters.

Albania and the countries that were part of Yugoslavia are left outside the sample because much of their data for the sample period are missing, partial, or affected by the region's wars. Similar considerations apply to Armenia, Azerbaijan, and Georgia, which formally are covered by the EU's neighborhood policy. Thus, these three countres are left out of the sample too. It is also doubtful whether these three countries seriously belong to the political economy of the wider Europe region. Finally, the United States is included to allow a comparison between the US dollar and the euro as anchor currencies in the wider Europe region.

To achieve its purpose, this chapter constructs and estimates an indicator of adjustment to an external anchor similar to the one used in Chapter 7. Wherever possible, the same variables and instruments are used, but some alterations in the model are imperative, given the nature of the political economies of the EU's neighbors. Specifically, because many of these added countries are not democratic, the model drops partisanship, political business cycle correlation, and cabinet duration (along with its instruments). Forecasts of the adjustment burden indicator are made this time against the group of current euro zone member states for each of the other sample countries for selected years during the period 1975–2004. This facilitates a dynamic analysis of the costs of adopting the euro in these countries.

This chapter mostly repeats the procedures presented in the previous chapters, so theoretical and technical aspects are only briefly discussed. Most of the discussion is devoted to description of a few new variables and instruments, and to the results of the statistical estimation. Unless otherwise specified, raw data are again taken from the IMF's *Direction of Trade Statistics* and *International Financial Statistics*.

Economic and Political Costs

This section describes the features of the countries that are included in the large sample but not in the small one, and studies the relationships among economic and political variables and instruments that are expected to affect adjustment. Again, these include bilateral trade, business cycle correlation, and bilateral disparities in inflation. The discussion skips over the relationship between openness and its instrument because this relationship is quite similar in the large sample to the one captured in Equation (4.4). In addition, this section discusses regime duration as a new determinant of adjustment.

Table 8.1 reports estimation results for a gravity equation explaining bilateral trade ratios among the forty-four sample countries. Equation (8.1) follows the same specification as in Equation (4.3). The dependent variable is the logarithmic transformation of *TRADE* (see Chapter 4 for technical details). It is explained by distance, language similarity, free trade agreements, adjacency between the partners, and a lack of sea access.

Table 8.1 Ordinary Least Squares Equations of Bilateral Trade (*TRADE*)

Equation number:	(8.1)	(8.2)	(8.3)
CONSTANT	4.75***	4.08***	4.62***
	(0.86)	(0.78)	(0.72)
ln.*DISTANCE* (−)	−0.82***	−0.66***	−0.73***
	(0.11)	(0.11)	(0.10)
LANGUAGE (+)	−0.002	0.01***	0.01***
	(0.003)	(0.004)	(0.003)
FREETRADE (+)	1.58***	1.13***	1.06***
	(0.12)	(0.11)	(0.11)
ADJACENCY (+)	0.71***	0.66***	0.90***
	(0.25)	(0.23)	(0.18)
LANDLOCKED (−)	−0.96***	−1.31***	−1.46***
	(0.22)	(0.20)	(0.19)
ARAB		−2.23***	−1.91***
		(0.27)	(0.26)
ARAB-ISRAEL (−)			−4.98***
			(0.91)
LIBYA (−)			−0.49
			(0.36)
Number of observations	945	945	945
Sum of Squared Residuals (SSR)	2682	2447	2251
R^2	0.25	0.31	0.37
F-statistic	61.2***	70.9***	67.8***

Notes: Estimates are corrected with White heteroskedasticity-consistent standard errors and covariance. Standard error values are indicated in parentheses. * $.05 < p \leq .10$. ** $.01 < p \leq .05$. *** $p \leq .01$. The signs by the names of the independent variables indicate their expected relationship with the dependent variable. The "ln" prefix denotes a logarithmic transformation of the variable.

As can be seen in Table 8.2, *TRADE* is on average lower in the large sample compared with the small sample. In other words, relative to GDP, bilateral trade involving the neighborhood countries was smaller in the 1990s than that among EU member states and the transition economies. Being a periphery, the neighborhood countries are also characterized by the great distances between them and their major trade partners in the EU. However,

Table 8.2 Descriptive Statistics of Dyadic Values

	Sample								
	26 EU member states and candidate countries				44 EU member states, candidate and neighborhood countries, and the US				
Variable/ Instrument	Mean	Std.	Min.	Max.	Mean	Std.	Min.	Max.	Units[a]
Dependent variables in the GMM procedure:									
ERV	0.070	0.083	0.001	0.378	0.108	0.119	0.001	0.562	RC
RERV	0.047	0.038	0.005	0.150					RC
ADJUSTMENT	0.220	0.238	0.026	1.249	0.316	0.283	0.038[b]	1.723	RC
RADJUSTMENT	0.146	0.144	0.003	0.685					RC
Economic endogenous variables of the structural (second-step) equation:									
OPEN[c]	88.4	27.0	42.6	171.6	81.0	25.4	28.6	171.7	percent
CYC	0.060	0.035	0.011	0.255					RC
CYCA					0.046	0.029	0.006	0.154	RC
INFLATION	6.7	7.5	1.0	40.2	7.1	8.7	1.0	57.7	ratio
Alternative measures of cabinet duration:									
ELECTION[c]	3.68	0.38	2.83	4.91					years
SHARE[c]	2.98	0.67	1.40	4.53					years
ALL[c]	2.85	0.70	1.29	4.46					years
RESHUFFLES[c]	2.72	0.86	1.21	5.34					years
Exogenous variables of the structural (second-step) equation:									
PARTY[c]	0	0.67	-1	1					index
POLICYC	0.61	0.11	0.19	0.85					DC
DURATION					32.5	27.1	1.3	166.5	years
Instruments:									
DISTANCE	1440	736	48	3768	2107	1439	48	9208	KM
LANGUAGE	0.02	0.10	0	0.88	0.05	0.18	0	0.99	index
FREETRADE	0.33	0.43	0	1	0.22	0.37	0	1	index
ADJACENCY	0.10	0.30	0	1	0.07	0.26	0	1	dummy
LANDLOCKED[c]	0.15	0.25	0	1	0.16	0.26	0	1	dummy
AREA[c]	166	111	3	526	879	1983	3	13119	1000 SK
BANK	1.27	0.25	1	2.45					ratio
DEMOCRACY[c]					0.81	0.21	0.05	1.00	index
AGE[c]	30	18	2.5	77					years
FRELIGION[c]	0.37	0.16	0.02	0.80					index
THRESHOLD[c]	11.9	7.5	0.3	37.5					percent
CONSTRUCTIVE[c]	0.24	0.29	0	1					dummy
HEADVETO[c]	0.46	0.35	0	1					dummy

(*continues*)

Table 8.2   continued

	Sample								
	26 EU member states and candidate countries				44 EU member states, candidate and neighborhood countries, and the US				
Variable/ Instrument	Mean	Std.	Min.	Max.	Mean	Std.	Min.	Max.	Units[a]
Other dyadic variables not used in the GMM procedure:									
FISCAL	4.53	3.98	0.50	28.1					percent
INDCONC[c]	0.11	0.03	0.07	0.23					index
INDSIM	0.64	0.12	0.25	0.88					index
TRADE	2.0	3.3	0.02	22	1.2	2.3	0.0002	22	percent
TRANSPOSE[c]	0.49	0.31	0	0.95					index
F[c]	0.72	0.07	0.52	0.86					index
FETHNICITY[c]	0.21	0.11	0.01	0.57					index
FLANGUAGE[c]	0.22	0.11	0.02	0.55					index
MAJORITARIAN[c]	0.13	0.23	0	1					dummy
SEATS100[c]	0.12	0.22	0	1					dummy
PRESIDENT[c]	0.06	0.14	0	0.73					dummy
EARLY[c]	0.04	0.13	0	0.50					dummy
LINKAGE[c]	0.08	0.18	0	1					dummy
FREQUENCY[c]	4.17	0.33	3.36	5.00					years
ARAB					0.18	0.27	0	1	dummy
ARAB-ISRAEL					0.01	0.09	0	1	dummy
LIBYA					0.05	0.21	0	1	years

Notes a. DC = difference in coding; KM = kilometers; RC = rate of change; SK = square kilometers.

b. The weight of each of *ADJUSTMENT*'s components changes from one sample to the other. Thus, the minimum value in the large sample is higher than in the small one.

c. Dyadic values are simple averages of two national values. For dyadic values of other variables and instruments, see definitions in the text.

to a great extent, *DISTANCE* figures in Table 8.2 reflect the inclusion of the United States in the sample. Jordan and the United States are the most distant pair of countries in the sample. Certain groups of neighborhood countries are characterized by very high levels of language similarity among them. This is especially the case of Belarus, Russia, and Ukraine, on the one hand, and the Arab countries, on the other hand. The greatest language similarity is observed between Egypt and Tunisia. Thus, on average, the large sample exhibits greater language similarity than the small sample.

The large sample also adds three landlocked countries (Belarus, Moldova, and Switzerland) to the four that are included in the small sample. The average value for *ADJACENCY*, however, is lower in the large sample compared with the small one. This reflects the fact that, relative to the sample size, there are fewer adjacent countries in the EU's periphery than in its core, which is expected given that Arab countries are separated from Europe by the Mediterranean Sea.

As for free trade agreements, the average value of *FREETRADE* in Table 8.2 shows that in the period 1992–1994, on which this variable is based, these were much less common among the neighborhood countries than among the EU member states and the transition economies that are included in the small sample.

Some of the Euro-Mediterranean association agreements that were signed in the 1990s and 2000s followed on free trade agreements that were signed in the 1970s. This is the case for Algeria, Egypt, Israel, and Syria. The agreements signed with these countries in the 1970s were not based on reciprocity. They allowed the Mediterraneans to keep shielding their industries from European competition even after their exports were allowed duty-free entrance into the EU, which occurred much before the beginning of the sample period. Israel is an exception to this trend, having fully removed its tariffs from EU imports by 1989.

The Euro-Mediterranean agreements committed the southern partners to trade liberalization but allowed them a lengthy transition period of more than ten years. Thus, they had no direct effect on trade during the sample period nor, of course, during the shorter period of 1992–1994, on which the free trade instrument is based. For Jordan (2002), Lebanon (2003), Morocco (2000), and Tunisia (1998), the Euro-Mediterranean agreements were the first attempt at creating a free trade area with the EU.

Two special cases in the array of Euro-Mediterranean agreements are Turkey and Israel. Since 1996, Turkey has been the only non-EU country besides Cyprus and Malta, that participates in the EU's customs union in industrial goods. This means that goods trade duty-free between the two parties. After a transition period ending in 2001, Turkey fully adopted the EU's tariff book and assumed all of the EU's trade agreements with third parties. Prior to 1996, Turkey was very slowly implementing a free trade agreement it had signed in 1963 with the EU (then the European Economic Commuity, or EEC). By the early 1990s the transition period granted by this agreement was almost over anyway.

Before 2001, when the EU tariff book became fully binding on it, Turkey signed free trade agreements with a number of sample countries, including EFTA (before Austria, Finland, and Sweden left it for the EU in 1995), ten transition economies (those included in the small sample), and Israel. These agreements had short transition periods, for obvious reasons, but only the one with EFTA affected the period 1992–1994.

Israel also has an extensive set of free trade area agreements. Aside from the EU and Turkey, Israel's free trade partners in the sample include the United States, EFTA, and seven of the small sample's transition economies. The agreements with the United States and EFTA were signed, respectively, in 1985 and 1992 and have been fully operational since 1990 and 1994. Israel's agreements with the transition economies allowed for great development in its trade ahead of some of these countries' accession to the EU, but did not affect the period 1992–1994.

Two other agreements involving countries of the large sample establish a free trade area between Jordan and the United States and between Estonia and Ukraine. The former was signed in 2001 with a ten-year transition period, and the latter was signed in 1996 effective immediately. Finally, since 1993, Belarus, Russia, and Ukraine have belonged to the free trade area of the Commonwealth of Independent States.

The equations in Table 8.1 generally support the arguments made in Chapter 4 regarding the determinants of trade. When considering trade agreements and adjacency in the 1990s, Equation (8.1) shows a more pronounced effect when the neighborhood countries are considered than does Equation (4.3), which is based on the small sample. However, distance seems to have a somewhat smaller effect on trade in the large sample compared with the small sample, and language similarity turns out to be highly insignificant in the large sample, with a negative rather than a positive coefficient.

Equation (8.2) introduces a dummy variable (*ARAB*) that scores 0.5 for the 288 dyads that include one Arab country and 1 for the 28 dyads of two Arab countries. The introduction of this control variable greatly improves the significance of language similarity as a factor explaining bilateral trade, and turns the sign of its coefficient, which means that during the sample period, Arab countries traded less than one would expect given their shared language. However, *LANGUAGE*'s coefficient remains very low. The effects of distance and trade agreements on trade are lower when Arab trade is controlled for, which means that Arab countries have traded less than their geography merited but more than could have been expected given the trade agreements they had signed. Finally, *ARAB*'s coefficient in Equation 8.2, when exponentially transformed, means that Arab countries' trade relative to GDP in the 1990s was only about 10 percent of its potential. This could be attributed to the efforts of Arab governments to control their economies as well as the obstacles that exist there for private business.

Equation (8.3) introduces two more control variables. *ARAB-ISRAEL* is a dummy variable for eight dyads involving Israel and any Arab country. It is supposed to control for the Arab official and unofficial boycott of Israel. Indeed, when the coefficient of this variable is exponentially transformed Arab-Israeli trade is found to have amounted in 1992–1998 to less than 1 percent of its potential, even after the relative economic isolation of Arab economies is controlled for.

LIBYA is a dummy variable for the forty-three dyads involving Libya.

Sanctions imposed by the UN on Libya in 1992 and 1993 limited aircraft movements to or from Libya, banned the sale of aircraft equipment and parts, halted the operations of Libyan national airlines abroad, banned the sale of arms and military equipment to Libya, limited the presence of diplomatic staff in Libya, froze Libya's assets abroad, and banned the sale of oil-related equipment to that country. This sanctions regime was suspended in 1999 and finally removed in 2003.

Although implying that Libya's trade was indeed 40 percent lower than its potential during the sample period, however, LIBYA's coefficient is of low statistical significance. The only major difference in the estimated coefficients in Equation (8.3) compared with Equation (8.2) is the rise in the effect of adjacency on trade, which probably reflects the near lack of trade between Israel and its immediate neighbors.

As in Chapter 4, it is hypothesized again that instrumented trade could be either negatively or positively associated with business cycle correlation, depending on the type of trade that develops between the partners. In Chapter 4, CYC served as a proxy for business cycle correlation and was calculated with quarterly data for industrial production, GDP, or employment. Many of the countries in the large sample, however, have no reliable quarterly data. Therefore, while essentially being calculated with the same formula used for CYC, CYCA uses annual real GDP data.[1] This makes it difficult to compare CYCA with CYC.

Developed countries are expected to engage in intra-industry trade and experience greater business cycle correlation among them than do other countries. However, the rate of transposition of internal market directives, which is applied in Equation (4.2), might not clearly distinguish between developed and developing countries in the large sample, which includes rich non-EU countries such as Iceland, Norway, Switzerland, and the United States. Instead, Equation (8.4) uses OECD, which is a dummy variable for ninety-one dyads of two member states of the Organization for Economic Cooperation and Development (OECD) as of 1995. This dummy is also interacted with instrumented trade, which is based on fitted values for Equation (8.2).

$$(8.4) \quad \ln.CYCA = -3.10 + 0.04 \times \text{fit.}\ln.TRADE - 0.81 \times OECD$$
$$\qquad\qquad (0.03)\ (0.02) \qquad\qquad\quad (0.06)$$

$$\qquad\qquad - 0.11 \times \text{fit.}\ln.TRADE/OECD$$
$$\qquad\qquad (0.05)$$

$R^2 = 0.19$; 944 dyadic observations; sum of squared residuals = 330; F-statistic = 74.0; $p < 0.05$ for all estimated coefficients; $p < 0.0001$ for the sum of coefficients of fit.ln.TRADE and fit.ln.TRADE/OECD, and for the sum of coefficients of OECD and fit.ln.TRADE/OECD.

The results of Equation (8.4) are generally in line with those of Equation (4.2), although the effect of trade on the business cycle is smaller in the large sample. Trade fostered cycle correlation among *OECD* countries in the 1990s, but hampered correlation among other countries. Business cycles among *OECD* countries were more correlated irrespective of trade, but became more correlated with trade.

How do the countries of the large sample perform in terms of bilateral inflation disparities? The neighborhood countries were generally characterized in the 1990s by higher consumer price inflation than in either the EU member states or the transition economies that acceded in 2004. The average annual rate of inflation in the large sample is 33 percent, up from 20 in the small sample. Hyperinflation was observed in ex-Soviet economies, with an average annual rate (in percent) of 426 in Belarus, 152 in Russia, and 156 in Ukraine. Other sample countries with high rates of inflation were Lebanon (24 percent) and Turkey (83). Table 8.3 reports results for ordinary least squares equations of the transformed rate of inflation (*D*).

The specification of Equation (8.5) draws on Equation (4.5). Detailed data on legal central bank independence is not provided here for all countries for brevity's sake. The following is a brief summary of the data. Legal central bank independence is on average lower in the large sample (0.51)

Table 8.3 Ordinary Least Squares Equations of the Transformed Rate of Inflation *(D)*

Equation number:	(8.5)	(8.6)
CONSTANT	0.17***	−0.01
	(0.05)	(0.09)
CBI (−)	−0.24**	0.49
	(0.09)	(0.38)
TRANSITION (+)	0.31***	0.29***
	(0.06)	(0.06)
DEMOCRACY (+)		0.24
		(0.14)
CBI/DEMOCRACY (−)		−0.82*
		(0.41)
Number of observations	44	44
Sum of Squared Residuals	0.82	0.74
R^2	0.53	0.57
t-statistic for sum of coefficients of *CBI* and *CBI/DEMOCRACY*		12.5***
t-statistic for sum of coefficients of *DEMOCRACY* and *CBI/DEMOCRACY*		6.27***
F-statistic	23.1***	13.2***

Notes: Estimates are corrected with White heteroskedasticity-consistent standard errors and covariance. Standard error values are indicated in parentheses. *** $p \leq .01$; ** $0.01 < p \leq 0.05$; * $0.05 < p \leq 0.10$. The signs by the names of the independent variables indicate their expected relationship with the dependent variable.

compared with the small one (0.61). Many of the countries in the large sample had average *CBI* levels for the sample period of below 0.40, which seems compatible with the higher average rate of inflation among them discussed above. However, some countries seem to spoil this trend. For example, Norway's *CBI* value was 0.16, but its rate of inflation was only 2.1. Belarus had a *CBI* value of 0.54, which does not seem to explain its hyperinflation. Syria is assumed to have had a *CBI* rate of 0 because no legal document concerning the independence of the central bank and applying for the period 1992–1998 is publicly available, but its rate of inflation was only 8 percent.

CLI in Equation (4.5) is replaced by *TRANSITION* in Equation (8.5) as a control instrument for the higher rates of inflation associated with the transition to market economy in ex-Communist countries. *TRANSITION* is a dummy variable for transition economies. *CLI*'s advantage is that it is based on indices of price liberalization and allows a more sensitive reading of the liberalization process. *CLI* is unavailable, however, for many of countries in the large sample, which cannot be assumed to have fully liberalized prices. Equation (8.5) is robust, with results roughly similar to those obtained in Equation (4.5) in terms of the signs of the coefficients and their level of significance.

These results may very well be spurious, however, because the rule of law in many of the large sample countries might be shaky and their decisionmaking processes may be lacking in transparency (Broz, 2002; Keefer and Stasavage, 2002). This concern applies especially to nondemocratic countries, where a single player or a very small group of players can change the law at will, with little negotiation or consultation with other interest groups. Similarly, interpretation and implementation of the law are carried out by authorities that cater to the same dominant player. Under such circumstances, interpretation and implementation are part of the dictator's policy, and the law does not serve to make government processes more transparent. Some parts of the law may be routinely ignored, whereas some established practices may not be legalized. Thus, the effectiveness of the law in securing the independence of the central bank from the government—and by implication its ability to reduce inflation—depend on the extent to which the political system can be regarded as democratic.

However, democracy also has distributive effects that influence the rate of inflation. As argued in Chapter 5, democracy exposes policymakers to pressure from interest groups and engages them in redistributive policies (Alesina and Drazen, 1991; Haggard and Kaufman, 1992). In contrast, autocratic rulers are more insulated from distributive demands of the citizenry (Leblang, 1999). Thus, it is argued that democratic countries are associated with greater fiscal deficits, greater reliance on monetization of debts and thus higher inflation than autocracies.

Equation (8.6) introduces two variables that attempt to capture the effect of democracy on inflation: *DEMOCRACY* and *CBI/DEMOCRACY*. *DEMOCRA-CY* is an index of institutionalized democracy, ranging from 1 for completely democratic regimes to 0 for completely autocratic regimes. *DEMOCRACY* is based on the *POLITY* variable in the Polity IV project database.[2] The project's original *POLITY* value for each country in each year is based on coded data reflecting the degrees of openness and competitiveness of political participation and executive recruitment, as well as the extent of constraints on the exercise of power by the executive. *DEMOCRACY* calculates for each country an average of the original *POLITY* score for the period 1992–1998 (Sadeh, 2004), and scales it on a 0 to 1 continuum.

Polity IV data are unavailable for Iceland, Lebanon, and Malta. Iceland and Malta are safely assumed to be perfectly democratic, as are all EU member states and OECD countries. Lebanon is assumed to have had scores identical to those of Syria because government processes in Lebanon were, at least until recently, heavily dominated by the Syrian government, turning the Lebanese government into no more than a provincial government. This indeed is the official Syrian policy with respect to Lebanon.

The large sample features great heterogeneity in political regimes. Whereas the western and central European countries are democratic, eastern European and southern Mediterranean countries have a greater tendency toward autocracy. On average, the regimes were 81 percent democratic during the sample period. Syria was the most autocratic sample country (along with Lebanon), with a score of 0.05. It is expected that *DEMOCRACY* is positively associated with D, reflecting the distributive effects of democracy.

CBI/DEMOCRACY is the product of *CBI* and *DEMOCRACY*. It is expected to be negatively associated with D, reflecting the positive effect that democracy has on the rule of law and on the effectiveness of legal central bank independence in reducing inflation. By the same token, a negative relationship between this interactive variable and D reflects the marginal effect of legal central bank independence on inflation for a given level of democracy.

Equation (8.6) is not as robust as Equation (8.5), with the coefficients of *CBI* and *DEMOCRACY* turning out to be of low statistical significance. The F-statistic, however, is still sufficiently robust (> 10) and the sum of squared residuals is actually lower than in Equation (8.5), suggesting an enhanced explanatory power. Importantly, all coefficients have the expected signs and the sums of the coefficient of the interactive variable with the coefficients of either *CBI* or *DEMOCRACY* are highly significant. These sums represent the marginal effect of these two instruments on inflation: –0.33 (= 0.49 – 0.82) for *CBI* in a fully democratic country, and –0.58 (= 0.24 – 0.82) for *DEMOCRACY*, given a fully independent central bank. In other words, in countries with a value of *DEMOCRACY* of 0.60 or greater, independent central banks are clearly effective in disinflation.[3] Similarly, given a central bank with a value of *CBI* greater than 0.29, democratization reduces inflation.

The last variable to be discussed in this section is regime duration. This variable is a substitute for cabinet duration, which was discussed in Chapters 5–7 as a determinant of the magnitude of adjustment. Many of the countries in the large sample are not democratic, so cabinet duration is a poor indicator for the stability of the government. In autocratic regimes, changes of cabinet may yet reflect a changing balance or power among competing interest groups, but because policy is much less a product of consultations and compromise in these countries than in democracies, it is also less sensitive to changing portfolios.

Regime change, defined as a significant change in a country's degree of democracy or the establishment of a new state, most often comes with a change of government; more important, however, it signals a change in the rules of the political game. As such, it may affect the extent to which the government engages in redistributive policies, if only because it changes the accessibility of decisionmakers to the public. It therefore follows that frequent regime changes are incompatible with long-term commitments such as currency links.

It is also important to recall that regimes, both democratic and autocratic, take time to institutionalize. As argued in Chapter 6, young democracies lack institutionalized parties, which enjoy greater discipline among their representatives in parliament and the support of a large core of loyal voters. These attributes are important for cabinet duration in democracies. But autocracies may also take time to tighten their control of power bases in the economy and society and to form established practices and routines. Thus, rapid regime change is expected to make policies more opaque and is once again incompatible with fixed exchange rates.

Rapid regime change is also simultaneous with corruption because incumbents have a greater incentive to abuse their power when they are not expected to stay in power for long. In highly autocratic regimes, corruption may not affect the stability of the regime; in democratic as well as mildly autocratic regimes, however, corrupt members of cabinet are at some point forced to step down, and thus corruption reinforces the instability of the regime. Finally, the political uncertainty that destabilizes governments in young regimes is reflected in risky financial markets and currency speculation (Sadeh, 2004).

Regime change, and certainly independence, is often coupled with the issuance of a new currency, so regime change is also a monetary event. Frequent changes of regime are associated with frequent monetary reforms. In contrast, currencies of durable regimes enjoy the benefits of inertia. Inertia in this context is the tendency to use a currency simply because it has already been used for a long time, even when there are good reasons to switch to another currency (Cohen, 2003). In other words, the use of an already accepted currency is likely to be perpetuated. The reason for this is that the uncertainty that is inherent in financial and monetary choices causes actors to minimize the perception of risk by repeating practices that are based on past experience. Perhaps more important, because the acceptability of a currency is based on a social norm, adoption of a new currency will not be cost-effective unless others are likely to use it extensively as well. The need for collective action in switching currencies slows the process. Finally, switching from one currency to another is costly because it involves technical financial adaptation.

Thus, populations and business communities operating under young political regimes may opt for some long-standing foreign currency as a medium of account and store of value if not as a medium of exchange. The more pervasive is the private use of a currency, the more detrimental to the local economy is the volatility in its value, and the more interested are the local authorities in its stability. Eventually, the authorities adopt it as a reserve currency. This, for example, is why outsiders are troubled when the US government follows a policy of benign neglect of the US dollar. As a result, it is expected that monetary authorities around the world do their best to stabilize the value of durable currencies.

Ideally, one would measure regime duration in the same way that Chapter 5 measures cabinet duration. However, regime change is not a frequent event and eventually did not occur in most of the sample countries between 1992 and 1998. Instead, DURATION is the dyadic average of each country's period-average of the number of years since the most recent regime change or independence. DURATION is based on the DURABLE variable in the Polity IV project database. Regime change is operationally defined as the establishment of a new state or a change of at least three points in the original national POLITY score (i.e., a change of 0.15 in the score of DEMOCRACY) over a period of three years or less (Sadeh, 2004).

Hypothesis 7: *Old regimes*
are associated with lower adjustment.

The large sample is heterogeneous in the maturity of its regimes. Whereas the transition countries in the sample are mostly young democracies only a few years old, as seen in Chapter 6, regimes in western Europe and the southern Mediterranean are decades old. The exception is Germany, which has been regarded as a new state since the unification of East and West Germany. Other relatively young regimes in Europe are Greece, Portugal, Spain, and Turkey, which abandoned autocracy in the late 1970s or early 1980s. France is considered to have undergone a regime change in 1968.

Sample countries with especially durable regimes that survived World War II are Ireland (74 years on average during the sample period), Sweden

(78), Switzerland (147), the UK (115), and the United States (186). The only sample countries to undergo regime change during the sample period are Algeria, Belarus, the Czech Republic, Romania, Russia, and Slovakia. Algeria and Belarus, which underwent two regime changes each during the sample period, have the lowest score, at 1.3 years. The regimes in the sample are on average 33 years old.

The Burden of Adjustment

This section presents results of the GMM procedure run on the large sample and forecasts of the adjustment burden. A few potential instruments are again dropped from the set at this point so as not to overidentify the model. These are *ARAB*, *OECD*, *CBI* (and its interactive variable), and *TRANSITION*. Their inclusion in the procedure increases the significance of the *J*-statistic and makes the results less reliable.

Table 8.4 details first-step ordinary least squares equations for the determinants of adjustment. The dyadic values of variables and instruments underscored with a dotted line are averages of their national values. The values of most other variables and instruments are identical to those used in the previous section. The only exception is *INFLATION*, which again is the ratio of the two countries' transformed annual rates of consumer price inflation (*D*), such that the lower rate is in the denominator.

Distance between trade partners and a lack of access to the sea have been shown in the previous section to reduce trade. The positive coefficients of the proxies of these factors in Equation (8.7) may be an indication that this reduction in trade was associated in the greater Europe region with enhanced business cycle correlation, which in turn suggests that these factors were associated mostly with intra-industry trade, driven by economies of scale.

Language similarity, trade agreements, and adjacency support trade. Their negative coefficients in Equation (8.7) can be interpreted again as indications that they were mostly associated with intra-industry trade. Unfortunately, the inability to include *ARAB* and *OECD* in Equation (8.7) makes it difficult to compare its results with those of Equation (8.4). Interestingly, though, the signs of the coefficients of distance, language similarity, and lack of access to the sea in Equation (8.7) are opposite to those obtained with the small sample in Equation (7.1).

Equation (8.8) studies openness. As expected, geographically large countries tend to be economically less open. A 1 percent more spacious country is estimated to have been 0.11 percent less open in the large sample. This effect is smaller than the one estimated in Equation (7.2).

Equation (8.9) focuses on bilateral disparity in national rates of inflation. The more democratic the two countries, the more the rates of inflation

Table 8.4 First-Step Ordinary Least Squares Equations of Determinants of Adjustment

Equation number:	(8.7)	(8.8)	(8.9)
Dependent variable:	ln.*CYCA*	ln.*OPEN*	ln.*INFLATION*
CONSTANT	−3.13***	4.94***	−0.95*
	(0.29)	(0.13)	(0.48)
Instruments:			
ln.*DISTANCE* (+/−)	0.11***	−0.01	−0.07
	(0.03)	(0.02)	(0.06)
LANGUAGE (+/−)	−0.002*	0.003***	−0.01***
	(0.001)	(0.001)	(0.002)
FREETRADE (+/−)	−0.44***	−0.20***	−1.23***
	(0.06)	(0.02)	(0.09)
ADJACENCY (+/−)	−0.005	−0.09**	−0.38***
	(0.09)	(0.04)	(0.12)
LANDLOCKED (+/−)	0.003	0.12***	−0.11
	(0.08)	(0.03)	(0.13)
ln.*AREA* (−)	−0.006	−0.11***	0.07***
	(0.01)	(0.01)	(0.02)
DEMOCRACY (+)	−0.15	0.35***	0.95***
	(0.11)	(0.05)	(0.18)
Exogenous source of adjustment:			
ln.*DURATION*	−0.22***	−0.07***	0.07*
	(0.02)	(0.01)	(0.04)
Number of observations	944	946	946
Sum of Squared Residuals	310	54.0	788
R^2	0.24	0.43	0.20
F-test	36.6***	88.8***	30.1***

Notes: Column entries are parameter estimates, and standard errors values are indicated in parentheses. Estimates are corrected with White heteroskedasticity-consistent standard errors and covariance. Instruments and variables underscored with a dotted line are calculated as bilateral averages of national values. The "ln" prefix denotes a logarithmic transformation of the variable. * $.05 < p \leq .10$. ** $.01 < p \leq .05$. *** $p \leq .01$. The signs by the names of the instruments indicate their expected relationship with one of the dependent variables; the boxed cells highlight the column of the relevant dependent variable in each row.

in the two economies diverged. This is expected, given the greater tendency discussed above in democracies to respond to allocational demands by various pressure groups. Autocracies are generally less responsive and feature more uniform rates of inflation; hence, the positive relationship between INFLATION and DEMOCRACY. Again, the inability to include CBI and TRANSITION in Equation (8.9) prevents more insightful comparisons with Equation (8.6).

The proxies for exchange rate variation (*ERV*) and overall adjustment (*ADJUSTMENT*) are calculated for observations in the large sample in a manner similar to that for observations in the small sample. The relevant fiscal data, however, are unavailable for Libya and Ukraine, and thus all dyads involving either of these countries are dropped. Due to lack of real exchange rate data for many of the countries in the large sample, it is impossible to construct RERV and RADJUSTMENT with meaningful country coverage.

As can be seen in Table 8.2 on page 144, on average the large sample features greater exchange rate variation (0.108) among its countries compared to the small sample. This is the standard deviation of quarterly changes in exchange rates during the period 1992–1998 for the average dyad. However, this mostly reflects the high exchange rate variation in the ex-Soviet countries, especially Belarus (with an average ERV value of 0.448 against the other sample countries) and Ukraine (0.355). Other non-ex-Soviet countries with average ERV values of more than 0.100 are Algeria, Bulgaria, Lebanon, Romania, and Turkey. Average ERV values for the rest of the countries hover between 0.066 and 0.082. The highest exchange rate variation was measured between Belarus and Bulgaria (0.562), and the lowest was again between Germany and the Netherlands.

Table 8.2 also shows that the large sample features, on average, greater adjustment (0.316) among its countries compared to the small sample. Again, transition economies lead with, for example, an average ADJUSTMENT value of 1.283 for Bulgaria and 0.912 for Belarus. Other economies with average ADJUSTMENT values of more than 0.400 are Lebanon, Lithuania, Moldova, Romania, and Russia. Average values for Algeria, Estonia, Jordan, Slovenia, Sweden, and Turkey are between 0.300 and 0.400, and these values are between 0.200 and 0.300 for all of the other sample countries. The greatest adjustment was recorded between Bulgaria and Slovakia (1.723), and the lowest was between Denmark and France (0.038).[4]

Table 8.5 details second-step GMM equations for two of the four indicators of adjustment. The lower number of observations in Equation (8.11) is due to missing fiscal data for some of the countries, as explained earlier. Results tend to support Hypotheses 1 through 3 from Chapter 4 and Hypothesis 7 in this chapter.

Hypothesis 1 argues in Chapter 4 that as business cycles become less correlated between European partners, adjustment between them rises. Indeed, the proxy for business cycle correlation is positively and robustly associated with both indicators of adjustment. Because this proxy is not based on the same type of data as CYC, it is difficult to draw comparisons with results for the small sample in Table 7.2.

Hypothesis 2 argues in Chapter 4 that the greater the openness, the smaller the nominal exchange rate variation but the greater the overall extent of adjustment between European economies. The first part of Hypothesis 2 relating to nominal exchange rate variation is definitely supported in Equation (8.10). The last part of Hypothesis 2 is not supported in Equation (8.11), however. Nevertheless, the smaller and weaker coefficient of the openness proxy in Equation (8.11) compared with that in Equation

Table 8.5   Second-Step GMM Equations of Adjustment Indicators

Equation number:	(8.10)	(8.11)
Dependent variable:	ln.*ERV*	ln.*ADJUSTMENT*
CONSTANT	4.86***	1.64***
	(0.83)	(0.62)
ln.*CYCA* (+)	0.64***	0.61***
	(0.20)	(0.14)
ln.*OPEN* (+) [(−) with *ERV*]	−1.08***	−0.15
	(0.14)	(0.09)
ln.*INFLATION* (+)	0.45***	0.28***
	(0.09)	(0.06)
ln.*DURATION* (−)	−0.48***	−0.26***
	(0.08)	(0.06)
Number of observations	943	858
Sum of Squared Residuals (SSR)	590	255
J-test	10.0	0.40
(*p* value)	(0.04)	(0.98)
Indicators of the reliability of forecasts:		
Theil Inequality Coefficient	0.13	0.17
Bias Proportion	0.00	0.00
Variance Proportion	0.03	0.01
Covariance Proportion	0.97	0.99

Notes: See notes in Table 7.1. Indicators of the reliability of forecasts are calculated for the forecasting of the sample's observations and rounded to two decimals. * $.05 < p \le .10$. ** $.01 < p \le .05$. *** $p \le .01$.

(8.10) suggests that in open economies, greater adjustment was taking place through the fiscal and monetary channels than through nominal exchange rates. In other words, these other mechanisms of adjustment compensated for the stability of exchange rates.

Hypothesis 3 argues in Chapter 4 that greater bilateral disparity in rates of price inflation increases adjustment between European countries. This hypothesis is strongly supported by *INFLATION*'s positive and robust coefficient in both equations in Table 8.5. Hypothesis 7 is supported as well. For every 1 percent increase in regime duration, nominal exchange rate variation and the comprehensive measure of adjustment decline, respectively, by 0.5 and 0.25 percent.

Equation (8.11) scores a little worse than Equation (8.10) on the Theil inequality coefficient, but better on the variance and covariance proportions. By far, the advantage of Equation (8.11) is in its *J*-test. The *p* value of this test means that it is very safe to assume that the instruments used are exogenous to the independent variables in the table, and to *ADJUSTMENT*. Thus, Equation (8.11) is selected for the purpose of forecasting the adjustment burden for adopting the euro or the dollar as a nominal anchor.

Three endogenous effects that fixed exchange rates are hypothesized to have on business cycle correlation, inflation, and cabinet duration are studied in Chapter 7 (see Table 7.3). Of these, cabinet duration is irrelevant to the large sample. The effect of fixed exchange rates on business cycle correlation is impossible to reliably forecast on the large sample with the model used here because in a GMM procedure the number of instruments must exceed the number of independent variables in the second-step equation. Thus, there would not be enough instruments to run a GMM procedure with *CYCA* as a dependent variable and the determinants of trade as independent variables. Many of the instruments used in the estimation of Equation (7.16) are dropped from the model, along with cabinet duration.

The GMM procedure is available for forecasting bilateral inflation disparities due to the small number of variables in the second-step equation. The results are unreliable, however, because the coefficient of exchange rate variation turns out to have low statistical significance and because the *J*-statistic is robust, which means that the equation is overidentified. These results are not presented here, to spare the reader from excess tables and numbers.

Table 8.6 presents forecasts of the adjustment burden of the countries of the large sample to the current euro zone (i.e., with eleven member states in addition to Luxembourg). The forecasts are made for seven different periods since the 1980s. Each such period spans seven years, ending in the year noted in the table. The forecasts are based on Equation (8.11) and real data for its independent variables in each period (see Box 7.5 for a more detailed technical explanation). Cells are empty whenever data are unavailable.

The third column from the right presents the ratio between the adjustment burdens to the euro and to the US dollar for the period 1992–1998. Values greater than 1 indicate that the euro would be cheaper as an anchor. This column is used to sort the countries in Table 8.6 from the highest to the lowest. The last column of the table presents the same euro/dollar cost ratio but assumes a coefficient of 0 for ln.*DURATION* in Equation (8.11). In this way, it clears the effect of regime duration on the forecasts and compares the two potential anchors based on economic variables alone. The period 1992–1998 is preferred over other periods as a basis for comparison between the euro and the dollar because it is the only period for which data are available for all sample countries.

Synthetic data for the euro zone, which obviously did not exist before 1999, is composed from national data of its member states. Annual changes in the sum of real national GDPs are used to calculate business cycle correlation between a euro zone member and a nonmember state. The euro zone's openness ratio, rate of inflation, and regime duration are each an average of the member states' national values, weighted by their real GDPs.

In the period 1992–1998, Denmark, Sweden, the UK, and the three EFTA countries had the lowest adjustment burden scores to the euro among

Table 8.6   Adjustment Burden to the Euro and the Dollar

	Considering the effect of regime duration								*Net of regime duration*	
	1982	1986	1990	1994	1998	2002	2004	1998 euro/dollar		1998 euro/dollar
Sweden	0.109	0.061	0.087	0.105	0.087	0.063	0.065	1.045	**Sweden**	1.331
Denmark	0.116	0.116	0.115	0.118	0.085	0.062	0.052	0.844	**Cyprus**	1.227
Cyprus	0.197	0.111	0.099	0.146	0.212			0.835	**Malta**	1.202
Malta					0.119	0.102		0.819	**Denmark**	1.136
Switzerland	0.144	0.094	0.086	0.090	0.066	0.046	0.056	0.816	**Estonia**	1.120
Syria	0.473	0.357	0.429	0.342	0.172	0.186		0.767	**Slovakia**	1.095
Iceland	0.156	0.199	0.229	0.171	0.145	0.101	0.074	0.737	Algeria	1.088
Morocco	0.185	0.192	0.201	0.210	0.300	0.234	0.173	0.722	Syria	1.082
Israel	0.214	0.187	0.263	0.225	0.188	0.136	0.100	0.713	Bulgaria	1.070
Estonia				0.388	0.321	0.202	0.076	0.694	Ukraine	1.067
UK	0.099	0.101	0.079	0.114	0.079	0.062	0.034	0.672	Romania	1.062
Lebanon				0.644	0.271			0.671	Belarus	1.056
Slovakia				0.325	0.287	0.200	0.147	0.671	**Latvia**	1.054
Bulgaria				0.566	0.638	0.711	0.334	0.668	**Czech Rep.**	1.027
Turkey			0.347	0.493	0.505	0.484	0.460	0.667	Morocco	1.024
Ukraine				0.891	0.859	0.346	0.138	0.661	Turkey	1.023
Algeria	0.178	0.103	0.276	0.301	0.239	0.161	0.088	0.660	Moldova	1.001
Latvia				1.124	0.913	0.177	0.158	0.654	Jordan	1.000
Romania				0.616	0.651	0.526	0.247	0.651	**Lithuania**	1.000
Libya					0.204			0.650	**Slovenia**	0.987
Belarus				0.309	0.912	0.454	0.289	0.641	Iceland	0.986
Czech Rep.					0.225	0.198	0.126	0.629	**Hungary**	0.968
Jordan	0.267	0.156	0.295	0.388	0.170	0.128	0.095	0.629	Switzerland	0.967
Moldova					0.371	0.362	0.361	0.620	**Poland**	0.967
Lithuania					0.528	0.273	0.260	0.620	Russia	0.965
Slovenia				0.417	0.297	0.096	0.074	0.612	Israel	0.963
Hungary	0.180	0.122	0.179	0.370	0.211	0.114	0.084	0.604	Lebanon	0.946
Poland	0.299	0.316	0.393	0.525	0.215	0.177	0.078	0.599	Libya	0.885
Russia				0.739	0.622	0.460	0.527	0.590	**UK**	0.818
Norway	0.082	0.086	0.147	0.144	0.100	0.120	0.062	0.541	Tunisia	0.772
Tunisia		0.153	0.195	0.204	0.155	0.129	0.082	0.492	Norway	0.727
Egypt	0.173	0.159	0.150	0.160	0.146	0.098	0.073	0.458	Egypt	0.625

Note: Thin double lines split the two sections of the table at the average value of "1998 eruo/dollar." Thin single lines split the two sections at the first and second standard deviations from the average of the "1998 euro/dollar."

the sample countries that do not participate in the euro zone (see the column for 1998 in Table 8.6). This seems obvious, given the high level of economic integration between these countries and the EU and their political stability. Equally obvious are the high forecasts of adjustment in the transition countries. The less obvious and more interesting finding is that the countries of the eastern Mediterranean have relatively low adjustment scores to the euro. The reason for this is the combination of relatively high business cycle correlation with the euro zone, moderate levels of inflation, and relatively high duration of political regimes in the region.

Most of the sample countries seem to be proceeding in a long-term process of reduction in the potential burden of adjustment to the euro, as they integrate with the EU, become more open, reduce their levels of price inflation, and mature politically. This trend has been especially strong since 1990, particularly in the transition economies. By 2004, transition economies such as Estonia, Hungary, Poland, and Slovenia reached EFTA-level adjustment burden values. Such levels are also forecast for most North African countries as well as Jordan (see the column for 2004 in Table 8.6). Exceptions, where no clear trend is observable, are Belarus, Cyprus, Moldova, Morocco, and Norway. Turkey actually shows the opposite trend of an increase in its potential burden of adjustment to the euro, reflecting a weakening of business cycle correlation with the EU in the 1990s compared with the 1980s, as well as higher rates of inflation.

However, for many countries in the wider Europe region, the potential adjustment burden is relatively low and decreasing not only against the euro but against the US dollar as well. The third column to the right in Table 8.6 shows that only for Sweden is the euro potentially cheaper as a monetary anchor than the US dollar. The average non-euro sample country has a euro/dollar ratio of 0.677, which means that the euro is 1.5 times more expensive as an anchor. Cyprus, Denmark, Malta, and Switzerland may be regarded as borderline cases, lying between two and three standard deviations from this average value, but even they lean toward the dollar. At the other extreme, the dollar is half as expensive an anchor as the euro for Egypt, Norway, and Tunisia.

A major factor working to the dollar's advantage is the extraordinary duration of the US regime. With an age of 186 years, on average, during the period 1992–1998, the United States dwarfs the average age of euro zone regimes, which is 26 years. This asymmetry would only be exacerbated if the EU or EMU would be considered as a regime in its own right, with the 1992 Maastricht Treaty perhaps as its founding document or at least a reflection of significant regime change.

The euro comes across as a much more attractive anchor for the European neighborhood once the effect of regime duration is neutralized in the last column of Table 8.6, which considers only economic factors. Under these conditions, most of the countries would find the euro easier to adjust to than the dollar, but many would do so by a thin margin. The only countries for which the dollar would decisively be a cheaper anchor (i.e., beyond one standard deviation from the average value of 1.008), solely on economic grounds, are again Egypt, Norway, and Tunisia, but more interestingly this time, the UK too.[5]

The euro zone's economic advantage over the United States lies mostly in its openness. The euro zone economies were, on average, 55 percent open in the period 1992–1998 compared with only 23 percent for the United States. This figure may be an overestimation of the euro zone's openness ratio because much of its member states' international trade was conducted with one another. The IMF's *International Financial Statistics* database suggests the contrary, however—that the euro area's openness ratio in 1998 was actually 63.1 percent (earlier data are unavailable, of course).

Otherwise, the euro zone and the United States have almost identical inflation rates for the period 1992–1998. In addition, their level of business cycle correlation with the non-euro sample countries is on average almost identical. In other words, in spite of the great geographic distance between the United States and many of the EU's neighbors, economic integration in the wider Europe region is not reserved for the EU. In a globalizing world, geographic proximity is not all that important.

Notes

1. At best there are only seven annual observations in the sample period, so it is also impossible to detrend the data. Real GDP data is based on annual products of population and real GDP per capita, which is taken from the *rgdpl* series in Heston et al. (2002), and is expressed in internationally comparable 1996 purchasing power parity (PPP) US dollars.

2. The Polity IV project database, managed by the Center for International Development and Conflict Management, University of Maryland, is available at: http://www.cidcm.umd.edu/inscr/polity/index.htm.

3. Substituting a value of a little less than 0.60 for *DEMOCRACY* brings the marginal effect of *CBI* on *D* (0.49 – 0.82 X *DEMOCRACY*) to zero.

4. Of course, the large sample cannot feature a lower maximum value or a higher minimum value than the small sample. *ADJUSTMENT* is an exception to this rule, however, because the weights of its three components are sample-sensitive.

5. Generally, neutralizing the effect of regime duration should work in the euro's favor. However, the UK's case is different because it is also characterized by a long regime duration.

9

Conclusion

The tranquility of the transition to the euro since 1997 contrasts dramatically with the previous tumultuous 1992–1996 period and with the longer history of monetary integration in Europe. Gone are the periodical exchange rate realignments and the political recriminations that often surrounded them. Have the member states converged sufficiently to make a monetary union among them natural? Or could it be that the seeming calm observed in Europe's monetary affairs since 1997 is as temporary as was the calm of the late 1980s?

The story of European monetary integration highlights the determination of policymakers and leaders in Europe to pursue this path regardless of the difficulties posed by political and economic diversity among their countries. The answer to political disagreement and market turmoil has often been the establishment of more institutions. However, political and economic diversity among the member states always had to be adjusted for at some point. Institutions could not stop such an adjustment from eventually taking place.

The main theme of this book is that EMU is socially expensive for many of its actual or potential member states.[1] The reason is that divergence in relevant economic and political idiosyncratic variables among EMU member states is still large, even when endogenous effects of currency union membership are considered. By using econometric tools and a dyadic cross-sectional dataset covering the period 1992–1998 and twenty-six European countries, the book develops a quantitative indicator of the political and economic burden to the societies of the member states of adjusting to actual or potential membership in the euro zone. This adjustment burden indicator is used to support the argument of the book, and to find which EU member state is potentially the cheapest anchor for the European currency area and whether the European currency is potentially a cheaper external anchor to the countries of the EU's neighborhood compared with the US dollar.

The Euro Is Expensive for Most of Its Members:
The UK Pound Would Be Cheaper

Bilateral macroeconomic diversity calls for adjustment between the two economies concerned. Adjustment is defined in this book as the realignment of economic variables in response to economic and political bilateral diversity, whether as a result of many individual decisions, as in the market, or as a result of government policies. This adjustment can take place through a number of mechanisms. Market-driven adjustment mechanisms include exchange rate adjustments, price adjustments, and labor and capital flows. Nonmarket adjustment mechanisms that can be applied by governments include fiscal and monetary policies.

If adjustment between diverging economies in a dyad does not take place through any of the above market- or government-driven mechanisms, some form of disequilibrium results in one of these countries or in both. In a recession-hit economy, such disequilibrium can be manifest in depressed economic activity and prolonged unemployment. In a booming economy, disequilibrium can take the form of higher price inflation or asset-price bubbles.

Market-driven adjustment mechanisms, which make sense from a liberal economic point of view, can be socially and politically costly from a mercantilist perspective or from the perspective of domestic vested interests. From a mercantilist perspective, migration is a loss of factors of production and represents relocation of production that weakens the state by reducing its economic base. Similarly, the state might view capital flows on a significant scale as undesired or at least suspicious. Capital outflows represent relocation of production, whereas capital inflows are accompanied by foreign ownership and control of factors of production. In addition, migration and immigration might challenge established perceptions of collective identity and change the ethnic composition of the population.

At the domestic level, important political economic cleavages might challenge adjustment. As a general rule, because a currency union encourages and even depends on mobility of factors of production among the member states, the less mobile factors or sectors are at a disadvantage when it comes to bargaining over their terms of trade, whether bargaining takes place at the individual level, as in a perfect market, or through collective bargaining.

EMU's adjustment burden indicator is based on forecasts of an index that is a weighted average of bilateral variations in the exchange rate and in fiscal and monetary policies. Other mechanisms of adjustment—namely, adjustment in prices and labor costs, and labor and capital flows—are shown to either play a minor role in adjustment in 1990s Europe, be poorly recorded, or introduce too much "noise" or variance that is unrelated to fundamental causes. The forecasts are based on an analysis of relationships between this index and economic and political variables during the sample period. Values of these variables for the period 1998–2004 are then substituted into the equation to yield forecasts, which also consider a few endogenous effects that the very establishment of a currency union has on adjustment.

The book draws on existing literature to raise a few hypotheses about the causes of adjustment. Based on the theory of optimum currency area, the first hypothesis is that the less correlated the business cycle is between European partners, the greater the adjustment between them. As far as business cycle correlation is concerned, Finland, France, Germany, and Spain formed a core in 1990s Europe. Unsurprisingly, the business cycles in the transition economies tended to be less correlated with those in the four major economies considered for comparison in this book (Germany, France, Italy, and the UK) than were cycles in the other sample countries. Slovenia performed better than the other transition economies in this respect, and Bulgaria, Lithuania, and Poland were the worst. None of the four majors had a significant advantage over the others as a potential anchor for the euro zone.

According to the endogenous optimum currency area theory, business cycles tend to get more correlated if enough intra-industry trade develops between the partners as a result of their currency union. However, if intra-European trade is mostly inter-industry trade, then the member states would become more specialized in their production as a result of a currency union among them. Thus, business cycles would become less correlated. Chapter 4 seeks which pattern of trade prevails in Europe.

Relative to GDP, Germany was the greatest trader among the four major EU economies in the 1990s. German trade was, on average, more important to the trading partners when conducted with transition economies than when conducted with euro zone member states. However, the opposite is true when it comes to French, Italian, and UK trade.

Based on a gravity model, bilateral trade is estimated to have decreased relative to GDP by 1.3 percent for every 1 percent increase in the distance between the partners, and by two-thirds between two landlocked countries. However, trade was greater relative to GDP between countries with perfect language similarity, partners of a free trade area, and adjacent countries by factors of 2.1, 3.6, and 1.2, respectively. Trade is found to have reduced business cycle correlation for nonmembers of the internal market, and membership in the internal market was associated with a tendency for trade to enhance cycle correlation.

The second hypothesis that the book raises, again based on the theory of optimum currency area, is that the more open an economy is to international trade and investments, the smaller the nominal exchange rate variation. Of course, openness does not reduce the extent of adjustment required between two countries in the wake of asymmetric shocks. If anything, highly open economies are ever more exposed to external shocks and resort to greater adjustments. The most open economy in the EU is Malta, and the least open are Greece and Italy, followed closely by France and Spain. Openness is, on average, higher among the ten transition economies in the sample than among the current euro zone member states. Among the four major EU economies considered, the UK is the most open. In addition, small countries are found to be more open than large ones.

The third hypothesis is that greater bilateral disparity in rates of price inflation increases adjustment between countries, and the fourth hypothesis is that greater nominal exchange rate variation increases bilateral disparity in rates of price inflation. All transition economies were characterized by high rates of inflation in the 1990s. Among the four major EU economies, France experienced the lowest rate of inflation and Italy experienced the highest rate. In addition, the study found that independent central banks achieved lower levels of inflation in 1990s Europe, and as liberalization proceeded in the transition economies, the price decontrol shocks receded and inflation was brought down.

Comparative politics literature argues that, compared with right-wing governments, left-wing governments are associated with softer exchange rate commitments in the long term but stronger commitments in the short term. Thus, partisanship is regarded in this study as an exogenous control variable, which can be positively or negatively associated with the extent of adjustment.

On average, neither left- nor right-wing parties dominated Europe, although there was a slight tendency to the right. There was a pronounced right-wing bias throughout the continent during the early 1990s, but this trend reversed in the late 1990s, producing in the end a mild left-wing bias. The absence of any difference in these patterns between the current euro zone member states and the other sample countries seems to be compatible with the common wisdom that the cause of (or opposition to) EMU was common to the left as well as to the right.

Based on comparative politics literature, the book's fifth hypothesis is that higher exchange rate variation reduces cabinet duration because fixed exchange rates serve as focal points for policy agreement and bargaining and help politicians manage intraparty and intracoalition conflicts. Conversely, the sixth hypothesis is that higher cabinet duration reduces the extent of adjustment. The reasoning behind this hypothesis is that maintaining a fixed exchange rate may require politically difficult adjustments, such as abandoning redistributive policies that directly benefit cabinet members or important interest groups for the sake of uncertain gains in the more distant future.

The transition countries are found to have featured significantly less durable cabinets than the other European countries in the 1990s. However, elections were about as frequent in western Europe as they were in central Europe. Among the four major EU countries, Germany and the UK stand out as having more durable cabinets. In the 1990s, reshuffles were the most frequent form of change in cabinets, replacing cabinets incrementally roughly once in every two years and eight months. Elections, taking place on average once in three years and eight months, were more frequent than coalition changes, meaning that they had some tendency to return incumbents to power. This is especially true with prime ministers and presidents, who were replaced on average almost once in every six years.

Thus, if personal leadership is important for a country's membership in EMU, then Denmark, Germany, and Spain seem to be potentially stable member states, whereas Estonia, Italy, and Latvia are less so. However, if EMU became politically contentious and sensitive to coalition changes and elections, then the distinction between compatible and incompatible member states, as far as cabinet duration is concerned, would change. Austria, Cyprus, and the UK would top the parade, and Denmark and Romania bring up the rear.

Finally, traditional political business cycle theory assumes that the economy is described by an exploitable Phillips curve and concludes that the incumbent government stimulates the economy prior to elections in order to create jobs and boost chances for reelection. In contrast, according to the rational political business cycle theory, politicians hold office in order to deliver benefits to favored interest groups, or for the sake of office perks. To get reelected, they hide these costs from the voters, avoiding pre-election inflation and devaluation, which, like a tax, erode the voters' purchasing power. After the elections the true size of the deficit is revealed, and inflation and devaluation ensue.

If two countries are similarly affected by their own political business cycles (i.e., both go through a traditional cycle or both go through a rational cycle), then it is expected that overlapping cycles in two countries would be associated with low values of the bilateral adjustment indicators. If, however, one country experiences a traditional political business cycle and the other experiences a rational cycle, then political business cycle correlation would be insignificantly associated with the dependent variables or even inversely associated with them.

Of course, the political business cycle in a given country is endogenous to its domestic politics and economics, not an idiosyncratic feature of the political system. Bilateral correlation of political business cycles is to a great extent a matter of coincidence, however. Because it is a random variable, political business cycle correlation, like partisanship, is regarded in this book as an exogenous control variable that can be positively or negatively associated with the extent of adjustment, as suggested above.

The discussion and empirical evidence presented in Chapter 6 supports arguments that durable cabinets are generally associated with mature and presidential democracies, social homogeneity, high entry thresholds to the legislature, small legislatures, constructive votes of no confidence, penalties for early elections, a multitude of veto players in cabinet dismissal games, and short constitutional parliamentary tenures.

The results of the analysis in Chapters 3 through 6 are used to specify the GMM equations estimated in Chapter 7. The results presented in Chapter 7 tend to support Hypotheses 1, 2, 3, and 6. A one percent improvement in business cycle correlation in 1990s Europe is found to have brought nominal exchange rate variation and other indicators of adjustment down by roughly one percent. A one percent increase in openness resulted in roughly a one percent decline in nominal exchange rate variation. In addition, it is confirmed that in open economies the fiscal and monetary mechanisms of adjustment compensated for the stability of exchange rates. The results further show that nominal exchange rates were only weakly related to differences in inflation between European countries in the 1990s, probably as a result of exchange rate policies. However, adjustment through the fiscal and monetary channels tended to offset inflation-driven price adjustments.

The estimated decline in the extent of adjustment required between European countries in the 1990s in response to a 1 percent increase in cabinet duration ranged between 0.87 and 2.36 percent. Nominal exchange rate variation appears to have been a little more sensitive to cabinet duration than were domestic price adjustments and fiscal and monetary adjustments. Left-wing governments are found to have been associated with more stable exchange rates than their right-wing counterparts in 1990s Europe. The estimated decline in the extent of adjustment required between two European countries governed by left-wing parties compared with two right-wing government countries ranged between 53 and 90 percent.

The effect of political business cycle correlation on adjustment is statistically weak. However, even by the lowest estimate of this effect, a hypothetical case of perfect political business cycle correlation is estimated to have been associated in 1990s Europe with an 80 percent decrease in adjustment compared with the average dyad in the sample. This trend was especially apparent in nominal exchange rates and in fiscal and monetary stances, but to a lesser extent, if any, in domestic price adjustment.

Chapter 7 also studies a few possible endogenous effects of EMU. Hypotheses 4 and 5 are supported and, in addition, lower exchange rate variation is found to have led to more correlated business cycles in 1990s Europe. Compliance with the Maastricht Treaty's stipulations on central bank independence is expected to lead member states to identical levels of legal central bank independence. In the average dyad, this chops 7.1 percent from the adjustment burden. Finally, reducing exchange rate variation from

7 percent in the average dyad to 0 is calculated to potentially improve business cycle correlation and cabinet duration by respectively 28 and 25 percent. However, forecasts of EMU's effect on cabinet duration are statistically not sufficiently reliable. Thus, this effect is not factored into the forecasts of the burden of adjustment.

As of 2004, the potential burden of adjustment to EMU by the EU member states is found to be much lower than observed levels of adjustment during the 1990s suggest. Business cycle correlation improved among most of the countries, especially whenever the transition economies were concerned. However, business cycles in Denmark, Greece, and especially Malta grew less correlated with the major EU economies. Perhaps the most important development was the deterioration of Germany's cycle correlation with all of the pre-2004 EU member states except Austria and Belgium.

Almost all European countries have grown more open since the 1990s. This is especially true for Hungary, Germany, and Poland. In contrast, in Latvia the openness ratio declined. Consumer price inflation was reduced in the 2000s in almost all of the sample countries. In Bulgaria, the Baltic countries, Poland, and Slovenia, inflation was brought down from double- and triple-digit annual rates to single-digit rates. Inflation remained high in Romania and rose marginally in Ireland, however.

Some slight improvement in the correlation of the political business cycles in the EU member states and candidate countries happened to take place after the launch of the euro. This tendency is especially observed in dyads involving France, perhaps as a result of the harmonization of presidential and parliamentary tenures in that country. However, elections in Belgium, Greece, Romania, and Slovenia tended to become less synchronized with those in the major EU member states. So far very little scholarly work has been carried out with respect to the causes of such trends in political business cycles correlation. Thus, it is probably best at this point to interpret these trends as coincidental.

Interestingly, the potential for adjustment between the transition countries (once they adopt the euro) and the four major EU member states is found to have diminished in recent years relative to the same potential for adjustment in the case of the current euro zone member states.

The transition economies' reduced potential for adjustment stems from the maturing effect of their democracies, which improves cabinet duration, as well as from the magnitude of EMU's calculated endogenous effect on business cycle correlation. This endogenous effect relieves the potential adjustment burden, especially that between Lithuania, Poland, and Romania, on the one hand, and France, Germany, and Italy, on the other. This effect also significantly affects the potential burden between Bulgaria, the Czech Republic, Greece, Poland, Romania, and Slovakia on the one hand, and the UK on the other.

A final observation in Chapter 7 is that among the four major EU member states, the UK emerges as the cheapest potential anchor country for the euro zone because the burden of adjusting to a currency link with it is on average lower than the burden of adjusting to a link with any other major country. This is true for the entire sample as well as for the current euro zone member states and the transition countries taken as separate samples. Unexpectedly, France comes second, followed by Germany and Italy, which are disadvantaged mostly by, respectively, deteriorating business cycle correlation and low cabinet duration.

When Germany is considered as an anchor country, more than half of the sample countries are found to be under pressure to adjust exchange rates that exceed the extent allowed before joining the euro zone. Had these countries continued to observe the ERM arrangement instead of launching the euro (thereby forgoing the endogenous effects of EMU) the pressure would have been even higher and they would have been forced into realignment of their exchange rates. Crucially, these countries include all of the current euro zone member states except for Finland and the Netherlands, and all of the major EU member states. Hence, the main theme of the book is supported.

To maintain their actual or potential membership in the euro zone many countries are either systematically breaking the stipulations of the SGP on fiscal discipline or experiencing adjustment in domestic prices. Indeed, recent evidence from Eurostat suggests that, since 1999, relative unit labor costs have risen in Italy and Spain by some 20 percent relative to Germany, where recession has had a downward pressure on wages (*Economist*, 2005). In contrast, when the UK is considered as an anchor country, only six countries are found to be under pressure for exchange rate adjustment that exceeds the extent allowed before joining the euro zone, including only one major country (Germany). These results again underscore the advantage of the UK's economy and politics as an anchor for the euro zone.

The Euro Is Not Better Than the Dollar
for European and Mediterranean Countries

Chapter 8 aims to find whether the euro is potentially a cheaper external anchor to the countries of the wider Europe region compared with the US dollar. To achieve its purpose, that chapter constructs and estimates an indicator of adjustment to an external anchor similar to the one used in Chapter 7, but this time with an expanded sample that includes the United States and forty-three European, North African, and Middle Eastern countries.

Wherever possible, the same variables and instruments are used, but some alterations in the model are imperative, given the nature of the political economies of the EU's neighbors. In particular, because many of these added countries are not democratic, the model drops partisanship, political business cycle correlation, and cabinet duration. Forecasts of the adjustment burden indicator are made this time against the group of current euro zone member states for each of the other sample countries for selected years during the period 1975–2004.

Relative to GDP, bilateral trade involving the neighborhood countries is found to be smaller than that among EU member states and the transition economies. Nevertheless, the analysis in Chapter 8 generally supports the arguments made in Chapter 4 regarding the determinants of trade. In addition, trade is found to have fostered business cycle correlation among OECD countries in the 1990s, but to have hampered correlation among other countries. Geographically large countries are found again to be economically less open. As for inflation, the neighborhood countries are generally characterized by higher consumer price inflation than in either the EU member states or the transition economies that acceded in 2004. Hyperinflation is observed in the 1990s in ex-Soviet countries. Other sample countries with high rates of inflation are Lebanon and Turkey.

Given that the 44-country sample includes many autocracies with a weak rule of law, inflation is explained in Chapter 8 as an outcome of an interaction of central bank independence and the extent of democracy. Democracy is argued, on the one hand, to be more inflation-prone due to its sensitivity to redistributive demands by various societal groups; on the other hand, democracy improves transparency and allows central banks to become truly independent from their governments. Analysis in Chapter 8 finds that in countries that are at least 60 percent democratic (based on the Polity IV project's ranking), independent central banks are clearly effective in disinflation. Similarly, given a central bank at least 29 percent independent (based on the Cukierman index), democratization reduces inflation.

Regime duration replaces cabinet duration in Chapter 8 as one of the determinants of adjustment. Regime change, defined as a significant change in a country's degree of democracy or the establishment of a new state, signals a change in the rules of the political game. As such, it may affect the extent to which the government engages in redistributive policies, if only because it changes the accessibility of decisionmakers to the public. It therefore follows that frequent regime changes are incompatible with long-term commitments such as currency links. It is also important to recall that regimes, both democratic and autocratic, take time to institutionalize. Thus, rapid regime change is expected to make policies more opaque and is once again incompatible with fixed exchange rates.

Regime change—and certainly independence—is often coupled with the launch of a new currency, so regime change is also considered as a monetary event. Frequent changes of regime are associated with frequent monetary reforms. In contrast, currencies of durable regimes enjoy the benefits of inertia—the tendency to use a currency simply because it has already been used for a long time—even when there are good reasons to switch to another currency. As a result, monetary authorities around the world are expected to do their best to stabilize the value of durable currencies. Thus, the seventh hypothesis raised in the book is that old regimes are associated with lower adjustment.

The maturity of the regimes varies significantly among the in the forty-four sample countries. On the one hand regimes in western Europe and North Africa are well established, but on the other hand the transition countries are young democracies. Southern European democracies are also relatively young. Sample countries with especially durable democracies that survived World War II, include Ireland, Sweden, Switzerland, the UK, and the United States. In contrast, the shortest-lived regimes in the sample are those of Algeria and Belarus, in each of which two regime changes took place in 1992–1998.

Results in Chapter 8 tend to support Hypotheses 1, 2, 3, and 7. Denmark, Iceland, Norway, Sweden, Switzerland, and the UK are found to have had low levels of potential adjustment burden to the euro in the period 1992–1998. This should not come as a surprise given that these countries are economically highly integrated with the EU, and their regimes are very stable. In contrast, the transition countries are forecast to feature higher potential adjustment burden were they to adopt the euro. Surprisingly, the countries of the eastern Mediterranean are found to have relatively low levels of potential adjustment burden. This is the result of relatively good business cycle correlation with the economies of the euro zone, moderate levels of inflation, and stable regimes.

This picture is admittedly static. Thus, Chapter 8 looks at the trends that the sample countries exhibit since the early 1980s. This analysis reveals a long-term process of decline in the potential burden of adjustment to the euro. It is true that in Belarus, Cyprus, Moldova, Morocco, and Norway integration with the EU seems to have stagnated recently. Turkey and the EU have even grown apart during the 1990s, as their business cycles became less correlated and their rates of inflation diverged. Nevertheless, with time European and North African countries seem to integrate with the EU, open up their economies, bring inflation down, and become more politically mature. This process has been especially pronounced since the early 1990s and especially in the transition economies. In recent years the potential adjustment burden in Estonia, Hungary, Poland, and Slovenia came down to levels more typical of EFTA countries. A similar trend is observed in most southern Mediterranean countries.

The decline in the potential burden of adjustment to the euro in the countries neighboring the EU may suggest that they are becoming better prepared to adopt the euro. Yet the euro may not be their obvious choice since a similar process is taking place against the US dollar. In fact, Sweden is the only country where the euro is potentially a cheaper monetary anchor than the US dollar; in Egypt, Norway, and Tunisia it is twice as expensive.

The dollar is benefiting from the great stability of the US political institutions. The United States is a much older political regime than those of the euro zone. The euro emerges as a much cheaper monetary anchor for the countries of wider Europe if political variables are cast aside and the analysis focuses only on economic ones. Under such a setting, for most countries the euro becomes easier to adjust too than the dollar. However, for many countries it would still be a close call. And for Egypt, Norway, Tunisia, and the UK, the dollar would still be a decisively cheaper anchor.

What makes the euro zone economically more advantageous to its neighbors compared with the United States? The answer is economic openness. Contrary to the way the EU is perceived in popular and media debates on these issues its member states are highly open to international trade. When it comes to other economic variables considered in this book the EU and the United States are on a par. The euro zone and the United States feature almost the same rates of inflation in recent years. Their business cycles are similarly correlated with the European neighborhood countries. Thus, many of the countries neighboring the EU are as economically integrated with the euro zone as they are with the United States in spite of the great geographic distance from the latter. In a globalizing world geographical proximity is not all that important.

Suggestions for Reforms

Twelve EU member states, eight of which have already adopted the euro, might find participation in the euro zone in its current membership to be very costly. These costs may take the form of unemployment, or quite the opposite—inflation. Such costs may not deter them from joining the euro zone or maintaining their membership in it if their governments and public deem that the benefits of membership, even if they are not tangible, outweigh the costs. And countries already in the euro zone should also consider the costs of withdrawing from the single currency. This book does not weigh such considerations. However, whatever the benefits of the euro, member states should attempt to reduce its costs. This section summarizes five ways in which the burden of adjusting to the euro can be reduced, as discussed in previous chapters.

First, governments should reduce their deficits and balance their accounts. Specifically, public deficits should not exceed 3 percent of GDP and must be temporary and balanced by surpluses of an equal frequency and magnitude. This would allow enough room for fiscal maneuver that governments could use to absorb occasional macroeconomic shocks.

Second, wages and prices must become more flexible in the EU's internal market and labor and capital flows must be encouraged. Greater financial integration could also improve business cycle correlation by smoothing consumption patterns. Unfortunately, recent political developments in Europe suggest that voters are more interested in isolating their political economies from external shocks than in allowing them more flexibility in adjusting to shocks. Further integration among EU member states is being rejected by important societal groups.

Third, countries should open their economies to international trade and factor flows. While some small European countries are fairly open, the trade turnover in others, notably most of the Mediterranean member states, is still low relative to GDP.

Fourth, cabinets must be made more durable. This is crucial for many of the transition countries but also for some of the old EU member states. The importance of stabilizing cabinets in France and Italy and reducing their turnover cannot be overstated. In order to increase cabinet duration a majoritarian electoral formula should be applied and parliamentary entry thresholds should be raised. These measures would reduce the fragmentation of national legislatures. In addition, calling early elections should be made harder, perhaps by giving the right to veto early dissolution of the legislature to some authority that is external to the coalition-building game. A requirement for a constructive vote of no confidence could also be helpful. And in general, because presidential democracies feature more stable cabinets than parliamentary democracies, perhaps a full presidential system is better for some of the member states. However, other potential aspects of such a fundamental institutional change should obviously be considered as well.

Finally, and this is the fifth suggestion for reform, EU member states adopting the single currency should try to commit to a synchronized electoral schedule and hold their elections simultaneously across the continent.

The challenge for neighborhood countries that are considering the euro as an external anchor is even greater, given the potentially destabilizing effects that democratization has on inflation (Haggard, 1991; 2000). Improving the rule of law, making central banks legally independent, concluding and swiftly implementing free trade agreements with the EU, and adopting the internal market's legislation could greatly reduce the costs of adopting the euro.

Epilogue

After all is said and done, an analysis of costs has only partial predictive power regarding the ability of a currency union to last many years. Since this book does not consider all of the aspects of sustainability it cannot provide a definite answer to this urgent question: How sustainable is the single currency? However, the research presented here can predict how much *more* sustainable the euro can become if the adjustment burden is reduced.

The fact that countries such as the twelve members of the euro zone, Estonia, Bulgaria, and Lithuania maintain exchange rate commitments in spite of the great potential for exchange rate variation shows that they are willing to bear the burden of the peg. In a unilateral small-country/large-country peg, the burden of adjustments presumably falls on the small country, which may consider the economic and political gains to be worth the pains. In other cases, multilateral arrangements are needed to redistribute the burden of adjustment among the member states. The EU can ease tensions raised by the single currency by enhancing fiscal mechanisms to assist depressed areas. Even the United States was not an optimal currency area for much of its history and relied on fiscal transfers to keep its union.

Thus, the sustainability of a currency union depends mainly on political factors, namely, the presence of a dominant state willing and able keep it, and/or a sense of solidarity among the member states. In this sense Franco-German leadership, rule keeping, and a sense of community among the EU member states are crucial for the sustainability of the euro. However, large countries cannot to be paid for staying in the euro zone. It is at this point that the costs of the single currency, underscored in this study, are transformed from merely putting a price tag on the euro to an actual sustainability issue.

Note

1. For an alternative view see Jones (2002).

Hypotheses

Hypothesis 1
The less correlated the business cycle is between European partners, the greater the adjustment between them (p. 47).

Hypothesis 2
The greater the openness, the smaller the nominal exchange rate variation but the greater the overall extent of adjustment between the European economies (p. 60).

Hypothesis 3
Greater bilateral disparity in rates of price inflation increases adjustment between European countries (p. 64).

Hypothesis 4
Greater nominal exchange rate variation increases bilateral disparity in rates of price inflation between European countries (p. 64).

Hypothesis 5
Higher exchange rate variation reduces cabinet duration in Europe (p. 80).

Hypothesis 6
Higher cabinet duration reduces the extent of adjustment in Europe (p. 81).

Hypothesis 7
Old regimes are associated with lower adjustment (p. 153).

Acronyms

2SLS	two-step least squares
BAFTA	Baltic Free Trade Agreement
CAP	Common Agricultural Policy
CBI	central bank independence
CEFTA	Central European Free Trade Agreement
CIS	Commonwealth of Independent States
CPI	consumer price inflation
EC	European Community
ECB	European Central Bank
ECOFIN	Council of Ministers for Economic and Financial Affairs
ECU	European Currency Unit
EEC	European Economic Community
EFTA	European Free Trade Association
EMCF	European Monetary Cooperation Fund
EMS	European Monetary System
EMU	Economic and Monetary Union
ERM	Exchange Rate Mechanism
ERV	exchange rate variation
EU	European Union
EUSA	European Union Studies Association
GATT	General Agreement on Tariffs and Trade
GDP	gross domestic product
GMM	generalized method of moments
IMF	International Monetary Fund
ISA	International Studies Association
IV	instrumented variables
MTFA	Medium Term Financial Assistance
OECD	Organization for Economic Cooperation and Development
PPP	purchasing power parity
RERV	real exchange rate variation
SGP	Stability and Growth Pact
SSR	sum of squared residuals

STMS	Short Term Monetary Support
UK	United Kingdom
US	United States
VSTF	Very Short Term Facility
WTO	World Trade Organization

Bibliography

Databases

Direction of Trade Statistics Yearbook, Washington, D.C., International Monetary Fund.

International Financial Statistics Yearbook, Washington, D.C., International Monetary Fund.

Annual Report on Exchange Arrangements and Exchange Restrictions, Washington, D.C., International Monetary Fund.

Government Finance Statistics Yearbook, Washington, D.C., International Monetary Fund.

International Yearbook of Industrial Statistics, Vienna , United Nations Industrial Development Organization.

Single Market Scoreboard, Brussels, European Commission.

Keesing's Record of World Events, Harlow, Longman.

The Statesman's Year-Book: Statistical and Historical Annual of the States of the World, London, Macmillan.

The World Factbook, Washington, D.C., Central Intelligence Agency.

Publications

Alesina, Alberto (1988), "Macroeconomics and Politics," *NBER Macroeconomics Annual* (Cambridge, UK: Cambridge University Press).

Alesina, Alberto, and Robert J. Barro (2002), "Currency Unions," *Quarterly Journal of Economics,* 117, no. 2, 409–436.

Alesina, Alberto, and Allan Drazen (1991), "Why Are Stabilizations Delayed?" *American Economic Review,* 81, 1170–1189.

Alesina, Alberto, and Nouriel Roubini (1994), "Political Cycles in OECD Economies," in Torsten Persson and Guido Tabellini (eds.), *Monetary and Fiscal Policy,* Vol. 2 (Cambridge, Mass.: The MIT Press).

Alesina, Alberto, and Nouriel Roubini (1997), *Political Cycles and the Macroeconomy* (Cambridge, Mass.: The MIT Press).

Alt, James E., and Gary King (1994), "Transfers of Governmental Power: The Meaning of Time Dependence," *Comparative Political Studies,* 27, no. 2, 190–210.

Amorim Neto, Octavio, and Gary W. Cox (1997), "Electoral Institutions, Cleavage Structures, and the Number of Parties," *American Journal of Political Science,* 41, no. 1, 149–174.

Andrews, David M. (1994), "Capital Mobility and State Autonomy: Toward a Structural Theory of International Monetary Relations," *International Studies Quarterly*, 38, no. 2, 193–218.

Apel, Emmanuel (1998), *European Monetary Integration: 1958–2002* (London: Routledge).

Armingeon, Klaus, Philipp Leimgruber, Michelle Beyeler, and Sarah Menegale (2004), *Comparative Political Data Set 1960–2002* (Berne, Switzerland: Institute of Political Science, University of Berne). Available at: http://www.ipw.unibe.ch/mitarbeiter/ru_armingeon/CPD_Set_en.asp.

Artis, Michael J., and W. Zhang (1995), "International Business Cycles and the ERM: Is There a European Business Cycle?" Center for Economic Policy Research Discussion Paper No. 1191 (London: Center for Economic Policy Research).

Artis, Michael J., and W. Zhang (2001), "Core and Periphery in EMU: A Cluster Analysis," *Economic Issues*, 6, no. 2, 39–60.

Balke, Nathan S. (1990), "The Rational Timing of Parliamentary Elections," *Public Choice*, 65, 201–216.

Barber, Charles (1998), "Creating a Mediterranean Community: Euro-Maghrebi Cooperation," *Mediterranean Quarterly*, 9, no. 4, 159–172.

Bartels, Larry M. (1991), "Instrumental and 'Quasi-Instrumental' Variables," *American Journal of Political Science*, 35, no. 3, 777–800.

Bayoumi, Tamim, and Barry Eichengreen (1997), "Ever Closer to Heaven? An Optimum-Currency-Area Index for European Countries," *European Economic Review*, 41, no. 3–5, 761–770.

Bayoumi, Tamim, and Barry Eichengreen (1998), "Exchange Rate Volatility and Intervention: Implications of the Theory of Optimum Currency Areas," *Journal of International Economics*, 45, 191–209.

Beck, Thorsten, George Clarke, Alberto Groff, Philip Keefer, and Patrick Walsh (2001), "New Tools in Comparative Political Economy: The Database of Political Institutions," *World Bank Economic Review*, 15, no. 1, 165–176.

Bénassy-Quéré, Agnés, and Amina Lahrèche-Révil (1999), "The Euro as a Reference Currency for Eastern and Southern Neighbors of the European Union," *Revue Economique*, 50, no. 6, 1185–1201.

Bénassy-Quéré, Agnès, and Amina Lahrèche-Révil (2000), "The Euro as a Monetary Anchor in the CEECs," *Open Economies Review*, 11, no. 4, 303–321.

Berglund, Sten, Tomas Hellen, and Frank H. Aarebrot (eds.) (1998), *The Handbook of Political Change in Eastern Europe* (Cheltenham, UK: E. Elgar).

Bernhard, William, and David Leblang (1999), "Democratic Institutions and Exchange-Rate Commitments," *International Organization*, 53, no. 1, 71–97.

Bernhard, William, and David Leblang (2002a), "Democratic Processes, Political Risk and Foreign Exchange Markets," *American Journal of Political Science*, 46, no. 2, 316–333.

Bernhard, William, and David Leblang (2002b), "Political Parties and Monetary Commitments," *International Organization*, 56, no. 4, 803–830.

Bernhard, William J., Lawrence Broz, and William Roberts Clark (2002), "The Political Economy of Monetary Institutions," *International Organization*, 56, no. 4, 693–723.

Bertola, Giuseppe (1989), "Factor Flexibility, Uncertainty and Exchange Rate Regimes," in Marcello De Cecco and Alberto Giovannini (eds.), *A European Central Bank? Perspectives on Monetary Unification after Ten Years of the EMS* (Cambridge, UK: Cambridge University Press, 1989).

Blomberg, Brock S., and Gregory D. Hess (1997), "Politics and Exchange Rate Forecasts," *Journal of International Economics*, 43, no. 1–2, 189–205.

Blomberg, Brock S., Jeffry A. Frieden, and Ernesto Stein (2004), "Sustaining Fixed Rates: The Political Economy of Currency Pegs in Latin America," working paper available at: http://www.people.fas.harvard.edu/~jfrieden/.

Brass, Paul R. (1977), "Party Systems and Government Stability in the Indian States," *American Political Science Review*, 71, no. 4, 1384–1405.

Brenton, Paul, Natalia Tourdyeva, and John Whalley (1997), "The Potential Trade Effects of an FTA Between the EU and Russia," *Weltwirtschaftliches Archiv*, 133, no. 2, 205–235.

Broz, Lawrence (2002), "Political System Transparency and Monetary Commitment Regimes," *International Organization*, 56, no. 4, 861–887.

Calvo, Guillermo A., and Carmen M. Reinhart (2001), "Fear of Floating," *Quarterly Journal of Economics*, 117, no. 2, 379–408.

Cameron, David Ross (1995a), "From Barre to Balladur: Economic Policy in the Era of the EMS," in Gregory Flynn (ed.), *Remaking the Hexagon: The New France in the New Europe* (Boulder, Colo.: Westview Press), 117–157.

Cameron, David Ross (1995b), "Transnational Relations and the Development of European Economic and Monetary Union," in Thomas Risse-Kappen (ed.), *Bringing Transnational Relations Back In—Non-State Actors, Domestic Structures and International Institutions* (Cambridge, UK: Cambridge University Press), 37–78.

Cameron, David Ross (1996), "Exchange Rate Politics in France, 1981–1983: The Regime-Defining Choices of the Mitterrand Presidency," in Anthony Daley (ed.), *The Mitterrand Era: Policy Alternatives and Political Mobilization in France* (New York: New York University Press), 56–82.

Cameron, David Ross (1997), "Economic and Monetary Union: Underlying Imperatives and Third-Stage Dilemmas," *Journal of European Public Policy*, 4, no. 3, 455–485.

Carr, Jonathan (1985), *Helmut Schmidt—Helmsman of Germany* (New York: St. Martin's Press).

Cohen, Benjamin J. (1993), "The Triad and the Unholy Trinity: Problems of International Monetary Cooperation," in Richard Higgott, Richard Leaver, and John Ravenhill (eds.), *Pacific Economic Relations in the 1990s: Cooperation or Conflict?* (North Sydney: Allen & Unwin), 133–158.

Cohen, Benjamin J. (1998), *The Geography of Money* (Ithaca, N.Y.: Cornell University Press).

Cohen, Benjamin J. (2000), "Beyond EMU: The Problem of Sustainability," in Barry Eichengreen and Jeffry Frieden (eds.), *The Political Economy of European Monetary Unification*, 2nd edition (Boulder, Colo.: Westview Press).

Cohen, Benjamin J. (2003), "Global Currency Rivalry: Can the Euro Ever Challenge the Dollar?" *Journal of Common Market Studies*, 41, no. 4, 575–595.

Commission of the European Communities (1990), "One Market, One Money," *European Economy*, 44.

Commission of the European Communities (2000), "Communication from the Commission to the Council and the European Parliament to Prepare the Fourth Meeting of the Euro-Mediterranean Foreign Ministers: Reinvigorating the Barcelona Process," COM(2000) 497 final.

Commission of the European Communities (2002a), "Communication from the Commission to the Council and the European Parliament to Prepare the

Meeting of Euro-Mediterranean Foreign Ministers, Valencia 22–23 April 2002," COM(2002)159 final.

Commission of the European Communities (2002b): "Conclusions of the Presidency—Euro-Mediterranean Ministerial Conference on Trade—Toledo, 19 March 2002," *Euromed Report*, 38.

Commission of the European Communities (2002c): "Vth Euro-Mediterranean Conference of Ministers of Foreign Affairs—Valencia Action Plan," *Euromed Report*, 42.

Commission of the European Communities (2003), "Communication from the Commission to the Council and the European Parliament: Wider Europe Neighbourhood—A New Framework for Relations with Our Eastern and Southern Neighbours," COM(2003) 104 final.

Commission of the European Communities (2004), "Communication from the Commission: European Neighbourhood Policy: Strategy Paper," COM(2004) 373 final.

Cukierman, Alex (1992), *Central Bank Strategy, Credibility, and Independence: Theory and Evidence* (Cambridge, Mass.: MIT Press).

Cukierman, Alex, Geoffrey P. Miller, and Bilin Neyapti (2002), "Central Bank Reform, Liberalization and Inflation in Transition Economies—An International Perspective," *Journal of Monetary Economics*, 49, no. 2, 237–264.

Cukierman, Alex, Steven B. Webb, and Bilin Neyapti (1992), "Measuring the Independence of Central Banks and Its Effect on Policy Outcomes," *The World Bank Economic Review*, 6, no. 3, 353–398.

De Grauwe, Paul (1994), *The Economics of Monetary Integration*, 2nd revised edition (Oxford: Oxford University Press).

De Grauwe, Paul, and Yunus Aksoy (1999), "Are Central European Countries Part of the European Optimum Currency Areas?" in Paul De Grauwe and Vladimir Lavrač (eds.), *Inclusion of Central European Countries in the European Monetary Union* (Boston: Kluwer), 13–36.

de Melo, Martha, Cevdet Denizer, and Alan Gelb (1996), "From Plan to Market—Patterns of Transition," *World Bank Policy Research Working Papers*, No. 1564 (Washington, D.C.: World Bank).

Deutsche Bundesbank (2004), *Exchange Rate Statistics—Statistical Supplement to the Monthly Report 5* (Frankfurt am Main, Germany: Deutsche Bundesbank).

Directorate General for Research (1999), *EMU and Enlargement: A Review of Policy Issues* (Luxembourg, Belgium: European Parliament).

Dodd, Lawrence G. (1976), *Coalitions in Parliamentary Government* (Princeton, N.J.: Princeton University Press).

Dyson, Kenneth (1994), *Elusive Union: The Process of Economic and Monetary Union in Europe* (London: Longman).

Dyson, Kenneth, and Kevin Featherstone (1999), *The Road to Maastricht: Negotiating Economic and Monetary Union* (Oxford: Oxford University Press).

Economist, The. (2005), "Economic Focus: The Real Picture," February 19, p. 67.

Edison, Hali J., and Michael Melvin (1990), "The Determinants and Implications of the Choice of an Exchange Rate System," in William S. Haraf and Thomas D. Willett (eds.), *Monetary Policy for a Volatile Global Economy* (Washington, D.C.: The AEI Press), 1–44.

Edwards, Sebastian (1996), "The Determinants of the Choice Between Fixed and Flexible Exchange Rate Regimes," Working paper 5756 (Cambridge: National Bureau of Economic Research).

Eichengreen, Barry, and Marc Flandreau (eds.) (1997), *The Gold Standard in Theory and History*, 2nd edition (London: Methuen).

Eichengreen, Barry, and Jeffry A. Frieden (eds.) (1994), *The Political Economy of European Monetary Unification* (Boulder, Colo.: Westview Press).

Eichengreen, Barry, Andrew Rose, and Charles Wyplosz (1995), "Exchange Market Mayhem: The Antecedents and Aftermath of Speculative Attacks," *Economic Policy*, 10, no. 21, 249–312.

Eijffinger, Sylvester C. W., and Jakob De Haan (1996), "The Political Economy of Central-Bank Independence," *Special Papers in International Economies*, No. 19.

Emminger, Otmar (1977), "The D-Mark in the Conflict Between Internal and External Equilibrium, 1948–75," *Princeton Essays in International Finance*, No. 122.

Erickson, Christopher L. (1995), "Regional Wage Differentials: A Comparison of the European Union and the United States," in Barry Eichengreen, Jeffry Frieden, and Jürgen Von Hagen (eds.), *Monetary and Fiscal Policy in an Integrated Europe* (New York: Springer) 166–181.

European Central Bank (1999), *Monthly Bulletin*, October.

European Monetary Institute (1998), *Convergence Report. Report Required by Article 109 j of the Treaty Establishing the European Community* (Frankfurt, Germany: EMI).

Flam, Harry (2004), "Turkey and the EU: Politics and Economics of Accession," *CESifo Economics Studies*, 50, no. 1, 171–210.

Frankel, Jeffrey A. (1997), *Regional Trading Blocks* (Washington, D.C.: Institute for International Economics).

Frankel, Jeffrey A., and Andrew K. Rose (1998), "The Endogeneity of the Optimum Currency Area Criteria," *Economic Journal*, 108, no. 449, 1009–1025.

Frankel, Jeffrey A., and Andrew K. Rose (2002), "An Estimate of the Effect of Common Currencies on Trade and Income," *The Quarterly Journal of Economics*, 117, no. 2, 437–466.

Fratianni, Michele, and Jürgen Von Hagen (1993), "On the Road to EMU," in Mario Baldassarri and Robert Mundell (eds.), *Building the New Europe—The Single Market and Monetary Unification*, Vol. 1 (New York: St. Martin's Press), 253–279.

Frieden, Jeffry A. (1997), "The Dynamics of International Monetary Systems: International and Domestic Factors in the Rise, Reign and Demise of the Classical Gold Standard," in Barry Eichengreen and Marc Flandreau (eds.) (1997), *The Gold Standard in Theory and History*, 2nd edition (London: Methuen), 207–227.

Frieden, Jeffry A. (1998), "The Euro: Who Wins? Who Loses?" *Foreign Policy*, 25–40.

Frieden, Jeffry A. (2000), "Making Commitments: France and Italy in the European Monetary System, 1979–1985," in Barry Eichengreen and Jeffry A. Frieden (eds.), *The Political Economy of European Monetary Unification*, 2nd edition (Boulder, Colo.: Westview Press).

Frieden, Jeffry A. (2002), "Real Sources of European Currency Policy: Sectoral Interests and European Monetary Integration," *International Organization*, 56, no. 4, 831–860.

Frieden, Jeffry A., and Erik Jones (1998), "The Political Economy of European Monetary Union: A Conceptual Overview," in Jeffry Frieden, Daniel Gros, and Erik Jones (eds.), *The New Political Economy of EMU* (Lanham, Md.: Rowman and Littlefield), 163–186.

Frieden, Jeffry A., Piero Ghezzi, and Ernesto Stein (2001), "Politics and Exchange Rates: A Cross-Country Approach to Latin America," in Jeffry A. Frieden and

Ernesto Stein (eds.), *The Currency Game: Exchange Rate Politics in Latin America* (Baltimore, Md.: Johns Hopkins University Press).

Garrett, Geoffrey (1995), "Capital Mobility, Trade, and the Domestic Politics of Economic Policy," *International Organization*, 49, no. 4, 657–687.

Giavazzi, Francesco, and Marco Pagano (1988), "The Advantage of Tying One,s Hands: EMS Discipline and Central Bank Credibility," *European Economic Review*, 32, no. 5, 1055–1075.

Goodman, John B. (1992), *Monetary Sovereignty: The Politics of Central Banking in Western Europe* (Ithaca, N.Y.: Cornell University Press).

Gordon, Raymond G., Jr. (ed.) (2005), *Ethnologue: Languages of the World*, 15th edition (Dallas: SIL Internatinonal), Online version at www.ethnologue.com.

Grilli, Vittorio, Donato Masciandro, and Guido Tabellini (1991), "Political and Monetary Institutions and Public Financial Policies in the Industrial Countries," *Economic Policy*, 13, 392–441.

Grofman, Bernard (1989), "The Comparative Analysis of Coalition Formation and Duration: Distinguishing Between Country and Within-Country Effects," *British Journal of Political Science*, 19, no. 2, 291–302.

Gros, Daniel (1996), "A Reconsideration of the Optimum Currency Area Approach: The Role of External Shocks and Labor Mobility," *Centre for European Policy Studies Working Paper No. 101* (Brussels: Centre for European Policy Studies).

Gros, Daniel, and Niels Thygesen (1998), *European Monetary Integration*, 2nd edition (Essex, UK: Longman).

Haggard, Stephen (1991), "Inflation and Stabilization" in Gerald M. Meier (ed.) *Politics and Policy Making in Developing Countries: Perspectives on the New Political Economy* (San Francisco: ICS Press), pp. 233–249.

Haggard, Stephen, and R. Kaufman (1992), "The Political Economy of Inflation and Stabilization in Middle-Income Countries," in Stephen Haggard and R. Kaufman (eds.), *The Politics of Economic Adjustment* (Princeton, N.J.: Princeton University Press).

Hallerberg, Mark (2002), "Veto Players and the Choice of Monetary Institutions," *International Organization*, 56, no. 4, 775–802.

Hallerberg, Mark, Lúcio Vinhas de Souza, and William Roberts Clark (2002), "Political Business Cycles in EU Accession Countries," *European Union Politics*, 3, no. 2, 231–250.

Harmel, Robert, and John D. Robertson (1986), "Government Stability and Regime Support: A Cross-National Analysis," *Journal of Politics*, 48, 1029–1040.

Heisenberg, Dorothee (1999), *The Mark of the Bundesbank: Germany's Role in European Monetary Cooperation* (Boulder, Colo.: Lynne Rienner).

Heston, Alan, Robert Summers, and Bettina Aten (2002), *Penn World Table Version 6.1*, (Philadelphia, Penn.: Center for International Comparisons at the University of Pennsylvania (CICUP)).

Hibbs, Douglas A. (1977), "Political Parties and Macroeconomic Policies," *American Political Science Review*, 71, no. 4, 1467–1487.

Hollis, Martin, and Steve Smith (1990), *Explaining and Understanding International Relations* (Oxford: Clarendon Press).

Jones, Erik (2002), *The Politics of Economic and Monetary Union: Integration and Idiosyncrasy* (New York: Rowman and Littlefield).

Kaltenthaler, Karl (2002), "German Interests in European Monetary Integration," *Journal of Common Market Studies*, 40, no. 1, 69–87.

Keefer, Philip (2002), "Politics and the Determinants of Banking Crises: The Effects of Political Checks and Balances," in Leonardo Hernández and Klaus Schmidt-

Hebel (eds.), *Banking, Financial Integration and International Crises* (Santiago: Central Bank of Chile), 85–112.

Keefer, Philip, and David Stasavage (2002), "Checks and Balances, Private Information, and the Credibility of Monetary Commitments," *International Organization*, 56, no. 4, 751–774.

Kenen, Peter, and Dani Rodrik (1986), "Measuring and Analyzing the Effects of Short-Term Volatility in Real Exchange Rates," *Review of Economics and Statistics*, 68, 311–315.

Kennedy, Ellen (1991), *The Bundesbank—Germany's Central Bank in the International Monetary System* (London: The Royal Institute for International Affairs).

King, Gary, James E. Alt, Nancy E, Burns, and Michael Laver (1990), "A Unified Model of Cabinet Dissolution in Parliamentary Democracies," *American Journal of Political Science*, 34, no. 3, 846–871.

Klein, Michael W. and Nancy P. Marion (1997), "Explaining the Duration of Exchange Rate Pegs," *Journal of Development Economics*, 54, no. 2, 387–404.

Krasner, Stephen D. (ed.) (1983), *International Regimes* (Ithaca, N.Y.: Cornell University Press).

Kratochwil, Friedrich V. (1989), *Rules, Norms, and Decisions—On the Conditions of Practical and Legal Reasoning in International Relations and Domestic Affairs* (Cambridge, UK: Cambridge University Press).

Krugman, Paul (1991), *Geography and Trade* (Cambridge, Mass.: The MIT Press).

Kurian, George Thomas (ed.) (1998), *World Encyclopedia of Parliaments and Legislatures* (Washington, D.C.: Congressional Quarterly).

Laakso, Markuu, and Rein Taagepera (1979), "Effective Number of Parties: A Measure with Application to West Europe," *Comparative Political Studies*, 12, no. 1, 3–27.

Laver, Michael, and Kenneth A. Shepsle (1996), *Making and Breaking Governments—Cabinets and Legislatures in Parliamentary Democracies* (Cambridge, UK: Cambridge University Press).

Leblang, David (1999), "Democratic Political Institutions and Exchange Rate Commitments in the Developing World," *International Studies Quarterly*, 43, no. 4, 599–620.

Leblang, David (2002), "The Political Economy of Speculative Attacks in the Developing World," *International Studies Quarterly*, 46, no. 1, 69–91.

Leblang, David (2003), "To Devalue or to Defend? The Political Economy of Exchange Rate Policy," *International Studies Quarterly*, 47, no. 4, 533–559.

Leblang, David, and William Bernhard (2000), "The Politics of Speculative Attacks in Industrial Democracies," *International Organization*, 54, no. 2, 291–324.

Lijphart, Arend (1968), *The Politics of Accommodation* (Berkeley, Calif.: University of California Press).

Lijphart, Arend (1999), *Patterns of Democracy: Government Forms and Performance in Thirty-Six Countries* (New Haven, Conn.: Yale University Press).

Lobo, Bento J., and David Tufte (1998), "Exchange Rate Volatility: Does Politics Matter?" *Journal of Macroeconomics*, 20, no. 2, 351–365.

Lohmann, Susanne (1998), "Federalism and Central Bank Independence: The Politics of German Monetary Policy, 1957–92," *World Politics*, 50, no. 3, 401–446.

Loriaux, Michael (1991), France After Hegemony: International Change and Financial Reform (Ithaca, N.Y.: Cornell University Press).

Ludlow, Peter (1982), *The Making of the European Monetary System—A Case Study of the Politics of the European Community* (London: Butterworth Scientific).

Lupia, Arthur, and Kaare Strøm (1995), "Coalition Termination and the Strategic Timing of Parliamentary Elections," *American Political Science Review*, 89, no. 3, 648–665.

MacRae, Duncan (1977), "A Political Model of the Business Cycle," *Journal of Political Economy*, 85, no. 2, 239–264.

Macridis, Ray C. (1959), "Cabinet Instability in the Fourth Republic," *Journal of Politics*, 14, 643–658.

Martin, Lisa L. (1993), "International and Domestic Institutions in the EMU Process," *Economics and Politics*, 5, no. 2, 125–144.

Masson, Paul, and Mark Taylor (1993), "Currency Unions: A Survey of the Issues," in Paul Masson and Mark Taylor (eds.), *Policy Issues in the Operation of Currency Areas* (Cambridge, UK: Cambridge University Press), 3–51.

McKinnon, Ronald (1963), "Optimum Currency Areas," *The American Economic Review*, 53, no. 4, 717–725.

McNamara, Kathleen R. (1998), *The Currency of Ideas—Monetary Politics in the European Union* (Ithaca, N.Y.: Cornell University Press).

Milner, Helen (1995), "Regional Economic Cooperation, Global Markets and Domestic Politics: A Comparison of NAFTA and the Maastricht Treaty," *Journal of European Public Policy*, 2, no. 3, 337–360.

Moravcsik, Andrew (1998), *The Choice for Europe: Social Purpose and State Power from Messina to Maastricht* (Ithaca, N.Y.: Cornell University Press).

Mundell, Robert (1961), "A Theory of Optimum Currency Areas," *The American Economic Review*, 51, no. 4, 657–665.

Nordhaus, William (1975), "The Political Business Cycle," *Review of Economic Studies*, 42, no. 2, 169–190.

Ordeshook, Peter C., and Olga V. Shvetsova (1994), "Ethnic Heterogeneity, District Magnitude, and the Number of Parties," *American Journal of Political Science*, 38, no. 1, 100–123.

Pauly, Louis W. (1992), "The Politics of European Monetary Union: National Strategies, International Implications," *International Journal*, 47, no. 1, 93–111.

Pindyck, Robert S., and Daniel L. Rubinfeld (1991), *Econometric Models and Economic Forecasts*, 3rd edition (New York: McGraw-Hill).

Popper, Karl R. (1966), *The Open Society and Its Enemies*, Vol. 2 (London: Routledge and Kegan Paul).

Power, Timothy J., and Mark J. Gasiorowski (1997), "Institutional Design and Democratic Consolidation in the Third World," *Comparative Political Studies*, 30, no. 2, 123–155.

Prodi, Romano (2002), "A Wider Europe—A Proximity Policy as the Key to Stability," speech delivered at the Sixth ECSA-World Conference, Brussels, 5–6 December 2002.

Rae, Douglas W. (1971), *The Political Consequences of Electoral Laws*, 2nd edition (New Haven, Conn.: Yale University Press).

Rae, Douglas W., and Michael Taylor (1970), *The Analysis of Political Cleavages* (New Haven, Conn.: Yale University Press).

Robertson, John D. (1983a), "The Political Economy and the Durability of European Coalition Cabinets: New Variations on a Game-Theoretic Perspective," *Journal of Politics*, 45, 932–957.

Robertson, John D. (1983b), "Inflation, Unemployment and Government Collapse: A Poisson Application," *Comparative Political Studies*, 15, 425–444.

Rodrik, Dani (1998), "Why Do More Open Economies Have Larger Governments?" *Journal of Political Economy*, 106, no. 5, 997–1032.

Rogoff, Kenneth (1990), "Equilibrium Political Budget Cycles," *American Economic Review*, 80, no. 1, 21–36.

Rose, Andrew (2000), "One Money, One Market: The Effect of Common Currencies on Trade," *Economic Policy*, 30, 7–46.

Rose, Andrew (2001), "Currency Unions and Trade: The Effect Is Large," *Economic Policy*, 33, 433–462.

Sadeh, Tal (2004), "The Potential for Anchoring MNMCs to the Euro Block," in Peter Xuereb (ed.) *The European Union and the Mediterranean—The Mediterranean's European Challenge, Volume V* (Malta: University of Malta) 569–593.

Sadeh, Tal (2005), "Who Can Adjust to the Euro?" *The World Economy*, 28, no. 11, 1651–1678.

Sandholtz, Wayne (1993), "Choosing Union: Monetary Politics and Maastricht," *International Organization*, 47, no. 1, 1–39.

Sandholtz, Wayne (1996), "Money Troubles: Europe's Rough Road to Monetary Union," *Journal of European Public Policy*, 3, no. 1, 84–101.

Sayek, Selin, and David D. Selover (2002), "International Interdependence and Business Cycle Transmission Between Turkey and the European Union," *Southern Economic Journal*, 69, no. 2, 206–238.

Sherman, Heidemarie (1990), "Central Banking in Germany," in Heidemarie Sherman, Richard Brown, Pierre Jacquet, and DeAnne Julius (eds.), *Monetary Implications of the 1992 Process* (New York: St. Martin's Press), 16–50.

Sorensen, Bent E., and Oved Yosha (1997), "Income and Consumption Smoothing among U.S. States: Regions of Clubs?" Center for Economic Policy Research Discussion Paper No. 1670 (London: Center for Economic Policy Research).

Stein, Ernesto H., and Jorge M. Sterb (1999), "Political Stabilization Cycles in High-Inflation Economies," *Journal of Development Economics*, 56, no. 1, 159–180.

Story, Jonathan (1988), "The Launching of the EMS: An Analysis of Change in Foreign Economic Policy," *Political Studies*, 36, no. 3, 397–412.

Story, Jonathan, and Marcello de Cecco (1993), "The Politics and Diplomacy of Monetary Union: 1985–1991" in Jonathan Story (ed.), *The New Europe: Politics, Government and Economy Since 1945* (Oxford: Blackwell), 328–354.

Strøm, Kaare (1984), "Minority Governments in Parliamentary Democracies—The Rationality of Non-Winning Cabinet Solutions," *Comparative Political Studies*, 17, no. 2, 199–227.

Strøm, Kaare (1990), *Minority Government and Majority Rule* (New York: Cambridge University Press).

Strøm, Kaare (2000), "Delegation and Accountability in Parliamentary Democracies," *European Journal of Political Research*, 37, 261–289.

Strøm, Kaare, and Stephen M. Swindle (2002), "Strategic Parliamentary Dissolution," *American Political Science Review*, 96, no. 3, 575–591.

Strøm, Kaare, Ian Budge, and Michael J. Laver (1994), "Constraints on Cabinet Formation in Parliamentary Democracies," *American Journal of Political Science*, 38, no. 2, 303–335.

Talani, Leila Simona (2000), *Betting For and Against EMU: Who Wins and Who Loses in Italy and in the UK from the Process of European Monetary Integration* (London: Ashgate).

Tavlas, George S. (1993), "The 'New' Theory of Optimum Currency Areas," *The World Economy*, 16, no. 6, 663–685.

Taylor, Michael, and Valentine H. Herman (1971), "Party Systems and Government Stability," *American Political Science Review*, 65, no. 1, 28–37.

Tovias, Alfred (2003), "Israeli Policy Perspectives on the Euro-Mediterranean Partnership in the Context of EU Enlargement," *Mediterranean Politics*, 8, no. 2–3, 214–232.

Tsebelis, George (2002), *Veto Players: An Introduction to Institutional Analysis* (Princeton, N.J.: Princeton University Press).

Tsoukalis, Loukas (1977), *The Politics and Economics of European Monetary Integration* (London: Allen & Unwin).

Tsoukalis, Loucas (2000), *The New European Economy Revisited* (Oxford: Oxford University Press).

Ungerer, Horst (1997), *A Concise History of European Monetary Integration—From EPU to EMU* (London: Quorum Books).

Vanthoor, Wim F. V. (1996), *European Monetary Union Since 1848—A Political and Historical Analysis* (Cheltenham, UK: Edward Elgar).

Verdun, Amy (1996), "An 'Asymmetrical' Economic and Monetary Union in the EU: Perceptions of Monetary Authorities and Social Partners," *Journal of European Integration*, 20, no. 1, 59–81.

Verdun, Amy (1999), "The Role of the Delors Committee in the Creation of EMU: An Epistemic Community?" *Journal of European Public Policy*, 6, no. 2, 308–328.

Walsh, James I. (2000), *European Monetary Integration and Domestic Politics: Britain, France and Italy* (Boulder, Colo.: Lynne Rienner).

Walsh, James I. (2001), "National Preferences and International Institutions: Evidence from European Monetary Integration," *International Studies Quarterly*, 45, no. 1, 59–80.

Warwick, Paul (1979), "The Durability of Coalition Governments in Parliamentary Democracies," *Comparative Political Studies*, 11, no. 4, 465–498.

Warwick, Paul (1994), *Government Survival in Parliamentary Democracies* (New York: Cambridge University Press).

Wendt, Alexander (1987), "The Agent-Structure Problem in International Relations Theory," *International Organization*, 41, no. 3, 335–370.

White, Gregory (1999), "Encouraging Unwanted Immigration: A Political Economy of Europe's Efforts to Discourage North African Immigration," *Third World Quarterly*, 20, no. 4, 839–854.

Wooldridge, Jeffrey M. (2002), *Econometric Analysis of Cross Section and Panel Data* (Cambridge, Mass.: The MIT Press).

Youngs, Richard (1999), "The Politics of the Single Currency: Learning the Lessons of Maastricht," *Journal of Common Market Studies*, 37, no. 2, 295–316.

Index

Adjacency. *See* trade

Adjustment, 13, 19–20, 22–23, 32, 42, 44, 47, 50, 60, 63–65, 69, 71–72, 74–75, 77, 81, 89, 91–93, 111–116, 119–124, 127, 131–135, 140, 143, 152–157, 160, 163–168, 170–174; burden of, 13, 15, 17, 19–20, 22–23, 26–27, 29, 32, 36–37, 39, 44, 60, 82, 109, 111, 124, 127, 130–133, 135, 137, 139, 142, 154, 157–160, 163–164, 168–173, 175; evidence of, 1, 6–7, 12, 34, 37–42, 44–45, 48, 69, 92–93, 119, 122–123, 130, 156, 164, 169; forecasts of, 19 124, 127–129, 133–135, 138, 142, 154, 157–159, 168–169, 171; indicators or measures of, 17, 23, 29, 32, 35–37, 39–42, 44, 48, 60, 77, 79, 82, 89, 91–92, 95, 109, 111–112, 119–124, 127–129, 133–135, 138, 142, 144–145, 155–157, 161, 163–164, 167–168, 170–171; mechanisms or channels of, 13, 20–23, 29, 32, 36, 38–45, 47, 71, 79, 93, 122–124, 132–135, 157, 164, 168, 170; potential for, 27, 41, 63, 131, 137–138, 160, 168–169, 172. *See also* bilateralism, Economic and Monetary Union, euro, euro zone, exchange rate variation, Optimum Currency Areas, prices

Algeria, 146, 154, 156, 159, 172. *See also* Arab countries, European Union, Mediterranean countries or economies, North Africa

Anchor currencies, 6, 9, 13, 17, 48, 64, 68, 89, 131, 133–135, 141–142, 157–158, 160, 163, 165, 170, 173–174. *See also* euro zone, European Monetary System, exchange rate commitments, Exchange Rate Mechanism, Optimum Currency Areas

Arab countries, 143, 145–147, 154. *See also* Algeria, Egypt, European Union, Jordan, Lebanon, Libya, Morocco, Mediterranean countries or economies, North Africa, Palestinian Authority, Syria, Tunisia,

Asymmetric shocks, 21–22, 45, 60, 136, 166. *See also* business cycles, Optimum Currency Areas

Austria, 10, 24, 30–31, 34, 40–44, 48–51, 53, 55, 57–58, 61, 67, 76–77, 79, 86, 88, 93, 97–98, 103, 128, 130, 134, 137, 146, 167, 169. *See also* Euro zone, European Union, landlocked countries

BAFTA. *See* Baltic Free Trade Agreement

Balkan countries, 140. *See also* Bulgaria, Croatia, Romania, Turkey

Baltic countries, 31–32, 37–38, 55–56, 75, 119, 122, 124, 130, 169. *See also* Baltic Free Trade Agreement, Estonia, Latvia, Lithuania, transition countries or economies

Baltic Free Trade Agreement (BAFTA), 56. *See also* Baltic countries, trade, transition countries or economies

Barcelona process, 139–140, 142. *See also* Euro-Mediterranean association agreements, European Union, Mediterranean countries or economies

Belarus, 140–141, 145, 147, 149–150, 154, 156, 159–160, 172. *See also* European Union, landlocked coun-

Credibility. *See* central bank independence, inflation, Optimum Currency Areas

Crises: in balance of payments, 6; in domestic politics, 92, 96; in exchange rates, 1, 8, 10; in Stability and Growth Pact, 11; international, 1, 12, 73. *See also* European Monetary System, Exchange Rate Mechanism, exchange rates, Stability and Growth Pact

Croatia, 140. *See also* Balkan countries

Currency boards. *See* exchange rate commitments

Currency unions, 15–16, 21–23, 25, 32, 47, 60, 64, 72, 82, 132, 135, 137; and endogenous effects, 1, 13, 15–16, 18–19, 51–52, 58, 124, 163, 165; in Europe, 1, 3, 7–12, 16, 24, 135, 137, 163; and sustainability, 12, 15, 17, 25, 137, 174–175; theories of, 18, 22, 51–52, 58, 72, 124, 132, 164–165. *See also* exchange rate commitments, Optimum Currency Areas, sustainability

Customs unions. *See* trade

Cyprus, 11, 30–32, 34, 40–41, 43, 49, 51, 53, 55, 61, 67, 76–77, 86, 88, 92–93, 96–98, 100, 102–104, 128, 134, 146, 159–160, 167, 172. *See also* European Union, Mediterranean countries or economies

Czech republic, 30–31, 34, 40, 43, 49–53, 55–57, 61, 67–68, 76–77, 86, 93, 97, 103, 128, 131, 134, 154, 159, 169. *See also* European Union, landlocked countries, transition countries or economies

Democracy. *See* cabinet duration and the age of democracy, exchange rate commitments and democracy

Denmark, 3, 8–11, 30–31, 34, 39–41, 43, 49, 51, 53, 58, 61, 67, 70, 76, 86, 88, 93, 97, 99, 102–103, 105, 128, 130, 134, 156, 158–160, 167, 169, 172. *See also* European Union

Deutsche Bundesbank. *See* Germany and German Bundesbank

Divergence, 1, 12, 20, 23, 41, 110; economic, 1, 3, 10, 12, 20–21, 24, 47–48, 117, 155, 163–164, 172; indicator of,

5; political, 1, 4, 12, 20, 100, 114, 163–164. *See also* bilateralism, European Monetary System, exchange rates

Diversity. *See* divergence

Dollar. *See* United States

Domestic political institutions, 4, 13, 16, 20, 23, 47, 64, 68, 71, 77–79, 91, 95, 107, 110, 113, 128, 137, 151–152, 171, 173–174. *See also* cabinet duration

EC. *See* European Community

ECB. *See* European Central Bank

ECOFIN. *See* Council of Ministers for Economic and Financial Affairs

Economic and Monetary Union (EMU), 1–2, 5, 7–13, 15–19, 23–25, 27, 29, 32, 39, 47, 65, 67, 70–74, 77, 79, 88, 125, 127, 129–131, 135, 138, 160, 163, 166–170. *See also* adjustment, European Central Bank, multilateralism, the Snake, Stability and Growth Pact, sustainability, Treaty of Maastricht, the Werner report

ECU. *See* European Currency Unit

EFTA. *See* European Free Trade Association

Egypt, 145–146, 159–160, 173. *See also* Arab countries, European Union, Mediterranean countries or economies, North Africa

Electoral cycles, 23, 64, 83, 88, 90–92, 117, 124, 137, 167. *See also* political business cycles.

EMS. *See* European Monetary System

EMU. *See* Economic and Monetary Union

Endogenous effects of membership in currency unions. *See* Optimum Currency Areas

ENP. *See* European Union

ERM. *See* Exchange Rate Mechanism

d'Estaing, Valéry Giscard, 5–6.

Estonia, 11, 24, 30–31, 34, 40, 43, 45, 49, 51–53, 55–56, 61, 67–68, 76, 86, 88–89, 93, 97, 99, 102–103, 128–129, 131, 134, 147, 156, 159–160, 167, 172, 175. *See also* Baltic countries, European Union, transition countries or economies

About the Book

The tranquility of the European Union's transition to the euro in 1999 contrasted dramatically with the preceding tumultuous decades of exchange rate crises and political upheavals. But have the EU member states in fact converged sufficiently to make monetary union a stable alternative? Or is Economic and Monetary Union (EMU) in Europe an institutional lid on a simmering pot of diverse economies in which tensions are building to a future blowup? And if the latter, what can be done to remedy the situation?

Arguing that EMU is disproportionately socially expensive for many of the present and potential member states, Tal Sadeh's rigorous analysis focuses on the problematic implications of the EU's economic and political diversity. Sadeh is particularly concerned with the domestic structural and institutional reforms that will be necessary to sustain EMU. His supporting quantitative data cover forty-three countries: all of the EU member states, the candidate countries, the United States, and the EU's neighbors in the Middle East, North Africa, and Eastern Europe.

Tal Sadeh is assistant professor of political science at Tel Aviv University. He is coauthor of *The Future Relations Between Israel and the European Communities: Some Alternatives.*

7 Day